CW01183122

Beyond Emasculation

Beyond Emasculation is based on long-term ethnographic research with *hijra*s, the emblematic figure of South Asian sexual and gender difference, in Dhaka, Bangladesh. It proposes the hijra as a counter-cultural formation that embodies not only a direct contrast to hegemonic patterns of masculinity but also as an alternative subculture offering the possibility of varied forms of erotic pleasures and practices otherwise forbidden in mainstream society. While most studies view hijras as an asexual, emasculated, third sex/gender, this book calls into question the phallocentric logic that obscures alternative sites and sources of bodily power and pleasure, emphasizing how hijras craft their own subject position. Ethnographically rich and theoretically engaged, this book will cause a new, global re-examination of both hijras in particular and the wider range of 'male femininities' in general.

Adnan Hossain is Assistant Professor of Gender Studies and Critical Theory at Graduate Gender Program, Utrecht University. His research concerns gender and sexual diversity, heterosexualities, masculinities, transgender and intersex studies, race and ethnic relations, bodies, nationalism, de/post-colonial studies and global inequalities in knowledge production.

Beyond Emasculation
Pleasure and Power in the Making of *Hijra* in Bangladesh

Adnan Hossain

CAMBRIDGE
UNIVERSITY PRESS

CAMBRIDGE
UNIVERSITY PRESS

University Printing House, Cambridge CB2 8BS, United Kingdom

One Liberty Plaza, 20th Floor, New York, NY 10006, USA

477 Williamstown Road, Port Melbourne, vic 3207, Australia

314 to 321, 3rd Floor, Plot No.3, Splendor Forum, Jasola District Centre, New Delhi 110025, India

103 Penang Road, #05–06/07, Visioncrest Commercial, Singapore 238467

Cambridge University Press is part of the University of Cambridge.

It furthers the University's mission by disseminating knowledge in the pursuit of education, learning and research at the highest international levels of excellence.

www.cambridge.org
Information on this title: www.cambridge.org/9781316517048

© Adnan Hossain 2021

This publication is in copyright. Subject to statutory exception and to the provisions of relevant collective licensing agreements, no reproduction of any part may take place without the written permission of Cambridge University Press.

First published 2021

Printed in India by Thomson Press India Ltd.

A catalogue record for this publication is available from the British Library

Library of Congress Cataloging-in-Publication Data

Names: Hossain, Adnan, author.
Title: Beyond emasculation : pleasure and power in the making of hijra in Bangladesh / Adnan Hossain.
Description: Cambridge, United Kingdom ; New York, NY : Cambridge University Press, 2021. | Includes bibliographical references and index.
Identifiers: LCCN 2021030236 (print) | LCCN 2021030237 (ebook) | ISBN 9781316517048 (hardback) | ISBN 9781009037914 (ebook)
Subjects: LCSH: Gender-nonconforming people—Bangladesh. | Masculinity—Bangladesh. | Sex role—Bangladesh. | Gender identity—Bangladesh. | BISAC: SOCIAL SCIENCE / Gender Studies | SOCIAL SCIENCE / Gender Studies
Classification: LCC HQ73.85.B3 H67 2021 (print) | LCC HQ73.85.B3 (ebook) | DDC 306.76/8095492—dc23
LC record available at https://lccn.loc.gov/2021030236
LC ebook record available at https://lccn.loc.gov/2021030237

ISBN 978-1-316-51704-8 Hardback

Cambridge University Press has no responsibility for the persistence or accuracy of URLs for external or third-party internet websites referred to in this publication, and does not guarantee that any content on such websites is, or will remain, accurate or appropriate.

For abba and amma

Contents

List of Figures	ix
Acknowledgements	xi
Introduction: Pleasure, Power and Masculinities	1
1. Kinship, Community and *Hijragiri*	26
2. Class-Cultural Politics and the Making of *Hijra*s	52
3. *Hijra* Erotic Subjectivities: Pleasure, Practice and Power	82
4. The Paradox of Emasculation	111
5. Practices and Processes of Gendering	134
6. Love and Emotional Intimacy: *Hijra* Entanglement with Normative Bangla Men	157
7. Contemporary Transformation of *Hijra* Subjectivities	181
Conclusion: Shifting Meaning and the Future of *Hijra*s	205
Glossary	210
References	215
Index	224

Figures

1.1 *Bagicha koti*s at a cruising site in Dhaka engaging in *ulu jhulu* 33
1.2 *Gamchali hijra*s posing for a photo for the author 35
1.3 Jomuna *hijra* with their *cela*s in Hridoypur on a lazy afternoon 41
2.1 *Hijra*s performing *badhai* in a working-class neighbourhood in Dhaka 63
3.1 Sex-worker *hijra*s at a public garden in Dhaka 94
4.1 A senior *hijra* preparing the altar to pay respect to Maya Ji and Tara Moni on the occasion of the *baraiya* ritual 122
5.1 *Hijra*s in Hridoypur dressed up and posing with the author for a photo 146
6.1 A senior *sadrali hijra* seated next to their *parik* with *cela*s standing in the back 170
6.2 A *parik* adorning his *hijra* partner with bangles in his own residence 178
7.1 A banner pinned to the front of a bus for a picnic organized by Badhon Hijra Shongho 193

Acknowledgements

This book has benefited both directly and indirectly from my engagement with myriad people over the last twenty years that I have been researching the *hijra* subject. In the course of this study, which is still ongoing, I have befriended several *sadrali hijra*s as well as trans and hijra activists who not only served as my interlocutors and informants, but also became entwined with my personal life in various capacities. Names that deserve special mention are Kala hijra, Payeli aka Habib, Joya Sikder, Ivan Ahmed Katha and Annonya Banik. I am eternally indebted to them all for their love, hospitality and friendship over the years. At the University of Amsterdam, colleagues that encouraged my research on gender and sexuality include Tina Harris, Kristine Krause, Francio Guadeloupe, Shifra Kisch, Eileen Moyer, Saskia Wieringa, Filippo Bertoni, Swasti Mishra, Mark Hann, Daniel Guinness, Domenica Gisella Calabrò, Nuria Rossell, Willem Van Schendel and Annemarie Mol. At Vrije Universiteit Amsterdam, Ellen Bal and Younes Saramifar took interest in my work. I thank them all. Many scholars also either read bits and pieces of my manuscript or listened to my presentations and provided comments at various platforms; I am particularly indebted to Rachel Spronk, Lawrence Cohen, Paul Boyce, Filippo Osella, Thomas Hendriks, Niko Besnier and Sino Esthappan in that regard. I also acknowledge Mark Johnson for his overall guidance and mentorship to bring to fruition the first iteration of this project in the form of a dissertation. I also want to acknowledge Serena Nanda, Momin Rahman and Michael Peletz for their encouragement and generous endorsement of my monograph. I have very fond recollections of time spent with Shipon, Mukti, Yousuf and Tuku Munshi whose support at various points of my fieldwork in Dhaka and beyond was invaluable. Special thanks are also due to Tanvir Alim for his work on the cover art. I want to thank Sumaiya Fareshta Islam for always believing in me, along with my parents, who have always been unconditionally supportive of my research. Finally, I owe a special debt of gratitude to Sidratul Muntaha, my niece, and my two daughters, Suhaila Hossain and Safwana Fatiha Islam, for being part of my life.

Introduction
Pleasure, Power and Masculinities

In Bangladesh, as in many parts of South Asia, gangs of *hijra*s adorned in saris and gaudy make-up are often seen swaggering down the busy streets, clapping and demanding alms at traffic lights or from the sellers in the bazaars. Like any typical Dhaka-dweller, I grew up viewing the hijras as not only starkly different from the normative mainstream, but also as neither men nor women. I have always been intrigued by the way people's attitude towards hijras tends to be a mixture of fear, pity and amusement. As popular public figures putatively devoid of functioning (male) genitals, and therefore occupying a liminal third space, hijras both arouse pity and incite laughter and mirth. At the same time, however, they are feared because they challenge mainstream society's notions of respectability and social protocols of appropriateness by engaging in activities ranging from sexually charged public cursing to exposing their putatively missing or defective genitals.

Upon close observation, one cannot help noticing the fact that hijras are perhaps the only group of people who are simultaneously asexual and hypersexual. Popular imagination across South Asia conflates genital ambiguity with asexuality or lack of sexual desire. Yet everyday interaction between hijras and ordinary people, especially men, is typically peppered with erotic banter, as hijras not only verbally shame the men with sexualized slurs, but also often directly fondle their genitals in a bid to coerce them into meeting their demands. The belligerence with which hijras typically communicate with the public (often accompanied by incessant hand clapping and body movements) is nothing short of being hyper-masculine in its aggressiveness and entitlement; at the same time, hijras emphasize their feminine comportment, which includes heavy make-up and nasalized speech, that enacts a caricature of femininity. Hijra practices thus raise the question of how to make sense of a social group that exemplifies values and practices that would seem to contradict each other.

This book focuses on these cultural paradoxes and contradictions in the production of the hijra subject position in Bangladesh and contends that hijra is an alternative space that one joins in order to be able to explore varied erotic, gender and sexual possibilities otherwise unavailable to normatively masculinized subjects both in Bangladesh and beyond. That an alternative hijra space had to be invented is emblematic of a broader politics of masculinity and the dominance of certain types of masculine hegemonies that operate to delegitimize a form of desire, culturally deemed to be incommensurate with certain styles of heterosexual masculinity. In this book, I foreground the cultural and scholarly politics of masculinity that frames the hijras as a third sex or third gender in the first place. I hope to demonstrate that while, on the one hand, hijras decentre and dismantle the phallus (the manifestation of masculine dominance both at the level of representation and practice) as the only and primary site of pleasure, power and masculinity, they also, on the other hand, paradoxically enforce and reinforce those ideals and politics of masculinity otherwise employed to socioculturally delegitimize them.

Pleasure and desire: rethinking the hijra subject position

Hijras are popularly described as 'neither men nor women' (Nanda 1999), or a third gender or third sex. More recently, hijras have come to the forefront of regional and international attention with several South Asian countries recognizing them as a legal category of a third or distinct gender (Hossain 2017). 'Hijra' is an Urdu word, widely used only after the Mughal invasion; its meaning stems from ninth-century Turko-Persian influence (Reddy 2005a). However, 'hijra' is also a Bengali word the lexical meaning of which incorporates ideas of impotency, being a eunuch, being someone born with genital ambiguity and asexuality. Its meaning, however, has shifted over time in response to various colonial and postcolonial notions of gender and sexuality. For example, the various ways the British constructed hijras during colonial rule reflected the British colonial establishment's intention to set themselves apart as morally superior to the Mughals, a process that served to facilitate British colonial governance of India (Gannon 2009; Hinchy 2019). As noted earlier, hijras across South Asia publicly present themselves as people born with defective or missing genitals and above sexual desire. It is in terms of this hijra insistence on their being asexual and public understanding of such that hijras are socioculturally institutionalized in South Asia.

Anthropological literature often depicts hijras as people who ritually remove or sacrifice their male genitals in return for spiritual power to bless newlyweds and the newborn (Nanda 1999; Reddy 2005a). It is through such ritual jettisoning of the penis and the scrotum, or emasculation, that hijras in South Asia acquire the status of a third gender or a third sex. One of the first anthropological debates on hijras appeared on the pages of *American Anthropologist* in the 1950s. Typical of the 'culture and personality' school of the time, this debate drew on deeply reductive theories of oedipal anxieties to explain the hijra practice of emasculation and transposed this on to the general Indian male personality structure (Agrawal 1997; Cohen 1995). In other words, the hijra practice of emasculation is read here as indicative of Indian males' generalized inability to reconcile their oedipal anxieties. Nanda (1999), one of the first ethnographers of hijras in India, departs from this psychoanalytically grounded reading and embeds emasculation within various Hindu mythological narratives to contend that the very loss of the penis paradoxically transforms the hijras into a universal source of fertility. In a similar vein, latter ethnographers contend that the ritual of emasculation is not simply central to the production of the hijra subject position, but that it is through a ritual sacrifice of male genitals that one becomes an authentic hijra (Reddy 2005a).

In this conceptual and cultural framework, obtaining such a special status also entails an active renunciation of erotic desire: those who get rid of their penises are also said to lose their masculinity and become asexual. Loss of the penis is equated with the loss of desire. What is often left unexamined is the reason why hijras present themselves as asexual and above desire, and how the adoption of a third sex/third gender works to erase desire. This book contends that it is not only the desire for normatively oriented masculine men that motivates one to become a hijra, but, more significantly, it is the abject and forbidden nature of desire that is central to the social marginalization and cultural abjection of hijras.[1] It is this contradiction between the public (re)presentation of hijras as asexual and above desire and the internal recognition of their being erotically inclined that lies at the heart of their lived lives and cosmologies.

---

[1] See Besnier (2004) for a similar argument in the context of Tongan gender-variant subjects' entanglement with mainstream Tongan men.

Foregrounding desire in the constitution of hijra subjectivity is not to reduce the hijras to gender and sexual difference alone. Throughout this book, I highlight a panoply of factors including class, kinship and religion in terms of which gender and sexual difference are configured and conceived. Rather, my point here is that the gender and sexual difference that hijras embody cannot be fully comprehended without an adequate examination of the desire that brought the hijra universe into being. In other words, while understanding how gender and sexual differences are refracted through other forms of social difference allows us to decipher the multiply inflected and complex configuration of gender and sexuality (Reddy 2005a); too often desire tends to be subordinated to other cultural refractions of difference. My concern here is to indicate how desire often gets subsumed under other factors of social difference rather than being central in the crafting of hijra subjectivities, even though desire is precisely what is at stake. The common theorization of hijra as an identity that derives its cultural legitimacy through the wider societal understandings of hijras as both above and beyond desire illustrates this representational effacement. Contemporary scholarship tends to focus on the public (re)presentation of hijras as asexual and above desire and the wider societal understanding and engagement with it in terms of the culturally valorized ideals of renunciation and asceticism (for example, Nanda 1999; Reddy 2005a). While situating hijras within wider cultural ideals of renunciation and detachment offers useful insights for contextualizing and historicizing hijras, failure to adequately engage with desire and its abjection not only inhibits us from comprehending hijra subjectivities, but also works to further the social marginalization of hijras.

My point here is that it is penile politics that produces the current forms of representation of hijras as not only a third sex, but also as a subject position above and beyond desire. It is precisely because of this phallocratic interpretive framework that hijras are placed outside the procreative heteronormativity as well as the economy of phallic pleasure. While this critical focus on the penis foregrounds the politics of hegemonic and subordinate masculinities, analytical approaches are often locked in a binary framework cast in terms of the appearance and disappearance of the penis, with the effect that those who get rid of their penis are denied not only masculinity, but also the power of pleasure. The very abjection of hijras is not only the result of societal understanding about hijras being people born with defective or missing genitals, but also of the popular understanding about hijras being outside the economy of desire and pleasure.

Anal thinking and the hijra as an alternative erotic space

Extant ethnographic literature reveals a problematic tendency to attribute defect, deficit and inadequacy in terms of gender and desire in the representation of hijras. Put differently, it is as if one becomes a hijra by default, that is, it is on account of having defective male genitals or failure to be sufficiently normatively masculine that one enters the hijra community. Against this narrative of deficit and inadequacy, most powerfully encapsulated in the now famous expression 'neither men nor women', this book demonstrates that the very act of an individual's identifying as a hijra also entails a conscious disapproval and disavowal of normative masculinities. That is, one joins the hijra community not because of one's failure to excel in masculine performance, but rather in order to be able to explore varied gender, erotic and ritual possibilities that are otherwise unavailable to the normatively masculinized subjects in Bangladesh.

According to the hijras, only those who renounce the privileges of heterosexual masculinity are entitled to varied forms of bodily pleasure. Desire is framed in terms of hetero-gendered idiom: those who penetrate are by definition men, as opposed to hijras who are always essentially receptive and therefore feminine, or 'female-like'. While such a penetrated/penetrator framework is often reversed in practice, this configuration of desire is not simply mimetic of heterosexuality. Rather, the reason why hijras lionize and strictly police this paradigm is because, according to my hijra interlocutors, being penetrated is a lot more pleasurable than penetrating. In other words, it is within this hetero-gendered framework that hijras maximize their erotic delights. Furthermore, hijras believe that only those who are part of the community as hijras are entitled to such pleasures. This does not, however, require hijras to be permanently detached from heterosexual affiliations. Rather, there are both hijras who are heterosexually married as well as those who are feminine-identified on a permanent basis; however, once one becomes a hijra, one is required to 'publicly' identify receptivity as the only legitimate form of sexuality. Because the anus in the mainstream view is not only culturally devalued, but also unspeakable, hijra space functions as an alternative site for actualizing and performing varied forms of erotic and bodily gratification.

Scholars often question the validity of cultural models that bifurcate people in male-to-male sexual intercourse into rigidly penetrative and receptive roles or categories. Such models often fail to acknowledge the complexities and fluidities of sexual behaviours and identities. The unwritten assumption is not just that pleasure is centred in the penis, but also that penile pleasures are superior to other forms of pleasures, a point that feminists have long made. Grosz (1994) underscores the way non-phallic body parts can be re-signified by same-sex attracted people as zones of pleasure. Reclamation and restoration of the erotically devalued body parts by non-heterosexuals, she contends, work to advance the possibility of a new order of pleasure. She further holds that it is through imagining the male body to be simultaneously engaged in insertivity and receptivity that a new order of pleasure can be established. While her suggestion is insightful and intriguing, I feel that she underestimates the pleasures of receptivity and its power. This is not to deflect our attention from the relations of power inequalities within which penetration and reception are structured. Nor am I indicating that erotic acts are non-political. Rather, what I emphasize here is that acts of penetration are neither more powerful nor automatically more pleasurable than those of receptivity.

The centrality of the penis is also evident in critical scholarship in the way non-penile body parts and most notably the anus are eroticized and reclaimed. For example, in her paper on the conceptualization of gender and sexuality in nineteenth-century Iran, Najmabadi (2008) contends that a system of hierarchical gradation of body parts was central to people's understanding not only of gender and sexuality, but also pleasure, wherein the anus (both of male and female) was considered superior to the vagina as an object of penetration. While such historical insights trouble the modernist narratives of gender and sexuality, here again the hierarchization of the body parts is often conceptualized through the standpoint of the penetrator, or the phallus. Furthermore, accounts of anal receptivity often uncritically equate receptivity with a loss of manhood. In a similar vein, albeit in a different context, Kulick (1998) contends that the Brazilian transgendered sex workers whom he studied derived their gender from their partners, by whom they were penetrated, while they derived erotic pleasure from their clients, whom they penetrated. The dominant underlying assumption informing this interesting body of scholarship is that pleasure inheres in and flows from the penis, much like the way the very lack of a penis among hijras works to consolidate hijras as asexual and above desire. Against this overarching penis-centred approach, this book foregrounds and asserts anal power and agency through hijra narratives of the anus as not only an object of desire, but also an active desirous subject.

The failure of imagination and scholarship to recognize and adequately and critically envision non-penile possibilities of pleasure is the direct corollary of how we as social scientists view erotic pleasures and relate to self, others and the ethnographic field. That is, ethnographers' understanding of pleasure and power is configured within particular socio-historically specific economies of desire, in terms of which both our understandings of the other as well as the knowledge we produce are framed.[2] Given that the epistemic template scholars of hijras specifically and gender and sexual diversity more generally adopt is penis-centred, analysis inevitably forces questions of body, pleasure, power, erotic practice, and agency back to the penis. In much contemporary writing on male-to-male sexual subjectivities or hijras as well as further afield, the penis often emerges as the uncontested cultural totem at the centre of erotic pleasure.

Given the cultural valorization of the penis in South Asia as well as in the Western world (Stephens 2007), it is not surprising that so much attention has been paid to a group of people who are alleged to obtain power and status on account of sacrificing male genitals. In other words, this conceptual and representational privileging of emasculation is the direct corollary of and paradoxically contributes to the hegemony of not only the penis, but also the phallus (Roth 2004; Stephens 2007). While I acknowledge the complexities of this relationship, I use the term 'phallus' to indicate the cultural manifestation of masculine hegemony. As my ethnography indicates, the hijra subject position is produced at the interstice between the magical appearance and disappearance of the penis and the way one's ability to claim authentic hijra status depends on one's ability to master this special art. Furthermore, emasculation represents an uneven distribution of the phallic power wherein the accommodation, if not acceptance, of hijras in the Indian social structure comes at the cost of emasculation (Agrawal 1997; Cohen 1995). My point is that as a social institution hijras have been conceptualized within a penis-centred frame of reference, even though the very absence of a penis is precisely what has been posited to be the truth about them.

The limits of a third sex/third gender framework and masculinities as an alternative approach

The most dominant lens in the study of hijras has been a third gender or a third sex framework (Nanda 1999). Several critical anthropologists have

---

[2] See Kulick (2006) on masochist ethnographic interest in the powerless and the libidinal structure within which ethnographic interest in the powerless is produced.

responded to this problematic and exotifying 'third sex' gaze on to the hijras and foregrounded the multiply configured and context-specific construction of hijra subjectivities (for example, Agrawal 1997; Cohen 1995; Reddy 2005a). The third sex/gender framework fails to account for the complex interaction among gender, sexuality and the social, economic and political context in which hijras are implicated. Critical scholarship has drawn our attention to the misleading conception about the emancipatory potential of multiple genders and the simplistic idea that more genders denotes greater freedom or acceptance. Instead of being an emblem of acceptance, the consignment of some people to the status of a third gender can be read as a form of gender failure on the part of those who fail to be either sufficiently masculine or feminine (Agrawal 1997). The hierarchical order of genders further complicates and hides the socio-political power relations that facilitate the formation of a third gender while naturalizing the existing two-gender system. The third gender as a model is driven more by a desire to challenge the two-sex/gender system than by the lived lives of the people who constitute this 'third' (Hossain 2017). Furthermore, the idea that societies that accommodate third gender categories are more tolerant than the rest works to obfuscate the everyday struggle of hijras, who must constantly fight against the mainstream to demand a position within those societies (Hall 1997).

Against this background, I adopt masculinities as an alternative analytical cipher to complicate the hijra subject. Although social scientists, including anthropologists, have conventionally overlooked masculinity and favoured a third gender lens, as indicated earlier (Osella, Osella and Chopra 2004, 2), I argue that masculinities are central to the marginalization of hijras in contemporary Bangladesh (Hossain 2012). Adopting masculinities as an optic adds considerably to our understanding not only of the hijra subject in South Asia, but also of the production, reproduction and transformation of masculinities. 'Masculinities' as an approach also allows us to account for the extant cultural accommodation of thirdness and its recent official institutionalization in several South Asian countries. A focus on the way the politics of pleasure and power constitute masculinity brings to the fore the problematic preponderance of the penis and the phallus in the conceptualization of hijras. As I have already previously indicated, it is precisely because of this phallocratic interpretive logic that hijras are placed not only outside the procreative heteronormativity, but also beyond the (phallic) realm of pleasure.

One of the widespread, albeit problematic, translations of the term 'hijra' into English, widely deployed during British colonialism and contemporaneously in South Asia, is 'eunuch', a word that marks the hijras as made out of male bodies. Although in the popular press, as well as in scholarly representations, a plethora of divergent terms, such as androgyne, transsexual, transvestite, hermaphrodite, intersex, homosexual or transgender, is often simultaneously used to describe hijras, critical ethnographies of hijras often describe them as 'phenotypic male[s]' who sacrifice their male genitals in return for special power (Reddy 2005a). Furthermore, despite the centrality of emasculation in the production of the hijra body, ethnographies on Indian and Pakistani hijras also make the claim that there may also be a minority of hijras who are born intersex. However, in the context of Bangladesh, as I argue in this book, it is only male-born people who can qualify to become a hijra. In other words, hijras are typically those assigned a male gender at birth who later may identify as either non-male or female. That various ideas including genital ambiguity and various intersex conditions are popularly ascribed to the hijra by the mainstream populace at least partially stems from the fact that hijras too present themselves as people born with missing or ambiguous genitals. That hijras present themselves as such, or as neither men nor women and/or as above and beyond desire, works to account for the long-running cultural accommodation of this group within South Asia, including Bangladesh.

Furthermore, in everyday contexts, the word 'hijra' is also often used by the mainstream non-hijra populace to mark, police and describe digression from the normative protocols of masculinity. The very utterance of the word 'hijra' in the context of daily life also provokes laughter and jest alongside a deep sense of commiseration for a group of people believed to have been born with defective or missing genitals. Here, there is a popular association between genital ambiguity and asexuality. Not only are people with genital ambiguity relegated to the status of a liminal third gender/sex in popular imagination in contemporary Bangladesh, they are also deemed to be asexual and above desire on account of those associations. Against this backdrop, masculinities as an alternative approach brings into view the structural inequalities in the social configuration of gender and sexuality that produce the hijra subject in the first place. The continued lack of attention to masculinities also has repercussions for policy change and intervention in the context of achieving gender equality and sexual rights for a range of gender-variant subjects, including hijras, transsexuals and the intersex and transgender, who are often problematically conflated in contemporary popular cultural imagination (Hossain 2020).

In adopting masculinities as an optic, it may be useful to think through the usefulness of this concept. Throughout this book, I use masculinities rather than masculinity to indicate that there is no single model of masculinity. However, in pluralizing masculinity, it is important to recognize that these models or types of masculinities are not static. Rather, divergent models of masculinities are enacted in a complex interplay with a variety of factors—namely class, ethnicity, gender, power, desire, religion, kinship and transnationalism—and are subject to change.

There also remains a strong tendency to collapse men and masculinity into a causally linked proposition. Recent queer and ethnographic interventions have, however, strongly challenged such analytical conflation, urging us to conceptually de-link masculinities from maleness. A slew of ethnographies on female masculinities, in diverse settings, have clearly driven home the point that masculinities are qualities and styles that females can take on, thereby guarding us against the reification of masculinity as maleness (Blackwood 1998; Davies 2007; Halberstam 1998; Lai 2007; Sinnott 2007; Wieringa 1999). Thus, in speaking to masculinities, the book does not essentialize the hijras as men. Nor does it reify masculinities or femininities as intrinsic properties of biological maleness and femaleness respectively.

An important and widely used concept in this context is hegemonic masculinity, which can be defined as 'the configuration of gender practice which embodies the currently accepted answer to the problem of the legitimacy of patriarchy, which guarantees (or is taken to guarantee) the dominant position of men and the subordination of women' (Connell 2005). Hegemonic masculinity brings into view the relations among masculinities: hegemonic, subordinate, complicit and marginal. Hegemonic masculinity is not a fixed character type, always and everywhere the same. It is rather the masculinity type that occupies the most hegemonic position and is always contestable (Connell 2005). Attending to the multiplicity of differentiations through which masculinities are inflected foregrounds how such hegemonies paradoxically engender various counter-hegemonic trends. Nevertheless, very few men actually live up to the normative ideals of hegemonic masculinity, while an overwhelming majority become complicit in sustaining its dominance (Alsop, Fitzsimons and Lennon 2002; Cornwall and Lindisfarne 1994).

From the perspective of hegemonic masculinity as described here, hijra can be seen as a countercultural formation that emerged not only in rejection of and as a response to compulsory hegemonic masculinity, but also as an alternative subcultural community offering the possibility of varied forms of erotic pleasures and practices otherwise forbidden in mainstream society. Describing the various configurations of masculinities and ideological systems mobilized in support of those gender configurations is beyond the scope of this book, but suffice it to say that here the concept of hegemonic masculinity primarily refers both to a generalized model of male-bodied masculinity against which hijras are publically defined in mainstream discourse, and to the set of stereotypical traits and styles that hijras associate with men and masculinity. Yet the so-called ideal that hijras verbally valorize and associate with normative men rarely corresponds to the actual men with whom hijras are romantically or erotically involved. In fact, quite ironically, hijras produce and reinforce the hegemonic masculinity by tending to define men in strictly normative terms: a man is someone who is by definition penetrative, while hijras and females are receptive.

While the readymade espousal of a third gender lens in contemporary ethnographies of hijras works to sidestep masculinities as already previously alluded to, there is now a growing recognition of the role of masculinities in the historical marginalization of hijras (Gannon 2009; Hinchy 2014). For example, hijras posed a particular challenge to the British colonial masculinity. They were also classed as a special caste and a criminal tribe as part of the British civilizing mission (Gannon 2009; Hinchy 2014; Levine 2000). Agrawal (1997) brings into view the centrality of the body in colonial and anthropological construction of a third gender identity in India, arguing that the construction of a so-called third gender operates not in opposition to but within the framework of gender binaries, as even when Indian society allows for the transformation of a body into a third gender, it does so at the cost of bodily change or castration. In a similar vein, Cohen (1995) takes up the issue of castration and interrogates its centrality in the construction of hijra identity, particularly in terms of what is at stake for those undergoing this process, rather than treating this so-called third gender as some 'disembodied liminal markers of thirdness'.

Particularly relevant to this book is the trope that posits ideals of sexual renunciation and androgyny as alternatives to the dyadic imperial bifurcation of the colonizer and the colonized into hyper-masculine and effeminate respectively (Chowdhury 2001; Kalra 2009; Krishnaswamy 2002; Sinha 1995). Instructive in this regard is Nandy's (1989) study, which highlights the internalization of colonial principles by Indian elites and their role in the making of Indian selfhood in postcolonial India. Drawing on Gandhi's call for the feminization of masculinity in the anti-colonial movement, Nandy argues that Gandhian androgyny emerged as an alternative to the political binary of effeminacy and hyper-masculinity. Yet, as Cohen (1995) points out, in deploying Gandhian androgyny as an anti-colonial subjectivity, Nandy bypasses the materiality and historicity of the lived bodies of the people marked as 'third' in their daily lives. Cohen contends that the metaphorization of androgyny further disembodies the hijras and obscures the way androgyny is differentially experienced across the class spectrum. Cohen's insightful critique of the class-specific and elitist nature of Gandhian anti-colonial androgyny resonates well with one of the concerns that this book takes on board and sets out to unpack—namely that hijra subjectivities are forged in a complex interplay with varied class dynamics.

Masculinities operate at the ideological level and intersect with other domains of social life. For example, the hijra practice of emasculation can be located within the broader cultural logics of the Hindu ideal of renunciation and asceticism (Nanda 1999; Reddy 2005a; Taparia 2011). Although hijras are not classed as ascetics per se, hijras evoke masculine and semen anxieties. From this perspective, at least at the symbolic level, hijras can be read as an embodiment of superior Hindu masculine individualism. In contrast, very little is known about such masculine anxieties and the making of men and masculinities in Islamicate South Asia (see Ahmed 2006; Hossain 2019a; Marsden 2007; Mookherjee 2004; Walle 2004 for the various configurations and negotiations of masculinities in non-Indian Islamicate South Asian contexts). Emblematic of the underlying logic of colonial masculinity, a growing body of scholarship notes the simultaneous feminization and hyper-masculinization of Muslims in Hindu-dominated India post-partition. Here, the dominant theme is that Muslims are popularly relegated to the status of not only 'non-man', but also hyper-masculine/sexual in the dominant Hindu imaginary. Different forms of discursive abjections of the 'Muslim other' have been read as attempts to recuperate Hindu masculinity (Hansen 1996; Osella and Osella 2006; Ramaswami 2007; Reddy 2003). While such a lop-sided discursive distillation of the Muslim as simultaneously emasculate and hyper-masculine works to reify such differentiation as a form of naturalized distinction, such discourses also obscure the complex negotiation of such ascriptions in real-life settings by various marginal groups, including hijras, to which I now turn.

Male femininities and 'male femaling'

While focusing on masculinities brings into view the cultural devaluation of femininity and the ideological legitimation for the subordination of hijras, combining male femaling and male femininities with masculinities allows me to capture the enactment of various hijra practices in daily settings through which they craft their subject position. While male femininity as an approach recently has been variably used in the context of Western male-to-female transgender practices (Ekins 1996) and late-capitalist androgynous metrosexuality (Atkinson 2008), I use male femininity mainly to illustrate the various forms of corporeal and social transformational possibilities that the male-bodied, feminine-identified hijras seek and experiment with.

The heuristic utility of a 'male femininity' approach over that of a third sex framework is that it allows us to take into account the processual character of the identity formation of hijras. Against the predominant representation of hijras as locked in an intermediate third sex category, a male femininity approach moves us beyond such immobility and foregrounds the dynamic and fluid practices and processes of movement and shifts across and between various subject positions through which the hijra subject is produced. For example, hijras in Bangladesh (as this book demonstrates) are not a subculture into which male-bodied people incapable of being successful normative men enter. Rather, those who enter the hijra community also disavow normative heterosexual masculinities in a bid to navigate and explore varied erotic pleasures and possibilities that are otherwise unavailable to masculine men. Furthermore, unlike the stereotypical image of hijras as located outside the institutions of reproductive heteronormativity, there are hijras in Bangladesh who are simultaneously masculine house-holding men and feminine-identified hijras. 'Male femininity' as an approach is well equipped to account for such constant shifts between and across masculinities and femininities, in that it does not reify either.

'Male femininity' also allows us to read hijras beyond the dominant trope of emasculation. The extant scholarship not only views hijras through the optic of emasculation, but also considers emasculation to be the most coveted cultural 'truth' about hijras. My research, however, calls into question the centrality of emasculation in the production of hijras. There are both hijras with penises and those without; some who move between hijra and normative masculinity and others who live as hijra on a more permanent basis. Against a focus on the singular ritual act of bodily transformation, a male femininity approach shows that becoming a hijra is a complex process. It is an achieved status and not an ascribed one. Adoption of a hijra subject position entails the attainment of ritually sacrosanct skills and acumen about various forms of gender and erotic expressions and their dexterous and persistent demonstration before both fellow hijras and non-hijras on a daily basis.

The 'male femaling' processual approach also foregrounds various contestations and conflicts over authentic hijra status. While emasculation is often deemed to be the desideratum among hijras both in India and Bangladesh, such a position is not uncontested in Bangladesh, as hijras with penises often draw on the similar cultural idioms and resources of Islam and Hinduism to berate the emasculated hijras as well as assert their own positions within the hijra universe. In other words, the ethnography I present in this book further nuances the various, at times contested, forms of hijra subject that are embodied and practised in South Asia. The spatial shifts between masculine comportment, and in some instances house-holding status, and the feminine-identified hijra subject are but one part of a larger process of movement that typifies hijra life and work both in a geographical sense— where hijras routinely travel between and across national boundaries—and in the sense of moving between different sorts of social settings, occupational positions and ritual statuses (Hossain 2012).

While hijras, as the putative antithesis of men and masculinity, may be read as an outcome of an oppressive masculine hegemony, they ironically produce and reinforce such reifications by tending to define men in strict hegemonic terms: a man is someone who is by definition penetrative while hijras and females are receptive. Yet closer attention to the dynamics of the hijra/men relationship discloses more complex and nuanced gender dynamics than the concept of hegemonic masculinity allows for. For instance, although hijras generically demand that their male partners comport themselves in a stereotypically masculine manner, such attributions are contradicted by their own lived practices wherein hijras, rather than their masculinized partners, emerge as more dominant, as will be demonstrated later in this book. Thus, I contend that while hijras help us decouple masculinity from its popular naturalized association with maleness and heterosexuality, hijras also become complicit in consolidating and imposing hegemonic notions of masculinities in constituting themselves and men in general. In other words, how hijras talk about and are distinguished from their partners—masculine-identified men—provides insights into the complex configuration of masculinities, hegemonic, complicit and subordinate (Connell and Messerschmidt 2005). Furthermore, although hijras are often viewed as the abjected other of the hyper-masculine at the discursive level, the very adoption of a hijra subject position endows the member of the hijra community with an uncanny virulence that the mainstream normative imagination would gender as nothing short of 'hyper-masculinity'.

'Male femininity' also allows us to see the complex relationship between various gender discourses and practices. For example, hijras simultaneously take on and transcend idioms of mainstream masculinity and femininity. Here a male femininity approach does not distil hijras into male or female categories. Rather, it brings into view the concepts, styles and practical strategies that hijras adopt to do, redo and undo masculine and feminine genders. Attention to the processes and practices through which gender is operationalized in the lives of hijras further complicates notions of masculinity and femininity. Most significantly, male femininity here brings into view the way hijras can be simultaneously hyper-masculine and hyper-feminine.

A dominant trend within South Asian masculinities studies, and masculinities studies in general, is to attend to the way the production of masculinities entails the consequent de-masculinization of some other groups. While this relational approach to the formation of masculinities has unpacked systems of cultural and political inequalities and sharpened our understanding of the workings of masculinities, what is rarely interrogated is the way such one-sided, stereotypical representation of certain social groups as emasculate conceals the negotiation of complex processes and practices through which those deemed to be emasculate both gender themselves and are gendered (Osella and Osella 2006; Rogers 2008). Scholarly inability to engage with the processes and practices of marginalized members of society further contributes to such stereotypical projections and inhibits nuanced conceptualizations of masculinities. In this connection, the 'male femininity' approach can attend to such complex negotiations by accounting for the way in which the marginal subject, including hijras, variably engage with the non-hijra, most notably the middle- and upper-class populace in Bangladesh, who routinely demonize and vulgarize them. Hijras, in the cultural imagination of Bangladesh, are a class-specific category not least because only people from the working class enter the hijra community, but more importantly because of the way hijras are described and defined in terms of class-marked imageries of filth, foul smell and dirt. Such a middle-class representation, however, does not help us understand the variable negotiation of masculinities in real-life situations, where the very presence of hijras instantiates masculine anxieties and fear among the non-hijra populace. Here a male femininity brings into view the ways hijras imagine and construct themselves, rather than reading them in terms of the discursive abstraction of the middle-class imaginary.

A male femaling perspective also challenges the scholarly proclivity to read the hijras as either intentionally subversive or politically resistant to real or imagined structures of inequalities and repressive gender and erotic regimes. Put in other words, what a male femininity approach enables us to acknowledge and appreciate is that the enactment and instantiation of varied forms of gender and erotic pluralisms (Peletz 2009) by hijras are not some means to an abstract end of dismantling sex/gender dimorphism, but are very much the ends in themselves. That is, instead of reading hijras as either politically inclined subjects bent on resistance or some kind of a gender failure in the guise of an intermediate category, a male femaling perspective attends to the everyday lived arts and acts through which hijras construct themselves and are constructed by the wider society as both gendered and gendering subjects.

The use of transgender as an optic in the study of hijras

'Transgender' emerged as a term across South Asia at some point in the late 1990s with the advent of the HIV/AIDS epidemic, and its subsequent prevention programmes and activism. Today it is not just a popular word used by the mainstream to describe gender-variant people such as hijras in particular, but it has also become a mode of self-identification for many gender-variant people. However, the use of transgender as a universal signifier works to not only perpetuate Euro-America-centric assumptions about gender and sexuality, but also obscure the socio-historical and cultural contexts out of which sex/gender subjectivities in any locale emerge (Towle and Morgan 2002; Valentine 2007). More important, and particularly pertinent to this book, is David Valentine's observation that the rise to popularity of the term 'transgender' is a recent phenomenon rooted in a specific social history and power relation. 'Transgender' emerged as a collective category of personhood in the United States from an aprioristic distinction between gender and sexuality as discrete ontological domains. Valentine argues that people who do not fit into the gay and lesbian categories are relegated to the status of transgender, that is, while gay and lesbian are deemed to be sexual constructs, transgender is understood to originate in gender (see also Dutta 2013). It is this fundamental analytic distinction that works to impose fixity on the lived lives of people for whom experiences are not compartmentalized but are integrated. It is precisely because of such a de-sexualizing tendency that the adoption of transgender in the study of hijras can work to further deflect our attention from the structural inequalities of gender and sexuality that produces the hijra subject.

Another serious problem worth highlighting is the way transgender has become an umbrella reference point used solely to designate feminine-identified people typically assigned a male gender at birth, a cross-cultural pattern, often to the blatant exclusion of the female-born, male-identified people. While this is a serious omission that can be explained in terms of a generic cultural devaluation of femininity (Valentine 2007), the recent emergence of various non-hijra trans-feminine and trans-masculine groups further brings into view the problems of the narrow use of transgender as a global code for hijras. Furthermore, while the diffusion of the transgender category has allowed for new opportunities for hijras across South Asia to forge transnational alliances with other gender-variant groups elsewhere through conferences, networking and travel, it also works to engender a new hierarchy in which hijras become the embodiment of an indigenous and traditional, but also backward and non-respectable subject position when compared to the modern and modernizing transgender community (Dutta and Roy 2014; Hossain and Nanda 2020).

Ethnographic site, scale and critical regionalism

Much of the substantial scholarship on hijras is narrowly centred on India (Hossain 2018). One consequence of this Indo-centricity is that, in popular Western imagination, hijras are often deemed as iconic figures of Indian gender and sexual difference. There is also a growing body of scholarship on hijras in Pakistan (see, for example, Khan 2016; Pamment 2010, 2019a, 2019b), but in contrast very little research and publication concern hijras in Bangladesh.[3] More problematically, the lack of attention to hijras outside India works to perpetuate not only the spatio-intellectual hegemony of India within South Asian studies of gender and sexuality, but also forecloses new lines of analytical possibility (Hossain 2018).

In a significant departure from the conventional focus of studies on India, this ethnographic monograph grows out of an empirical research involving hijras in Dhaka, the capital of Bangladesh. Spread over 300 square kilometres and home to an estimated 18 million people, Dhaka is now a huge, fast-growing, modern metropolis.[4] With massive inequalities in wealth, slum-dwellers make

---

[3] However, there has been nascent research interest in hijras in Bangladesh in recent years. See, for example, Hossain (2012, 2017, 2020), Hussain (2013, ch. 3) and Khan et al. (2008).

[4] See https://worldpopulationreview.com/world-cities/dhaka-population (accessed 1 January 2021).

up around 40 per cent of the population.[5] The poor are crammed into sprawling shanty towns. Dhaka is a major hub of hijras, most of whom live in shanty towns. The actual number of hijras in Bangladesh is in dispute, with estimates ranging from 10,000 to 100,000.[6] People typically talk about Dhaka in terms of old and new Dhaka. According to my hijra interlocutors, old Dhaka, located on the banks of the Buriganga river, was the traditional stronghold of the hijras. But with time as the city expanded, the hijras too spread out. Today hijras are spatially distributed all over Dhaka.

Situated between the old and new Dhaka, Hridoypur, a pseudonym[7] I use to protect the identities of my interlocutors, has one of the largest concentrations of slums in the Dhaka metropolitan area. About fifty hijras live in this area. Although I conducted fieldwork with hijras all over Dhaka and beyond, the principal group of hijras I befriended and worked closely with was based in Hridoypur. Hijras in Hridoypur, like any other hijra group, did not live together in one house in an isolated manner. Rather, they were spread out within the area. Many from the hijra group in Hridoypur travelled not only to other parts of Bangladesh, but also to various cities in India. There were also hijras in Hridoypur who were part of hijra groups in various areas of West Bengal and Delhi in India. Although extant ethnographies of hijras often highlight country or nationwide networks of hijras within India, trans, inter- and intra-regional networks, flows and movement are rarely acknowledged as significant factors in the crafting of hijra subjectivity (Hossain 2018). Thus, while my focus is on hijras in Dhaka, Bangladesh, I am very much aware of the limits of an approach premised on either cultural particularism (Johnson 1998) or a national frame of reference (Hossain 2018). Rather, I approach the hijra subject as configured by various frequent comings and goings of symbolic and material forces across South Asia and beyond (Johnson, Jackson and Herdt 2000; Wilson 2006). While recent waves of

---

[5] See https://www.citiesalliance.org/newsroom/news/urban-news/climate-migration-drives-slum-growth-dhaka?fbclid=IwAR22i_7_TpSIe-kcjgFLY0wtUDgKTMoxaNk390XmxAZCQVf9UjrwUvujG6k (accessed 1 January 2021).

[6] While according to the ministry of social welfare, there are around 10,000 hijras in Bangladesh, my hijra interlocutors always disputed this figure and argued the total number of hijras to be nearing 100,000. See https://msw.gov.bd/ for further details on estimates by the government of Bangladesh.

[7] Throughout the text, I have used pseudonyms for all my interlocutors and the places they inhabit to protect their identities, except when they explicitly wished for their real names to be used.

globalization have brought to the forefront the role of flows and movement in the formation of hijra subjectivity, hijras in Bangladesh and India have long been connected through a transregional hijra network and have crossed borders to participate in various hijra rituals (Hossain and Nanda 2020). In other words, hijra conceptualization of ritual jurisdiction confounds various categorical boundaries, including the national cartographies of India and Bangladesh, forcing us to discard national or nationalist frames of reference in the study of gender and sexual diversity (Gopinath 2007; Hossain 2018).

On method and entanglement

I was exposed to the word 'hijra' as a child when a male-born person who did not conform to normative notions and practices of masculinity was employed as a cook in my house. Both relatives and immediate neighbours denigrated this person, labelling him as a hijra, a slur that eventually led to his leaving us without any notice. Some of my early recollections of hijras are from my childhood experiences in a football field next to which a band of hijras lived in a dilapidated tin house. Every afternoon, on my way to and from the playground, I would notice some of them sitting idly on the roof basking in the sun and casually combing each other's hair. As I grew older, I was exposed to hijras in public space and realized that 'hijra' was not only a term used specifically to designate 'effeminate' males in everyday settings, but also was employed to refer to publicly visible organized groups who were starkly different from the normative mainstream on account of their gender-variant sartorial presentation and their putatively missing or defective genitals. It was in around 1999, however, that I made efforts to connect with hijra groups as an undergraduate student with the curiosity to understand them.

While my informal interactions with various hijra groups have continued since 1999, I systematically conducted fieldwork with hijras in Dhaka between September 2008 and September 2009, followed by at least one or two short visits every year to date. Most of the data presented here is drawn from this extended period of my observation and interactions with hijras. During my one-year fieldwork in Dhaka, I visited Hridoypur three to four times per week. In the evenings, I also visited some of the popular cruising sites in Dhaka to meet people from other hijra groups. My main method of eliciting data was participant observation. However, it was not only the sites in which my interlocutors operated as hijras where I did my research. Rather, many hijras were also frequent visitors to my house in Dhaka and participated in social events and gatherings with my family and friends. Thus, the distinction between my personal life and professional ethnographic interest became blurred in the process of my research with hijras. In addition, the 'data' from my participant observation consisted both of ethnographic field notes and transcribed material from digital recordings of informal and directed conversations, as well as selected interactions and exchanges at public events. I wrote up field notes based on observations and recollections at the end of each day after returning to my home in Dhaka. I supplemented my field notes with transcriptions of recordings from a small digital recorder that I carried with me on a daily basis. The digital recorder was used to record informal and more directed conversations with hijras in Hridoypur, as well as some of their conversations with visiting hijras. I also made recordings of their performances and their interactions with people in the wider society in Hridoypur. My hijra interlocutors in Hridoypur consented to my using the recorder.

Unlike many ethnographers starting out in a new place and facing immense difficulties in finding the right connections, my entering into the lives of hijras to conduct systematic inquiry was not very difficult as I already had developed deep connections with several hijra groups in Dhaka. Here it is important to add while I entered the field as a male-born, male-identified, middle-class subject in Bangladesh, my subject position throughout my fieldwork also shifted depending on the socio-spatial location of my encounter with the hijras. In Hridoypur because of my long-term presence and regular visits, the majority of hijras thought I was a lover of one of the hijra leaders. Suspicions also grew among many hijras about the possibility of my being a *parik*, the hijra word for a partner or a husband, or a hijra myself, especially because of my being *pakki*, the hijra expression to refer to someone who is deeply aware of and trained in hijra practice and values.

Most significantly, hijras in Hridoypur initially refused to accept the fact that I was trying to research hijras. My initial attempts to clarify my position further intensified their belief that I was indeed a lover but a secretive one who stays away but makes occasional visits. While the very possibility of a putative romance with a normatively gendered and middle-class person at times worked to my advantage, especially when approaching a new hijra group, my refusal to engage in sexual activities with hijras led many to think that I was a hijra myself in the guise of a man. My mastery of Ulti, the clandestine hijra argot which signifies community membership or some sort of a loose association with hijras, aroused further suspicion that I might be a hijra. There were in fact several people attached to the hijra group in

Hridoypur who would dress like a male or publicly comport themselves in a normatively masculine manner, and because of societal pressure could not publicly identify as a hijra or be part of a hijra group.

While the dynamics of my interaction with the working-class hijras in Dhaka are variously elaborated in my chapters on class-cultural politics and erotic desire, here I just want to highlight one issue that recurred throughout my fieldwork. Having befriended hijras in Hridoypur and participated in many of their rituals, which are otherwise inaccessible to outsiders, I always felt extremely privileged to be a part of not only their quotidian lives, but also special ritually marked festivities. Yet time and again my closest hijra interlocutors explicitly instructed me to stay at a remove from them or pretend not to be with them, especially during some of the ritual practices in which either hijras of other areas or members of the wider society were present. Three such ritual events that I elaborate on in later chapters are *cholla*, the hijra collection of money from the bazaar; *badhai*, the acts of demanding gifts at birth; and *night kam*— that is, sex work in the public gardens. In the case of badhai, in which they performed before a mainstream audience and blessed newborn children, they often advised me to act like any other curious bystander gleefully gazing at their performance, while in the cruising sites I was specifically instructed to observe the events from a safe distance so that their clients did not become suspicious of my presence. There were also ritual occasions like *baraiya* (a festival undertaken to mark the rebirth of a newly emasculated hijra, which I discuss in my chapter on emasculation) when I was instructed to appear in the role of an amanuensis and write down the names of the guests and their gifts. What I briefly allude to here are some examples of 'distancing strategies' suggested by my interlocutors. While these strategies helped me to acquire more information about hijras, these strategies could also be read as examples of the rules set by the hijra group that I was expected to abide by in their space.

How the book unfolds

The first chapter, 'Kinship, Community and *Hijragiri*', situates the hijra category within the broader matrix of culturally recognized 'male femininities'. It not only focuses on the various groups of male-born, feminine-identified people, but also highlights the similarities and differences among these various groups. Although these variably situated groups are often embroiled in conflicts and contestations over authenticity, they share a similar working-class background and a desire for 'masculine' men. Over the life course, a male-born, feminine-identified individual may switch from one group to the other or may variably belong to all these groups simultaneously. One crucial difference between the *sadrali hijra*s, those following the occupation of the hijra goddesses, and that of the other groups is a difference in the degree of possession of ritual knowledge and formal affiliation. Yet these groups are entangled through a complex web of kinship networks with the sadrali hijras acting as the quintessential marker of hijras against and in relation to which other groups negotiate and assert their identities. Conflicts and contestations over authenticity among these groups underscore not only the micro-politics of power, but also the performative conquest of normative masculinity and its relation to claiming authentic hijra status within the public space.

Chapter 2, 'Class-Cultural Politics and the Making of *Hijras*', underlines the constitutive role of social class in the social production and construction of hijra as a category of abjection. Although hijras are a visibly organized public subculture in Bangladesh, not only are the middle and upper classes hostile to and prejudiced against hijras, but also hijras often become the language employed to speak about gender variance and lack of respectability. Hijras are a class-specific category comprising only working-class male-bodied, feminine-identified people. Hijras in Dhaka are spatially in tune with their working-class neighbours, who also act as their chief patrons. Elaborating two ritualized hijra occupational practices, namely badhai (demanding gifts at birth) and cholla (collecting money and foodstuffs from the bazaar), various sorts of agencies that hijras appropriate and exercise in soliciting recognition as hijras are highlighted. While the middle-class understanding of hijras is informed by flimsy media reportage and medicalizing discourses which work to de-masculinize and demonize hijras, this class-cultural abjection of hijras paradoxically confers on them a different sort of masculinity that calls into question the power of the stereotypical middle-class representation.

Chapter 3, '*Hijra* Erotic Subjectivities: Pleasure, Practice and Power', turns to erotic desire and its erasure in the conceptualization of hijras. Desire is not peripheral but central to the hijras' sense of selfhood. While desire is paramount to hijra subjectivity, it is through a particular manifestation of that desire in the form of anal receptivity that one can lay claim to authentic hijra status. There is, however, a major paradox pertaining to desire and its public proclamation. Although publicly hijras almost inevitably present themselves as people without and above desire, internally it is this publicly denounced desire that qualifies one to identify and be recognized as a hijra. This dilemma and ambivalence between internal knowledge and external projection is foregrounded in the hijra invention and use of a clandestine language known as Ulti. Ulti is a coded way of signalling communitarian belonging and a shared sense of desire for normative men. The very deployment of this semiotic system indexes the limits of Bangla, the predominant spoken language in Bangladesh, as an appropriate medium to convey those desires. Put differently, the very existence of Ulti and its use by hijras and other male-bodied, feminine-identified people bring into view the unspeakable nature of desire that hijras deem central to their sense of selves; that is, not just desire for 'masculine men', but more particularly for the pleasure of being anally penetrated by them. Navigating through the apparently inscrutable realm of Ulti complicates the popularly understood and scholastically sanctioned tropes of hijra asexuality and their resonance with the broader cultural politics of renunciation by calling our attention to the centrality of lived and embodied desire in the construction of hijras. Significantly, hijras view accessibility to these culturally forbidden pleasures in terms of a principle of (dis)entitlement whereby only those ready to forego the Bangla-defined masculinity, specifically penile pleasures, in encounters with other male-bodied people, are allowed to partake of the hitherto undiscovered anal pleasures.

Chapter 4, 'The Paradox of Emasculation', expands the conceptualization of the hijra subject position by taking on emasculation, the most dominant trope in the representation of hijras in extant scholarship. Underscoring myths, rituals, bodily transformation and functional factors bearing on emasculation, I detail the practice and concept of emasculation as acted out in the context of the lives of hijras in Dhaka. While emasculation is deemed to confer on the operated individual a ritually superior position, such a position is not uncontested. That is precisely because the very mythic tale invoked by the emasculated hijras to authenticate their position also offers resources for the *janana*, or hijra with a penis, to challenge such authenticity. Furthermore, because emasculation does not, as is frequently assumed, render one asexual, since erotic desire is deemed by hijras to be located in the anus and not in the penis, conflicts and contestation over authenticity between hijras with a penis and those without frequently occur. The dominant scholarly representation of hijras as inhering in and flowing from emasculation is deeply problematic, as it assumes automatic conflations between circumcision, emasculation and Islam that in the Indian context serves to reinforce the Hindu nationalist stereotyped construal of Muslim men as either effeminate or hypersexual.

Following from emasculation, Chapter 5, 'Processes and Practices of Gendering', discloses multiple processes of gendering that hijras in Dhaka practise and perform. This chapter focuses on hijra notions of masculinity and femininity and the variable and contextual meanings of those practices in terms of both the wider Bangla mainstream gender ideologies and hijra appropriation of those Bangla protocols. That is, the very act of their taking on feminine sartorial trappings is not permanent, but episodic, with regular switches across and between varied masculine positions and feminine identifications. In fact, central to being an authentic hijra is the mastery of this very art of movement between and across heterosexual masculinities and feminine-marked hijra identifications. This fluidity is best captured through *ligam potano*, the physical art of magically (dis)appearing the penis. Although a physical art that hijras with a penis master, ligam potano is indexical of various agentic 'vanishing' acts—involving not only the corporeal penis but also the Lacanian phallus, namely heterosexual masculinities, households and marriage—through which hijra subjectivity is constructed.

In another significant departure from previous ethnographic work on hijras, Chapter 6, 'Love and Emotional Intimacy: *Hijra* Entanglement with Normative Bangla Men', examines the role lovers play in the life of my hijra interlocutors. The normatively inclined 'masculine' male partners form a significant part of the lifeworld of hijras in Dhaka. Despite the rhetoric of those Bangla men being masculine in their erotic and affective interaction with hijras, Bangla men's interactions with hijras exemplify a kind of doubly hidden 'male femininity' evident not only in their being 'domesticated' by hijras, but also through their entrance into the hijra lineage as affine. Unlike mainstream heterosexual Bangla relations, where brides enter the houses of their masculine husbands, hijra relations with their pariks, or intimate partners, illustrate a reversal of such culturally valorized ideals of heterosocial structure. Furthermore, the mobility of the partners is seen to be restricted not only in terms of how and to what extent they can interact with both hijras and the normative Bangla society, but also in terms of what is and is not acceptable in erotic play with hijras. Furthermore, the Ulti universe enables not only accommodation, but also cultural recognition of hijra–parik relationships that are otherwise forbidden within the mainstream Bangla world. The ethnographic elaboration of hijra affective affinity for and entanglement with partners underscores the complex processes of the formation of masculinities wherein both hijras and their partners co-constitute each other's gender. Although partners are presented here mainly through the lens of hijras, partners' participation, albeit circumscribed, in the hijra communitarian rules and rituals complicates the conventionally assumed tightly drawn lines of demarcation between hijras and Bangla men.

Chapter 7, 'Contemporary Transformation of *Hijra* Subjectivities', focuses on the way non-governmental organizations (NGOs) and various transnational movements continue to shape the hijra subculture. In the wake of state and predominantly NGO interventions in Bangladesh, a plethora of often contradictory discourses and categories on same-sex sexualities and hijras have emerged. Two main significant phenomena are the emergence of various sorts of discourses pertaining to same-sex sexualities and hijras and the proliferation of various kinds of identity categories. Discourses pertaining to hijra sexuality as both criminal and pathological gained an added impetus on account of the recent exposure to hijra vulnerability to HIV/AIDS. Additionally, the efflorescence of these varied discourses has been linked with a proliferation of varied identity labels in contemporary Bangladesh, circulated mainly through the symbolic capital of NGOs. Specifically, the rise of transgender has reduced the hijras to a feminine-identified subject position, requiring male-bodied, feminine-identified people to publicly present themselves in a prescribed feminine manner. While the emergence of these varied but often contradictory discourses and categories is increasingly challenging not only the popular perception of hijras as asexual and disfigured, but even their very accommodation within the Bangladeshi social structure, hijras are not mere victims of these transnational governmentality and disciplinary regimes, but are active players in appropriating and adapting those newly available resources and idioms.

The conclusion, 'Shifting Meaning and the Future of *Hijras*', turns to the question of the likely transformation of the hijra subculture in the face of various ongoing processes and changes. The deeply embedded position of hijras within the Bangladeshi social structure, on the one hand, exemplifies a form of resolution of gender and erotic incommensurability. On the other hand, the cultural space occupied by the hijras also indexes supra-locality. Hijras are a part of the Bangladeshi social world, yet they are outside of the mainstream precisely on account of their inhabiting an alternative semiotic and symbolic space of desire that is neither readily accessible nor intelligible to the wider society. However, this present accommodation of hijras is now being challenged on multiple fronts. Reminiscent of British colonial policies, the conventional occupations of hijras are now targeted as archaic and criminal, as new initiatives to transform hijras into citizens worthy of rights and recognition proliferate. At the same time, hijras are increasingly being incorporated into the transnational world of LGBTI (Lesbian, Gay, Bisexual, Transgender and Intersex) movement, engendering both friction and new opportunities for the crafting of subjectivities.

1 Kinship, Community and *Hijragiri*

One afternoon I was in the house of Joynob, a *hijra guru*, in Savar on the outskirts of Dhaka. Suddenly a few *cela*s (disciples) of Joynob arrived after finishing their day's work. Handing Joynob cash and foodstuff collected from the bazaar, they[1] started talking about two people they had encountered there. The celas explained that while on their way back, they had met two *vabrajer chibry*s, that is, hijras born straight from the wombs of their mothers. Dubious, Joynob's celas inspected those two persons and found that they had genital ambiguity. Those two individuals had stopped the hijra group and wanted to join them. Joynob was enraged and warned their celas to stay away from such people. Later Joynob argued that those 'born hijras' are dangerous and even looking at their faces can spell disaster.

The vignette above underscores one of the central concerns of this chapter: what is a hijra? If, as Joynob contends, those born hijras are dangerous, then what is the status of Joynob? What are their celas like? Are Joynob and their celas 'real' hijras and if so, on what basis do they make the claim to be such? In this chapter, I navigate these questions to better understand the contestation over what it means to be a hijra in Dhaka and the various markers of authenticity and differentiation that hijras employ to assert their identities.

In her monograph, Reddy (2005a) offers a contextual ethnography of variably situated *koti* groups in the context of the south Indian cities of Hyderabad and Secunderabad. 'Koti' serves as a generic all-encompassing identity within which several non-normatively oriented groups, including the

---

[1] The third person singular pronoun in Bengali is uninflected by gender. Although scholars have conventionally used 'her' in the representation of the hijras, throughout this book, I use 'them' instead of 'her' (and also they/their instead of she/her) to demonstrate and capture the context-specific and fluid nature of hijra gender performativity and various movements in and out of masculinity and femininity that characterize the hijra subject position.

hijras, belong. She contends that while several groups of male-born, feminine-identified koti groups exist there, these various groups often assert their moral superiority over others in a bid to claim authenticity. Her main contention is that all these groups identify sexual receptivity as central to their sense of koti identity, as opposed to men, whom they define in terms of the penetrative role. Stressing the fact that these groups are not reducible to gender and sexual difference alone, Reddy foregrounds various markers of differentiation, namely religion, class, language and desire, kinship, occupation and bodily practice as salient to the contextual construction of 'thirdness' and competing claims over authenticity. To this important list of factors, Reddy adds what she calls 'a moral economy of respect' in terms of which these groups negotiate and claim authenticity. In deploying this trope of respectability, the most important rhetoric invoked by her interlocutors is that of emasculation and its associated image of asexuality. In other words, it is on account of emasculation and asexuality that the south Indian hijras claim to be the most superior and authentic of all the diverse groups within the koti universe. Reddy locates this trope of asexuality within the broader cultural valorization of renunciation and emasculation in the Indian context, arguing that this trope works to set hijras apart from other groups who, although often linked with hijras, are placed below them in a ladder of hierarchical valuations.

Reddy's analysis is particularly relevant to my discussion of various markers of authenticity deployed by several male-born, feminine-identified groups in Dhaka. A key distinction here is that although hijras in Dhaka too always inevitably invoke the trope of their being 'born that way' and asexual, respectability in the context of my fieldwork accrues from the ability to conduct *hijragiri*, or the occupation of hijras, regardless of one's genital status. While, as suggested in detail below, various markers of differentiation, namely occupation, ritual knowledge and formal affiliations, are variably employed by the male-born, feminine-identified groups in Dhaka, *sadrali hijra*s claim to be the most authentic of the hijra groups, not only because of their association with putatively missing or defective genitals, but also because of their possession of ritual knowledge and skills and the ability to demonstrate these before both fellow male-born, feminine-identified groups and society at large. In terms of authenticity, another key distinction worth underscoring is that emasculation in the Bangladeshi context does not resonate with cultural ideals of renunciation per se. Rather, emasculation, as I suggest in detail in chapter 4, primarily confirms one's status of being effeminate, asexual and disfigured.

Because of this popular conflation of hijras with missing or defective genitals, there is a widespread perception among the public that hijras forcefully abduct and castrate men to enhance their member base. Equally strong is the idea that hijras snatch newborn children with ambiguous genitalia by force during the performance of *badhai* (the practice of demanding gifts at birth and conferring blessings on the newborn, which I discuss in chapter 2) as a way to surreptitiously confirm said genital ambiguity. To the best of my knowledge, those who join hijras in Dhaka do so voluntarily. There is no element of coercion in recruitment, as is often claimed in the popular press. It is also worth pointing out that persons born biologically female but incapable of menstruating are not part of the hijra community in Bangladesh (cf. Nanda 1999, 15, 18). I never heard of a single case where a female, due to her inability to menstruate, became or was identified as a hijra. It is on account of neither embodied ambiguity nor a lack of penile prowess or sexual potency that one becomes a hijra. Rather, it is the desire for 'masculine' men that my interlocutors contend defines them as hijras. While I analyse the gendering of this desire in chapter 5, suffice it to say that when hijras talk about desiring 'masculine' men, they speak in terms of their desire to be anally penetrated, and it is this receptive desire that my interlocutors argued is what makes one a hijra, regardless of whether one is a part of a formal hijra group or not.

There are in contemporary Bangladesh several groups of people who in popular imagination are classed as hijras. While these various groups of male-born, feminine-identified people, as already suggested earlier, possess some shared commonalities, there is also subtle and at times pronounced distinction on the basis of which each of these groups seeks not only to legitimize its position, but in many cases also to assert its moral superiority over other groups. What are the shared similarities among these various groups of people? How are they different from each other, and, more importantly, what are the criteria on the basis of which such distinctions are drawn by hijras themselves? Can one be a part of different groups at the same time? In analysing these disjunctures and similitudes, I do not mean to impose any fixity onto any of these groups. Rather, my intention here is to demonstrate ethnographically how each of these groups talks about the others and the various idioms of distinction that each group deploys in a bid to assert their authenticity over the others.

The main analytical aim of this chapter, therefore, is to offer a broader picture of male-to-male gender and sexual variance in Bangladesh. It is in relation to this broader context of gender and sexual diversity that hijras become culturally intelligible subjects in Bangladesh. While these various groups, I suggest later, may not always identify themselves as hijras, more often than not they are embedded into the same spatio-cultural context where hijra-identified groups operate. Locating hijras within such contexts, therefore, pre-empts any tendency to distil hijras as a fixed category. Attending to the contextual cultural complexities within which hijra subjectivities are embedded allows me to nuance hijras not as some reified 'third', but as a prominent variant of 'male femininity' within the broader context of male-to-male homo-social configuration of Bangladesh. Here, a caveat is necessary. While I present these various groups separately, the actual empirical context in which I observed these groups defies such neat compartmentalization. In that sense, the artificial segregation of these various groups amounts to reducing the very complexities of the lives of the hijras that I am keen on unpacking. However, as will be made clear, it is precisely through paying attention to these differences and similarities that we may be able to make sense of hijras as a culturally constructed subject position.

In organizing this chapter, I first offer a brief discussion on the various ways hijras as a publicly recognizable group are defined and understood by the wider society. I draw a distinction between hijra self-definitions and that of the wider society, particularly highlighting the hijra-gendered view of the cosmos. I elaborate that although there are various male-born, feminine-identified groups, one commonality that binds all these groups is a shared desire for normative masculine men. Four such groups I elaborate are *dhurrani*, *gamchali*, *bagicha* and sadrali hijras; these groups are not only publicly recognizable but also have their own internal networks and rules. Finally, I draw attention to the fact that although these various groups can be distinguished from one another on the basis of various markers of differentiation, empirically there is considerable overlap not only in terms of rules and rituals, but also in terms of individuals' simultaneous membership of various groups.

The sadrali view on the social universe

In what follows, I describe the social universe as explained to me by my hijra interlocutors. I do so primarily through the lens of sadrali hijras, that is, those who conduct hijragiri, not least because they are the most organized and publicly visible of all the groups I describe here, but also because sadrali hijras deem themselves and are deemed by other groups to be the apotheosis of hijragiri. In hijra conceptualization, the universe is composed of three types of people. These are (*a*) *panthi*, or man, (*b*) *neharun*, or woman and (*c*) hijra/koti. I enlarge upon these categories in chapter 5; here, I only introduce how hijras define these types. It is also worth noting that this view also corresponds to the mainstream understanding of gender in Bangladesh, although the mainstream terms to describe those categories differ from those of hijras. A panthi, according to hijras, is someone who is inherently and essentially a penetrator, as opposed to a neharun or a hijra/koti, who are receptors. In this configuration, both neharuns and hijras are conceived in opposition to the penetrating panthi.

Given the popular and scholarly conceptualization of hijras as 'handicapped' and castrated, it is very difficult to imagine hijras without any reference to a discourse of biological defect or lack. I interrogate and challenge this view in chapter 2. Here, I would like to highlight that it is neither genital defect nor intersexual condition, castration or impotence for which one becomes a hijra. On the contrary, many of those who become hijras also define themselves as successful normative householding men. Yet they become hijras to be able to explore varied gender and erotic possibilities that are otherwise unavailable to normatively masculinized subjects in Bangladesh.

That genital defect or asexuality becomes the starting point for analysing hijras partly arises from the fact that hijras always present themselves accordingly in public. In reality, however, there are hijras with penises as well as those without; more significantly, those who get rid of their penises and scrotums do so neither because of impotence nor because of some genital ambiguity or deformity. All my interlocutors who underwent emasculation maintained that they had well-functioning male genitals and it was precisely on account of the functionality of their genitals, and an associated sense of embarrassment due to their having penises, that they underwent emasculation. Hijras in general, however, deny not only the functionality of their penises but, more importantly, the very fact of their being endowed with penises in the first place. While hijras make such claims to 'disfigurement' in public and often display intense pride on being born that way, my ethnographic materials suggest a different story. In a nutshell, one becomes a hijra not because of some inherent genital defect or one's inability to perform normative masculinity, but because of one's desire for normative men. And it is this shared desire for normative masculine men that binds the various male-born, feminine-identified people that I elaborate below.

Categorical fluidity and the debate over hijra versus koti

One evening I was strolling through a park with a few sadrali (those who wear feminine-identified clothes) hijras. As a group of middle-class males walked past from the other direction, my sadrali interlocutors cried out, 'Akkhar kholer koti!'—literally, 'koti of the rich household'. 'Koti' as a label denotes effeminate males. Sadralis claim it to be a hijra argot and use it to refer to any man whom they consider to be effeminate and desirous of other men. Another example leaps to mind. Once, a friend of mine came to visit Hridoypur, an area in Dhaka where I conducted prolonged fieldwork. Hijras in Hridoypur later wondered if he was a koti. When I asked why they had thought so, they argued that his bodily comportment and style of talking were typical 'koti-pona', that is, akin to the mannerisms of a koti. When I wondered why they thought he was a koti rather than a hijra, they argued that all hijras are koti, but not all kotis are hijra.

Hijras in Hridoypur and elsewhere would often address each other as koti. Sadralis explained that they called each other koti rather than hijra as the word 'hijra' has stigma attached to it. They also maintained that 'koti' is an alternative term for 'hijra' that they use to avoid being understood in public. Sadralis also often use the expression 'Bangla koti' to refer to those unschooled in hijra mores. Bangla is the predominant mainstream language. So a 'Bangla koti' is someone who desires men and is effeminate, but is unaware of the secret Ulti universe of hijras, a topic on which I expand in chapter 3. Another expression hijras often use is 'kari koti'—literally, a koti in the guise of a man. So to skeletonize, 'koti' in hijra argot is used as a generic term to refer to 'effeminate' males who desire other 'masculine' men, and it is on account of this desire that one is a 'koti', independent of any formal affiliation. While I expound on the gendering central to this construction later in this book, suffice it to say here that 'koti' as a generic label encompasses all male-born, feminine-identified people who desire normative masculine men. The complexities pertaining to the cultural context in which such labels are used as a mode of self and ascribed identification will become clearer in the discussion of four main groups of people below. It is, however, important to indicate that the main descriptive labels that I use are those articulated by the sadrali group, although the views of each of these groups also inform my elaboration. Sadralis spoke about these groups mostly in relation to my questions about the status of these other groups, while at times discussion emerged either when members of these non-sadrali groups attended some of the events organized by the sadrali hijras or during our casual encounter with these groups. Owing to a lack of documentation of these various groups in Bangla, the mainstream language wherein all these groups are popularly classed as hijra, the etymological trajectories of these terms are hard to determine. Yet members of some of these groups, as will be specified below, often trace their lineage to a long-running but unspecified past. In describing themselves, the non-sadrali groups on the one hand acknowledged many self-referential terms to be part of the sadrali hijra argot, while on the other resisted some of the labels used by sadralis to describe them.

Bagicha kotis

Dressed in normative male attire, troupes of youthfully flamboyant males congregate once or twice a week in a large public garden in Dhaka to enact feminine-gendered performance and cruise for men. The word 'bagicha' literally means 'garden', and is used by sadrali hijras to refer to these groups of kotis. These koti groups, however, describe themselves only as koti. Although these groups of kotis never explicitly self-referenced themselves as 'garden koti', I use this expression to describe them as it is mostly in such large garden premises that they act out their koti-like behaviours. Garden kotis gather in public gardens from afternoon onwards typically to undertake what they call 'ulu jhulu', which can loosely be translated as 'fun'. Garden kotis use this expression to refer specifically to experimentation with their bodies, dancing, singing and cruising for men. Garden kotis at times put on lipstick and makeup. Some also pad out their chest with 'ilu ilu'—condoms filled with water. Even though they are normatively attired, their tight-fitting clothes and choice of bright colours mark them out from other normative crowds in the garden.

More importantly, garden kotis speak Ulti, the hijra argot that I discuss at length in chapter 3. Relatively young in age, garden kotis live with their natal families and switch to a normative masculine mode once they leave these park or garden premises. My visits to such gardens always left me with the impression that there was never a shortage of such kotis, as old frequenters would be replaced by new faces within a very short span of time. For instance, kotis I befriended and saw to be present in one public garden regularly in 2009 were no longer around when I went back there in 2010. Many of the kotis I knew later joined the sadrali hijra group (see later), while others took up work in NGOs. Some were still frequenting the gardens but as casual visitors, while those with NGOs were acting as peer educators providing information about safe sex. There was also a strong contingent of a middle-class, gay-identified group in this public garden that I do not discuss here, but suffice it to state here that hijra and koti groups identify these middle-class gay men as kotis, though middle-class gay men consciously seek to distance themselves from kotis/hijras even as they cruise in the same area and seek sex with them. The divide here is primarily one of class, a thread I will pick up in chapter 2.

Garden kotis form a human ring while they dance in turn inside the circle to music playing from mobile phones. Bystanders, mostly male visitors, gather and watch while kotis make sexual overtures to them. All the kotis I spoke to argued that they were both kotis and hijras. Chanchal, who had been cruising in a park for the last two years, maintained that although they were not a sadrali hijra, their guru was. Aziz, another garden koti, once related, 'We are koti. We have many colours. Sometimes we are men, sometimes women and sometimes a bit of both.' In public gardens where kotis do *ulu jhulu* (Figure 1.1), the bystanders I spoke to always termed these kotis as 'hijra'. No one I interacted with knew the word 'koti'.

The majority of these garden kotis hail from lower-class backgrounds. Unlike the kotis in Delhi observed by Hall (2005), the garden kotis in Dhaka neither trace their lineage to Mughal times nor do they consider themselves

Figure 1.1 *Bagicha kotis* at a cruising site in Dhaka engaging in *ulu jhulu*
Source: Author.

to be a special group distinct from the hijra group. Rather, many of these kotis are intimately linked with hijra groups and are regular visitors to hijra households. The very first time I saw garden kotis was on the occasion of a *baraiya*. That garden kotis attend baraiya is significant, as hijras consider baraiya to be a quintessentially (sadrali) hijra ritual. Jomuna, a hijra guru in Hridoypur, pointing their finger at one of these garden kotis, once stated that they were their *puti cela* (great-grand-cela—see later on guru–cela relationship). Several hijras in Hridoypur were once regular frequenters of such gardens, but as they grew older and became full-time hijras they stopped visiting these 'dhurrani khol', the hijra expression for public gardens used to cruise for men.

Gamchali hijras

Groups of men dressed in *lungi* (a seamless tubular shape garment worn around the waist), *genji* (t shirts) and *gamcha* (a traditional Bangladeshi towel made up of thin, coarse, cotton fabric) are often seen to walk down the streets with swaying hips and exaggerated body movements. Although lungi, gamcha and genji are normative male attire, the gamchali group stands out by virtue of their crimson lips reddened from incessant chewing of betel leaves, plucked and threaded eyebrows and especially their style of wearing the gamcha. The way they wear the gamcha across the chest inevitably conjures up the image of the *orna*, a piece of cloth similar to a long scarf, worn across the breast by females in Bangladesh (Figure 1.2). Gamcha is the trademark of this group. It is important to note that despite gamcha being the distinctive marker of this group, they style themselves—and are popularly styled by the mainstream—as hijras. 'Gamchali' as an expression is used as a mark of differentiation within the wider community of male-born, feminine-identified people. I call them 'gamchali hijra' in line with the sadrali practice of describing them. While they generally do not identify themselves as gamchali hijra, they often highlighted their occupation and the visible marker of gamcha sartorial flourish as a way to set themselves apart from other groups. Gamchali hijras work in the burgeoning construction sites in Dhaka as cooks. Once a construction project is over, they move to a new construction site. Generally hailing from rural areas and low socio-economic backgrounds, most gamchali hijras are heterosexually married and their heteronormative families live in their home villages. They support their families with the income earned from cooking. In speaking of the origin of

Kinship, Community and *Hijragiri* 35

Figure 1.2 *Gamchali hijras* posing for a photo for the author
Source: Author.

this occupation, Mustafa, a gamchali guru, maintained that gamchali hijras are not a new phenomenon and have been in existence for a very long time. According to Mustafa, gamchali hijras were once considered a special group of people; they were routinely summoned to beat the roof of newly built houses with hyacinth, a practice that has become obsolete today (see also Gannon 2009, 188, for a discussion of hijras as cooks in historical documents).[2]

Gamchali hijras take pride in the fact that they do not beg or prostitute themselves but work for their living. Mustafa once related, 'Kormo koira khai'

---

[2] Some senior citizens in Dhaka also told me a similar story about hijras being summoned to beat the rooftop in the past. That hijras were summoned to undertake this task may very well have been the result of a wider societal conception about hijras being 'intermediate beings' with the power to connect the other-worldly with the worldly, and it was on account of such beliefs that they used to be summoned to sacralize the making of an abode. Such beliefs no longer persist in contemporary Bangladesh. Similar arguments have been advanced in relation to island Southeast Asia (Johnson 1997).

(We live by working). Hasina, another gamchali, stated, 'We are not like them. We do not take penis in the back like them. We work to earn money and live with it and we do not engage in sex work.' Gamchali hijras argue that they work as cooks as this is a 'soft' work that they as hijra are capable of doing, unlike men for whom hard work is reserved. Abida, another gamchali hijra, explained, 'I derive mental peace from cooking for men. Every day I cook twice for the workers in the site. Once in the morning and once in the evening. I go to the bazaar and buy foodstuffs. I also do the cleaning and I like my work.' There are about eight hundred of them in Dhaka, according to Mustafa, the leader of a gamchali hijra group. Mustafa maintains a register where they write the name of each newcomer to the group. Once a week, they all gather in a public park in Dhaka for rendezvous and dispute resolution. In line with the sadrali hijragiri (see later), Mustafa moderates such arbitrations. In the event/case of disrespecting one's guru, a *don* (compensation) is imposed. Mustafa maintains that although they are the main guru, there are others who are their *gothia*s (hijras of similar rank, that is, equal) but because of their efficiency and experience, they are the chief of this group.

Mustafa once related to me their story:

> My hijra life began back in my village. It was there I first learnt hijragiri [the hijra code of conduct]. During that time my guru used to come to Dhaka to work as a cook. They would stay in Dhaka for about five to six months and then come back. Once I went with my guru to Dhaka and worked with them. Later on as I got married in the village and fathered children, I stopped being a hijra openly. These days I come to Dhaka and work as a cook for a few months and then return.

Like Mustafa, there are several others in the gamchali group who were at some point affiliated on a full-time basis with a sadrali group. Zainal, another gamchali hijra, has been in this line of work for about twenty years now. They have a wife and three daughters living in the village whom they visit once a month. Shaon, another gamchali hijra, has been working as a cook for about ten years now. Prior to taking up cooking, they were a sadrali hijra in Medinipur, an area in India bordering Bangladesh. Shaon lived with the sadralis there for about six months and then came back as they could not cope with the hard work they had to do there. Although both Shaon and Zainal are now gamchali hijras, their first gurus, with whom they are still in touch, were sadralis. Both Shaon and Zainal stated that it is important to have a guru. 'How can you live without a guru? You may not be a sadrali but you need a guru,' related Zainal.

Sohel, also known as Soheli (Sohel is a male-identified name, while Soheli is female-identified), forty-five years of age, came to Dhaka recently from Chapai Nawabganj, a northern district in Bangladesh. Sohel was renamed Soheli by Kajol, a gamchali hijra, some twenty years younger than them. Kajol first chanced upon Sohel at a tea stall adjacent to a construction site. When I spoke to Soheli, they said Kajol was their guru, although they could not explain much about what this hierarchy meant. Being new to the hijra universe, Soheli had knowledge of neither Ulti nor the hijra code of conduct. When I inquired how Kajol had realized Soheli was one of them, Kajol explained that 'oisi akhhar dhurrani' (they are a big whore). Furthermore, Kajol maintained, 'When you look at someone you can tell whether that person desires a man or not.' In one of my regular visits to a bazaar where I would meet a gamchali group frequently, Rehana, a gamchali hijra, was initiating a new member into the group. I was told that although Abdul had been with the gamchali group for the last three months, they were yet to be made someone's cela. Rehana agreed to take Abdul as their new disciple. Rehana and I were sitting under a neon light in a tea stall sipping tea while Abdul, along with two other gamchali hijras, was sent off to buy a new gamcha for the initiation. Asking the hijras to be the witness, Rehana put the end of the gamcha on Abdul's head and a piece of sweet into Abdul's mouth. Then Rehana declared that from then on Abdul was their cela. Abdul then greeted Rehana with 'salamalaikum' (peace be on you), the standard Muslim greeting in Bangladesh.

Gamchali hijras denounced sex work vehemently. Kajol once related, 'We gamchalis do not need to do "night kam" [sex work], as we earn enough from cooking—but we all desire men (*panthi chis kori*) and that is why we are hijras.' They also maintained that gamchali hijras never take any men from the site of their work as *parik*, the hijra word for husband, as they do not want to lose their reputation as asexual in their workplace. Although gamchali hijras do not publicly dress like females, they do so on special occasions that they organize. In one such programme that a gamchali group in Dhaka arranged, several gamchali hijras dressed like females and danced and sang behind a construction site. One of the special guests of that programme was a sadrali hijra guru who turned up with a few of their sadrali members and blessed their gamchali hijra celas.

'Dhurrani' hijras

The word 'dhurrani' derives from the word 'dhur'—literally, 'to fuck'. 'Dhurrani' hijras are those who work as sex workers on a relatively permanent basis. 'Dhurrani', however, is not a self-referential term, but is used by all hijra groups to deride hijras associated with sex work. Hijras engaged in sex work refer to themselves simply as hijras, while the sadrali group (despite themselves being engaged in sex work) disparages the sex worker hijras as 'dhurrani'. The very first time I met a 'dhurrani' hijra was at a cruising site. Dressed in *salwar kameez* (a loose t-shirt and pyjama-style trousers), Mona was cruising in a public garden. Although there were several other hijras present, Mona seemed to be out of touch with the rest. Later I found out that Mona lives in a rented ramshackle apartment with five other 'dhurrani' hijras. All of them work as sex workers but in different locations. There are several such hijra groups in Dhaka whose members work as sex workers on a full-time basis.

The sadrali group (hijras with more elaborate rules and rituals who generally claim to be asexual) often condemn the 'dhurrani' hijras as 'the most despicable and fallen', and maintain that it is on account of the 'dhurrani' hijras that the reputation of sadrali or 'real' hijras has been damaged. 'Dhurrani' hijras, in contrast, argue that sadrali hijras are all 'velki', or fake. Tomali, a sex worker, once commented, 'There is not a single sadrali who does not have sex. Sadralis are more voracious sexually than us. They are the greatest whores (*bishoo dhurrani*). They just throw dust in the eyes of society so that they can earn money (*thappu*).'

'Dhurrani' hijras maintain some sort of a guru–cela hierarchy. For instance, Rikta, a full-time sex worker, once stated that they would never work in the *mazaar* (shrine) area as their celas work there. In some areas, however, I had discerned guru and cela to be cruising together, although often at a remove. 'Dhurrani' hijras dress like females during work and—unlike the bagicha koti discussed earlier—make their living exclusively through sex work.

While sadralis always publicly present themselves as asexual and above desire, the reality is that sadrali hijras too participate in sex work. In fact, there are 'dhurrani' hijras that are also part of the sadrali hijra group. For instance, both Rikta and Tomali, whom I have already mentioned, were full-time sadralis previously. Both of them are still linked with the sadrali group. There are also 'dhurrani' hijras who are sadrali by day, that is, they conduct ritually sanctioned work, namely *badhai* (demanding gifts at birth) and *cholla* (collecting money or foodstuffs from the bazaar), and sex workers by night. In

Hridoypur, several celas of Meghna, a sadrali guru, were full-time 'dhurrani' previously. There were also celas of Meghna who went to public gardens to sell sex at least twice a week. That celas of Meghna engaged in sex work was not unknown to Meghna, although initially they feigned ignorance. Later, when I grew close to Meghna, they spoke frankly about their celas' 'dhurrani' work. They insisted, however, that for hijragiri only money earned through ritually sanctioned means was used. Meghna maintained that as the guru, they had no right to the money that their celas earned though sex work. While sadralis publicly maintain a sharp distinction between themselves and the 'dhurrani' hijras and categorically deny any association with the latter, in reality one can be simultaneously sadrali and 'dhurrani'.

Sadrali hijras and their internal social structure

When people generally talk about hijras in Bangladesh, the image that leaps to mind is that of a group masculine in stature but feminine in attire walking down the busy streets of Dhaka clapping and demanding money and hurling raunchy comments at the public, especially men. This typical image corresponds most closely to the sadrali hijras. While the previously elaborated groups are also publicly recognizable, sadrali hijras are the most dominant and organized of all. In a way, the rules and regulations, including the use of Ulti, and the guru–cela hierarchy that the previously discussed groups observe, are all modelled on the sadrali practices. The word 'sadrali' literally denotes the state of being clad in a sari, or *sadra*.

Sadrali hijra argot is used to specifically single out this group of hijras. Sadrali hijras self-identify and are identified by other non-normative groups using that label. The import of sadrali here extends beyond the mere feminine-identified sartorial practices to refer to the ritual conduct of hijragiri—namely badhai and cholla, the two quintessentially sadrali hijra occupations. I elaborate these two practices at length in chapter 2; here, I simply highlight that it is on account of these ritually sanctioned occupational practices that the sadrali hijras distinguish themselves and are distinguished from other groups. Sadrali hijras believe that these occupational practices are the direct prescriptions of two primordial hijra archetypes—namely Maya Ji and Tara Moni, whom I discuss in chapter 4. Sadrali hijragiri is a 'way of life' centred on the occupation ordained by these two goddesses. Sadrali hijragiri entails a systematic mastering of rules and regulations and the ability to live up to those ideals on a daily basis. It is on the basis of formal initiation into this group and the subsequent acquisition of ritual acumen and practices that sadrali hijras make claims to be the real and most authentic hijras. One therefore has to learn the sadrali ways in a systematic manner through rigorous practice over time under a hijra's mentorship. In what follows, I unpack some of the organizational structuring principles of sadrali hijras.

Guru–cela hierarchy

Hijra social structure revolves around a guru–cela hierarchy. A guru has the role of a preceptor, and a cela is like a student or disciple. It is only under the aegis of a guru that a novice can be initiated into the hijra group. While a guru may have many celas under their command, celas too can in turn have celas under their discipleship. So important is this affiliation that a hijra is known throughout their life by the name of their guru. For instance, the very first question a hijra is asked when confronted by another hijra is, 'Whose cela are you?' or 'To whose *ghor* [house] do you belong?' Although ghor here signifies a symbolic lineage, what is essentially asked of a hijra is the name of the guru to whose house they belong. In other words, the guru becomes the marker of the ghor.

Hridoypur, where I spent a large amount of time during my fieldwork participating and observing the daily lives of hijras, is presided over by Jomuna, a nonagenarian hijra. Because of infirmity, Jomuna lives in another area along with their natal sister and brother-in-law. Jomuna inherited a small room from their natal family where they now spend their time. Jomuna has put Meghna, their cela, in charge of the *birit*, the ritual jurisdiction to which a hijra group is entitled in terms of performing cholla and badhai. Meghna, the cela of Jomuna, has around fifty hijras under their command, comprising not only their immediate celas but also *nati* and puti celas (grand-celas and great-grand-celas, as it were). While Meghna lives in a rented one-storey tin-shed room, their other celas live dotted across the area. Hijras in Hridoypur are all known as belonging to the ghor of Jomuna. Here, belonging to a ghor does not embody the physical habitation of a single household, but rather the symbolic lineage of Jomuna (Figure 1.3).

The reason Meghna has been given the task of overseeing the whole birit on Jomuna's behalf is not only because Meghna is the most trusted and loved of all Jomuna's celas but because of their capacity to manage the group. In order to become a guru, a sadrali hijra has to be able to manage the whole group, which entails being an expert in dispute resolution and, most significantly,

Kinship, Community and *Hijragiri*

Figure 1.3 Jomuna *hijra* with their *celas* in Hridoypur on a lazy afternoon
Source: Author.

possessing the knowledge of hijragiri. Within the sadrali hijra universe, status differentiation is not based on rigid, essential traits, such as age or socio-economic background. For instance, there are several celas of Meghna who are older than them. In hijragiri, one of the decisive factors for becoming a guru is not age but seniority, based on the time of one's entry into the group and subsequent acquisition of ritual knowledge and its skilful execution. In Dhaka, there are about twenty such houses, all of which are known by the name of the guru. Most of these gurus are gothias, or hijras of more or less similar rank. For instance, two celas of the same guru are gothias, while celas of celas of the same guru are their nati, or grand-celas. Although age is not technically a factor in becoming a guru, the twenty hijra ghors are all headed by older hijras.

Initiation rites

The entrance of a new cela is officiated in keeping with well-established rites of initiation. Typically, the ritual of initiation, or 'asla', as hijras call it, is conducted in the presence of the sponsoring guru, along with their existing celas and hijras from other houses. The word 'asla' derives from 'achol'—literally the end/hem of a sari. 'It is like being under the achol of your mother. Like mothers, gurus also keep the celas under their achol,' said Meghna, the hijra guru, during one initiation. 'Asla khawa', as hijras often say to refer to one's becoming a cela, is to come under the achol of a guru. Here, the word 'achol' is figurative, its meaning extending beyond the mere piece of cloth to encompass ideas of motherly care and nurturance. A guru bears all the expenses associated with the initiation rite. The sponsoring guru purifies a space on the floor and asks the initiand to sit on the 'purified space', before touching the head of the novice with the end of their sari. They then put a piece of sweet into the mouth of the novice, whereupon the initiand says 'salamalaikum' to the guru. From that moment onwards, the initiand becomes a cela and a new member of the hijra group. Typically, hijras from other ghors present during an initiation give out cash to the newly initiated, with the money going straight to the sponsoring guru. The invited guests are treated to rich food like *biryani* (oily rice cooked with fragrant spices and meat) and sweets on such occasions. Sometimes guests come from faraway places, including India. Usually, hijras close to the sponsoring guru are invited. The extent of the festivity of initiation varies depending on the economic situation of the sponsoring guru.

During my fieldwork, among many of the initiation rites I attended, one event in particular leaps to my mind, where I was given the task of being an amanuensis. Rani, a hijra guru, organized a festival on the occasion of the initiation of a new cela. Hijras from not only outside Dhaka, but as far afield as Barashat in India were invited. Since influential hijras from several different places were present and because some of them might object to the presence of an outsider like me, Rina asked me to write the contract for the initiation and keep a record of the amount of money given by the guests. As several *daratni*s—the hijra word for leaders—assembled in the room, Rina handed me a 100 taka (roughly US$1.26) notarized government stamp paper. A hijra named Siraj Master dictated while I scribbled. The contract, which I later photocopied from Rina, is reproduced below in translation, with the original names changed:

> I, Sadia hijra (Father: Moshrraf, Mother: Monira, Village: Mithakhali, District: Kurigram) hereby declare that I am accepting the discipleship of guru Trishna Hijra of 1/a, Topkhana Road, Segunbagicha, Dhaka-1000

Kinship, Community and *Hijragiri*

(Guru: Rina hijra, dad guru: Jomuna hijra,) and Nan guru: Rina hijra (Guru: Jomuna Hijra, 28/2, Sohag vila, 1 no college road, Asrafabad Kamrangirchar, Dhaka). I also declare that if I ever join another hijra house, leaving my guru and the house of Rina, I will be liable to pay a don of 100,000 taka in keeping with the hijra pon-pesha/code of conduct.

The above contract was signed by Nadia, the initiand, along with six hijra witnesses. The contents of the contract not only illustrate the importance of the guru in the life cycle of a hijra, but also the binding nature of such discipleship. Trishna, the guru of Nadia, is known by their guru and grand guru, as the contract shows, as is Rina, the guru of Trishna in whose household the festival took place. Although the hijra initiating a cela typically sponsors such an event, in this case it was Rina hijra, the guru of Trishna, who was the sponsor. The reason the initiation took place at Rina's *khol* (house) is because Trishna was not a full-time sadrali but a bagicha koti who lived with their natal family. The contract also shows that despite the binding nature of this contract, Nadia is allowed to change their guru and move into a new house—however, such a decision entails the settlement of the agreed don of 10,000 taka (around US$125).

Although a cela can change guru by paying the agreed amount, in the case of Nadia it may be very difficult, given the size of the amount. A 'don', the hijra word for penalty or compensation, can be much lower or higher than this. Hijras in Hridoypur maintained that it was around one lac taka (around US$1,000) in the case of their grand guru Jomuna, while the don for other initiations I attended ranged between 5,000 and 20,000 taka (roughly US$60–250). When a cela changes to a new house, the sponsoring guru pays the amount to the old guru. Celas, however, rarely change houses and when they do, it is often due to severe problems of adjustment. Although several of my interlocutors in Hridoypur did leave on occasion, they all came back eventually.

It bears noting that signing such a contract is not a widespread practice among hijras. Meghna, the hijra guru in Hridoypur who was also present during the aforementioned initiation, later explained, 'Agreements like this are entered only when there is a lack of trust. Since Rina is very bad-tempered and has lost several of their celas in the past, they now always use a written contract to ensure that celas do not leave them easily.' Meghna also maintained that the use of the government notarized stamp was merely symbolic, with no legal standing, as in the case of a cela leaving their guru, such matters are never referred to the court for resolution.

Ethnographers of Indian hijras noted that celas in India often change from one house to another (Nanda 1999; Reddy 2005a). For instance, Reddy maintains that there are seven hijra houses to which hijras all over India belong. In contrast, there are no such major symbolic divisions in the way hijragiri is organized in Bangladesh; rather, celas are all known by the name of their gurus. There are, however, three symbolic houses—namely Shambajariya, Ghunguriya and Machuya. Machuya is the smallest of the three and is a breakaway group from the Ghunguriya; some hijra gurus dismissed Machuya as a house altogether, saying that it does not exist. The word 'Shambajariya' derives from a bazaar known as Sham Bazaar, although hijras could not specify its exact location. In contrast, 'Ghunguriya' derives from the word 'ghungur'—literally, anklet. Ghunguriya, therefore, originated from a group of dancing hijras while Shambajariya is named after a place. Hijras in Hridoypur and elsewhere in Dhaka maintained that since Ghunguriya is associated with dancing, they have lower prestige. However, the fact is all hijra groups dance and sing and such a division is nominal, with very little bearing on how one group treats the other. There is practically no difference between these three major houses in terms of ritual practices. Nor were my hijra interlocutors sufficiently knowledgeable about the differences between these three houses. Unlike India, where a change of guru entails a change of house or symbolic descent line (Reddy 2005a), such divisions are of little practical significance to hijras in Bangladesh. A hijra can change to any other hijra group irrespective of this nominal tripartite division. Hijras in Dhaka rarely talk in terms of these symbolic divisions. Rather, the predominant marker of belonging is decided in terms of one's guru. With the exception of a few hijra gurus, most hijras had no clear conception either about these symbolic houses or about which of these houses they represented. Rather, the name of the guru, or guru's guru, is more important than these three symbolic divisions.

Reciprocity and power in guru–cela relationships

Hijragiri is a guru–centric institution. A novice may become a member of the hijra group only if an existing member is willing to take the novice as a cela. Gurus are highly venerated among hijras. When a guru grows infirm, the celas are expected to take care of them. Although Hridoypur, as already mentioned previously, is the birit of Jomuna, Meghna, the most trusted and dearest cela of Jomuna, oversees the group on their behalf. Once a week, Jomuna visits Hridoypur to supervise and get their share of the birit. If Jomuna is unable to visit, hijras from Hridoypur visit Jomuna with the cholla. Jomuna maintains that it is Meghna in whose name they conduct hijragiri. Jomuna contends that Meghna was like their father and mother and without their blessing, they would not be where they are today. Meghna once related, 'It is a relationship based on mutual trust, love and respect. If I did not respect my guru, they would not have conferred the birit on me. In a similar vein if my celas do not respect me, then they too will be denied their rightful share'.

Misconduct in relations with a guru is a severe offence for which stringent punishment is meted out. In almost every aspect of life, consultation with the guru is sought by the cela. The guru-centricity of hijra social organization was further evident to me when I started to frequent Meghna's house on a regular basis. Twice a week, celas would eat at Meghna's house. While celas of Meghna dropped by whenever necessary, they gathered at Meghna's house at least twice a week before setting out for cholla and badhai. After coming back from cholla and badhai, Meghna would eat with all their celas. Meghna, like a mother, would cook *dorma* and *khobra*, the hijra words for rice and beef, respectively. Celas would always seek permission from Meghna before eating. When celas see their guru, the first thing they do is greet the guru with 'salamalaikum', the standard Muslim greeting in Bangladesh. In the evening at the sound of the call for prayer, or *azan*, celas would greet their guru with 'sham bati salamalaikum' (an evening greeting). At the time of leaving, celas would say 'guru pao lagi'—literally, 'guru, I touch your feet', a reverential form of valediction. Touching of feet, or 'pao', is considered a way of showing respect to elders among hijras and in Bangladesh generally.

Another event leaps to my mind. Once I was in the house of Nasima, an influential guru in the old part of Dhaka. We were all sitting on the floor. Suddenly a next-door neighbour called out for Nasima from outside. Tania, Nasima's cela, was rushing out of the room to respond but accidentally their achol touched Nasima's head. Instantaneously Nasima stopped Tania and asked them to tear a thread from the hemline of their sari to give to them. Since the 'achol' is used to initiate a cela, a cela's achol is not supposed to touch the head of a guru. In case this happens, a thread is to be torn from the sari to be given back to the guru, to undo the guru–cela 'role reversal' believed to result from such a faux pas. Celas of Meghna argued that despite the hard work that they had to do as celas, like trawling through the streets and the bazaars in search of cholla under scorching heat and the strict code of conduct under which they have to act, their lives under Meghna were far better than their previous lives with their natal families. Ruposhi, another cela of Meghna, once related that they would have been on the street without a place to stay had they not been a cela of Meghna, who not only provided for them but also protected them from street thugs. Another cela of Meghna in Hridoypur explained, 'It is my duty to take care of my guru. Do you not take care of your parents? It is the same with us. If I do not take care of my guru now, when I grow old I will also be left uncared and without celas.' What emerges from the above is that the guru–cela relationship is central to the reproduction of the hijra social system. While the guru may seem like the tyrannical patriarch of a hijra house, the relationship between a cela and their guru is based on mutual respect, care, love and trust. Although the will of a guru reigns supreme in the hijra hierarchy, it is not an exploitative arrangement with gurus enjoying the benefits at the expense of the celas. Rather, this hierarchical configuration enables a division of labour with both guru and cela having a specific set of tasks, the undertaking of which is central to the maintenance of the hijra status quo.

While the guru–cela relationship is based on mutual respect and reciprocity, it is also at times fraught with tension. For instance, in the event of an infringement of a code of conduct, a hijra may be subjected to stringent punishment. The nature of the punishment hinges upon the severity of the offence. The accused is at best fined, or at worst excommunicated. During my fieldwork, I saw two such incidents. Once it so happened that a cela was found to be sexually involved with the husband of a guru. As a punishment, the accused had to have their head totally shaved before being kicked out of the group (I discuss the partners of the hijras in chapter 6). The second incident took place after a cela underwent emasculation without the permission of a guru but was later reincorporated by paying a 'don' or penalty (see chapter 4 on emasculation). Aside from such serious infractions, penalties for petty crimes include paying a don, or in some cases 'chol pani bondh' (an enforced period of fasting). Once *chol pani bondh* is imposed, it is only the guru who reserves the right to lift it. Once the ban is lifted, the guru embraces the cela and feeds them with their own hand.

Although the guru–cela relationship is modelled on a mother–daughter relationship, with the guru acting like a mother, the dynamics of this relationship also resonate with Hindu husband–wife relationships. While hijras do not read it along this line, some of the practices bespeak this symbolic similarity. For instance, when a guru dies, a cela, in line with Hindu mourning rites, breaks their bangles and puts on a white sari. The mourning cela also abstains from consumption of meat and fish for forty-one days. In addition, the cela continues to wear white clothes on major hijra occasions. Although a cela whose guru has died wears a white dress for the next forty-one days, a thin red wrist band is worn alongside the white. Hijras argue that this red amidst white is a way for a cela to go back to colourful dress or a state of normality at a later stage. The practices adopted by a cela after the demise of a guru may be seen to echo, at least at a symbolic level, the funerary rites that the wife of a deceased husband performs in Hindu culture. Although hijras strongly objected to such interpretations, I expound this possibility further in chapter 3.

'Milk daughter': A bond of permanence and unrequited love

Celas, I noted previously, can change from one hijra house to another. However, there is a kind of guru–cela relationship that transcends the typical conditionality of the guru–cela divide. Often spoken of in terms of the umbilical cord, a 'milk daughter', or *dud beti*, is a cela perpetually tied to the mother-like guru. Unlike other celas, a dud beti remains a cela for good and can never break this affective bond. Like a daughter who is fed by her mother, a dud beti is also a daughter to the hijra mother. Although not based on umbilical cord and breastfeeding, it is a bond based on unconditional love. A dud beti always remains thus to their hijra mother regardless of how bitter the relations may grow. 'It is like an unbroken bond that nothing on earth can dismantle,' related Meghna in speaking of their dud beti, Tulsi.

During Tulsi's initiation, an elaborate ritual was undertaken in Meghna's home amidst the presence of all their celas. Typically, the preparatory ingredients for this initiation include a plate, a glass, seven betel leaves and seven dots of vermilion. These ingredients serve as witnesses to the enactment of this sacramental bond. The initiand is made to sit on the lap of the guru and symbolically feed at their breast. The initiand does not literally suck the breasts of the guru; rather, the mother symbolically pours some milk into their dud beti's mouth. Meghna, after this initiation, explained that while a regular guru–cela relation or *asla* involves one knot, the relation between a dud beti and their mother is signified by five knots and hence is difficult to untie.

Interestingly, milk daughters are rarely seen to stay with their dud mothers. For instance, Tulsi, the dud beti of Meghna, is not part of the Hridoypur hijra group, although Tulsi would occasionally visit Meghna. Tulsi is what hijras in Hridoypur called a 'kari besher koti'—a hijra in the guise of a normative man. Tulsi, also known as Tola, is a heterosexually married man who works in a sweet factory. Tulsi had never been a part of a sadrali group, that is, they never undertook badhai and cholla. Even during the initiation, Tulsi was dressed in *panjabi* and *pyjama*, typical masculine attire in Bangladesh. This is not to suggest that dud betis are always heterosexually married and without any formal affiliation with the sadralis. Rina, another hijra, also has a dud beti who works as a sadrali in Barashat, in the state of West Bengal in India. During my fieldwork in Hridoypur, Sugondhi, Rina's dud beti, visited Hridoypur twice.

What emerges is that the relationship between a dud beti and their mother or guru is eternal. While a cela of a guru can change the hijra house, a dud beti's ties with their hijra mother are irrevocable. More interestingly, the case of Tulsi suggests that one does not have to be a sadrali to be a dud beti. Although Tulsi lives like a normative male, hijras in Hridoypur viewed them as a hijra. What kind of a hijra are they? In what follows, I present a system of classification that sadralis employ to talk about different types of hijras.

Sadrali internal classification

According to the sadrali hijras in Dhaka, there are basically three kinds of hijras. These are:

Janana: *Janana*s are hijras with a penis. As Dilu, a hijra from Hridoypur, once explained, 'It is like someone has a pen but no ink.' In other words, they have a penis but no use for it. While this statement may be taken to indicate the status of a person's erectile dysfunction or impotence, what it actually means is that they do not put their penis to use (see chapter 3 on erotic desire where I unpack this). However, hijras generically contend that those among them with a penis can neither get an erection nor produce sperm.

Chibry: *Chibry* hijras are those who have had their genitals (both penis and scrotum) completely removed. As hijras in Hridoypur would often put it, 'they neither have pen nor ink'. Hijras, including the chibrys, generally claim to have been born that way.

Vabrajer Chibry: *Vabrajer chibry* means 'born straight from the womb of the mother'. The words 'vab raj' in hijra argot denote 'pregnant women'; but when used in this context, it refers to those born with ambiguous or missing genitals. As Nina, a hijra guru, once explained,

> They are hijras with ambiguous genitalia. Many just have a hole to urinate. They are actually real hijras but are not part of the organized hijra group. They pass their lives in the guise of females in their natal families. Also females who never menstruate can be classed as part of this group.

While hijras have a category for the 'vabrajer chibry', they are, as the opening vignette of this chapter suggests, neither part of the hijra groups nor welcome to become members.

There are a few things to be noted here. First, the above system of classification that hijras deploy to describe the diversity within the hijra universe is primarily centred on genital status. It needs mentioning that while hijras publicly claim to be born that way, that is, born with defective or missing genitals, such a classificatory grid is employed only internally. For instance, 'janana' is rarely used as a self-referential address, nor does it constitute a separate hijra group. Furthermore, while people with missing or ambiguous genitals are marked as 'vabrajer chibry', they are not part of the hijra universe. Yet it is precisely this trope of defective or missing genitals that hijras invoke on a daily basis to seek recognition as real hijras. Second, sadrali hijra groups typically boast both janana and chibry as members. While monographs on hijras in India (Nanda 1999; Reddy 2005a) report status differentiation based on genital status, in the context of Bangladesh the state of being emasculated does not necessarily correlate with greater status, for reasons I explain in chapter 4. Third, the aforesaid system of sadrali classification centred on genital status is also employed by other non-sadrali groups, in that in speaking among themselves they often resort to the same sort of classification and language. Yet one important point to note here is that it is only among the sadrali group that chibry hijras are existent, while other non-sadrali groups boast only janana hijra as members. Fourth, while the trope of realness and authenticity is often invoked by hijras, realness or authenticity here entails the ability to master their sacrosanct rites and ceremonies, and the consequent performance of related skills and customs both before the public and fellow hijras. In other words, the attainment of a successful hijra status entails the ability to conduct hijragiri, regardless of one's genital status. In the words of Jomuna, the nonagenarian hijra guru in Hridoypur, 'One becomes a hijra by virtue of one's ability to converse (*bole*), earn money (thappu), maintain rules and rituals (*pesha* and *pon*), and arbitrate (*salish*).' This comment illustrates a critical point relevant to one of the wider arguments of this book: one becomes a hijra processually, regardless of whether one is a janana or a chibry.

Conclusion

In this chapter, I elaborated the various groups of male-bodied, feminine-identified people in Dhaka, highlighting similitude and disjuncture and the tendency on the part of these groups to censure each other on account of occupational practice, involvement with sex work and knowledge and conduct of ritual practices. Navigating through these distinctions and similarity foregrounds questions of authenticity and realness that each of these groups deploys to seek moral superiority over the others. Bagicha koti, gamchali hijra and 'dhurrani' hijra groups all approximate some of the practices of the sadrali hijras, evident in the way they maintain a guru–cela divide. While this is strictly enforced among sadrali hijras, other groups too acknowledged its centrality. Although bagicha kotis do not enforce such a strict guru–cela hierarchy in the garden premises, they are also often affiliated with sadrali hijras. While the sadrali hijras consider themselves superior to others on account of their ritual knowledge and adherence to the archetypal occupations of badhai and cholla, gamchali hijras seek to authenticate themselves on the ground of their occupation of cooking, which they regard as superior to sadrali work. Both the sadrali and the gamchali hijras publicly denounce sex work and argue that involvement in prostitution is emblematic of fake hijra status. 'Dhurrani' hijras, on the other hand, retort by saying that sadralis too are 'dhurrani', although they may deny it. Bagicha kotis, too, consider themselves to be hijras on account of their linkage with sadrali groups and their hijra-like performance in the garden premises. While these groups differ from each other in terms of space, occupation, sartorial practice, public presentation and kinship, such distinctions often collapse as many of my interlocutors belonged to all these groups simultaneously, while others switched from one group to another in the course of their life-historical trajectories.

More often than not, ethnographic discussion on hijras reduces the complexities of the cultural context by not positioning the hijra within the wider context of gender and sexual variance. In highlighting the complex and fluid cultural context of male-to-male desire within which hijras are embedded, Reddy (2005a) contends that the various groups, including that of the hijra she encountered, were actually part of a broader koti family. In other words, 'koti' in Reddy's account emerges as a generic moniker to encompass variably situated male-bodied people who desire masculine men. In a similar vein, Hall (2005) notes the presence of koti in Delhi and argues that it is distinct from the hijras and is a 'fourth breed'. Both Reddy and Hall contend that koti is no less authentic than the hijras and in some sense precedes the hijras as a subject position. In contrast, Boyce (2007) and Cohen (2005) argue that koti as a subculture is a by-product of recent AIDS-focused NGO activism. That is, the very organized groups of people that self-identify as koti in contemporary South Asia are a new phenomenon. Here my concern is not to resolve the debate over hijra versus koti firstness. Rather, what I would like to underscore is that hijras and kotis are not antithetical to each other. Following the lead from my interlocutors, I would argue that 'koti' as an expression originates in hijra argot, a view that all the aforesaid groups in Dhaka endorsed. Here I concur with Reddy in arguing that 'koti' is a generic label with which various male-bodied, feminine-identified groups identify, although the context of its use as a form of self-identification varies. Furthermore, while 'koti' as a word derives from hijra argot, unlike 'hijra', koti is an internal word and its use outside the non-mainstream groups is still rare.

Finally, my intention in this chapter was not merely to document the existence of several non-normative groups. Rather, I presented them with the aim of bringing into view the complex and fluid cultural contexts within which hijras are embedded. The elaboration of the cultural context that these various groups inhabit allows us to read hijras not as some reified category with fixed traits, but as a part of a continuum of 'male femaling' practices. In other words, each of these groups requires systematic mastery of various kinds of 'male femaling' knowledge and skills. Yet a point worth accentuating is that all these male-bodied, feminine-identified groups are concatenated through a shared desire for normative masculine men, regardless of their presentation to the contrary in public. I discuss the centrality of desire in the crafting of hijra subjectivity later in this book. Here, let me just contend that it is on account of this shared desire that these various groups consider themselves to be part of a similar universe of desire. This shared similarity is further reflected in their possession of knowledge of Ulti, the clandestine hijra argot, which works to assert a communitarian sense of belonging to this secret universe of desire. Another commonality that binds these groups is their shared lower-class background in the Bangladeshi social structure, which I discuss in chapter 2.

2 Class-Cultural Politics and the Making of *Hijras*

Ethnographies of *hijras* in contemporary South Asia have often projected hijras as a group lying outside the dominant markers of social differentiation—namely class, caste, religion and ethnicity (Reddy 2005a; Nanda 1999). Although hijras often crosscut such markers in terms of accepting people of various backgrounds, the class dimension of hijra identity has been largely ignored. My hijra interlocutors often emphasized what they styled as 'lutki kholer maigga'—literally, 'effeminate boys of the poorer families'—in describing the social standing of their natal families. 'It is not that hijras are not born to the upper and middle classes, but only those from the lower classes join the community,' commented Josna, a hijra in Dhaka. Moyna, another hijra, once stated, 'The upper- and middle-class hijras are called gay. They have their own societies but we are no different from them in essence.' This chapter brings into view specifically the role of class in the formation of hijra subjectivity. I argue that the public vilification of hijras is not reducible to their sex–gender difference alone, but inherent in this process is a class-cultural politics that works to reproduce such discursive and material abjections. In advancing my argument, I contend that class is not a static category but a social fact always in the making. Focusing on hijra spatial practices and location within the urban socio-cultural milieu, I bring into view the complex interplay between class, gender and sexuality in the production and reproduction of hijras.

Scholars within the field of critical gender and sexuality studies have noted the problematic tendency to overlook class in the formation of sex–gender subjectivities (Binnie 2011; Heaphy 2011; Hennessy 2000). While culturalist queer theory tends to reduce subjectivities to the level of discourse alone, the material queer strand calls for a re-materialization of sexuality studies. Material queer theorists argue that the very invocation of class as an analytical tool continues to be intellectually suspect in much of the cultural queer theoretical strand. The main criticism of the cultural queer body of scholarship is that the privileging of class has often resulted in the relegation of gender and sexual subjectivities to the status of a super-structural excess. That is, subjectivities have been read as superfluous derivations of an over-determined economic structure (for example, Morton 2001). On the other hand, the material queer strand tends to dismiss the culturalist queer point-blank for its inattention to the economic structures of inequality.

Notwithstanding this disagreement, I argue that these two positions are not necessarily antithetical to each other. To overcome this disjuncture, I follow Liechty (2002) in arguing that class and culture co-constitute each other. In his analysis of the burgeoning middle class in Kathmandu, Nepal, Liechty calls for an anthropology of class that shows adequate sensitivity to both the cultural practices constitutive of class and the unequal distribution of power and resources that disproportionately affect people's lives. Following Bourdieu (1984), Liechty argues that class is not a predetermined category, but a process always being made and remade through embodied spatial practices, or what he calls 'the class cultural process'. The usefulness of the class-cultural approach as proposed by Liechty lies in its ability to locate the spatial dynamics through which class is produced and reproduced on a daily basis. More significantly, as Liechty argues, a class-cultural analysis enables us to understand not only what class is, but also what it *does*. This insight is particularly useful for my analysis of the class-cultural abjection of hijras. Hijras in Bangladesh are not only censured on account of their positioning within the working class milieu, but, more importantly, are constantly produced and reproduced via middle/upper-class cultural imaginings. Middle- and upper-class cultural and spatial imaginings serve as powerful discursive tropes through which hijra bodies are continually and simultaneously desexualized and demasculinized. I argue that it is through a displacement of the middle-class cultural anxieties about morality, respectability and boundaries onto working-class bodies that the middle classes imagine their own class-cultural difference and superiority over their abjected working-class others. It is worthwhile to mention that in the normative scheme of gender relations generically talked about in terms of the categories of men, women and hijras, not only are hijra bodies defined as a 'failed' middle category, but they are also described in highly class-specific terms. That is, when a middle-class male is denigrated as 'hijra' by his class equals, it is not just a general transgressive gender expression, but rather an insult intended to imply associations specifically with the lower-class hijras for which such men are disparaged.

Morality tales, middle-class imagining and the spatial location of hijras in Dhaka

Dhaka, the capital of Bangladesh, is one of the fastest growing cities in the world, with a population size in excess of ten million. With a dense concentration of urban slums, the gap between the rich and the poor is one of the highest in the world. Hijras in Dhaka mostly live in these shantytowns. Hridoypur, my primary field site, is one of the poorest areas in Dhaka, and has a massive constellation of poor migrants and working-class people. Members of the hijra community in Hridoypur, like any typical hijra group, are spread across the area. Despite the stigma associated with hijras, they are not spatially ghettoized, but are seen to be living with the mainstream poor populace. My hijra interlocutors often argued that poorer sections of society are more approving and sympathetic towards them compared with the rich. Hijras predominantly hail from the same kind of socio-economic backgrounds as their mainstream neighbours. Hijras in Dhaka and elsewhere in Bangladesh often complain that it is the middle- and upper-class populace who are hostile to them. For instance, hijras in Hridoypur pointed out that even if they were in a position to afford to move, they would never be accepted in the middle- and upper-class neighbourhoods. Later in this chapter I discuss hijra entanglement with their class counterparts; here, I highlight the way the middle classes construe the hijras.

The term 'hijra' is often used by the middle classes not only to describe males who fail to be sufficiently normatively masculine, but also middle-class men who do not conform to the norms of respectable middle-class masculinity. As a middle-class Bangladeshi, I had never seen *hijras* come to any typical middle-class households either as guests or as performers. Nor had I heard any middle-class people talk positively about hijras. Although I grew up in an area with a hijra household nearby, it was not until I developed some interest in hijras that I started interacting with them in a personal capacity (in chapters 3 and 6, I go on to explore how my middle-class positionality in Bangladeshi social structure shaped my interaction and reception among hijras).

As a matter of fact, there is rarely any interaction between the middle classes and hijras, except for fleeting moments of confrontational encounter in public. My observation was that the middle classes entertain ingrained prejudices against hijras. The main clientele of hijras in Dhaka is not the middle or upper class, but those of working-class background. For instance, the sadrali hijras perform *badhai* only in the poor households (see later). In the Indian context, anthropologists noted that hijras perform badhai in both lower- and middle- or upper-class households; additionally, hijras are also seen to demand money in ceremonies like marriage and birthdays in middle/upper-class houses. In contrast, the mobility of the sadrali hijras in Dhaka is restricted only to working-class households. Older hijras often nostalgically related to me that formerly they had enjoyed a certain cachet as entertainers invited to perform in households and at celebrations); however, with the rise of other forms of outlets—namely media, television and satellite channels— the traditional cultural demand for hijras as performers has disappeared. Nanda (1999), for instance, opens her monograph with a description of a badhai performance in an upper-middle-class household. She notes that in the popular Indian imagination, hijras are conceptualized as specialist cultural performers. In contrast, there is no such popular perception of hijras being cultural performers in Dhaka. Unlike India where hijras are believed to possess sacred power which in turn entitles them to perform and bless the newborn, there is no such corresponding belief in hijra ability to either bless or curse among the non-hijra Bangladeshi populace in general. My interlocutors often pointed to this difference in cultural attitude as the reason for the wide income disparity between hijras of India and those of Bangladesh. Here, I reproduce a few highlights from newspapers in Bangladesh as a way to demonstrate how the middle classes read hijras.

On 25 June 2009, the *Daily Star*, an English-language newspaper, carried a report titled 'Hijra Panic Grips City Dwellers'. The report contains several vignettes of the reported harassment faced by the mainstream middle and upper classes. Excerpts from the news are as follows:

> City dwellers remain in a state of panic nowadays due to frequent attacks of [the] hermaphrodite (hijra) populace who suddenly come to the houses or make attacks on individuals at different signal points for money or other goods. Hijra attacked Shamima Akhter, mother of a two-month-old son, at her Gulshan residence where she lives with her husband. She said, 'I went to the veranda after hearing [the] shouting of my guard around 11:00 am yesterday and found some five to six hijra beat up my guard as he refused to allow them [entrance] to the house. I got panicked and called my husband, who was also harassed by the group of hijra[s]. They demanded Tk 5,000 (around US$60) for our kid's welfare, otherwise they would kidnap my son,' said Shamima. The doting mother also said, 'We finally paid them Tk 2000 after much hard bargaining. We have already decided to change our house

from this area as they [hijras] frequently come.... Hijra[s] also attacked the commuters at different signal points where cars and other vehicle stopped for [a] few minutes, said a victim, who recently lost a mobile phone and a wallet from his own car at Mohakhali. 'Suddenly they come to the car and try to enter the vehicle by force or start to scold in very offensive language and gesture.'

On 24 March 2010, the same daily ran another report titled 'Panic Attack by Hijra at Uttara: Two Hurt'. The article follows:

A group of hijra[s] (hermaphrodites), who were engaged in raising extortion money from different houses by intimidation, attacked a house at Uttara sector 5 yesterday and injured two security personnel. The group, consisting of five to six hijra[s], was chased away by the local people with canes and brickbats. During the short chase, one hijra was injured. Hijras, however, returned to the area with 20–25 ones [*sic*] of the community immediately and attacked people and some houses located on Road No. 3 of the sector. On [receiving this] information, Uttara police rushed to the spot and tried to take control of the situation, but hijras ignored their presence and launched their attacks, creating [a] public nuisance. Hijras made phone calls to their friends to 'send more hijra[s]' to the scene. Panicky residents stayed within their homes while the police tried to calm down the agitating hijra[s], who claimed that one of their comrades was killed. Traffic movement came to a halt for almost one hour. With the interference of the police, hijras finally left the area. Locals said a small group of hijra[s] stormed a six-storey house, [and] went to the second floor, where a family with small children resides, to seek money. The security guards of the house tried to push two hijra[s] from the stairway. At that time, other hermaphrodites waiting outside the building attacked the security men....

There are a few things to be noted here. First, the news items above underscore one of the central contentions of this chapter: hijras in Bangladesh are not recognized as sacred and religiously powerful cultural performers in middle-class imaginaries as is generally the case in India. Hijras, as one of the news items would hysterically have it, demanded money for the welfare of a two-month-old child; while another hijra group stormed into a house to approach a family with small children. That the middle classes do not recognize badhai (the practice of demanding gifts at birth) is also evident in the way they variously described the hijras' demand for money as 'extortion', 'criminal' and a 'public nuisance'. While I am not able to ascertain the veracity of these specific allegations, the hijras' encounter with these middle-class households appears to have been confrontational. Hijras, as I previously noted, are not welcome in middle-class households or areas to demand badhai. Second, the news items indicate a class-specific way of representing hijras. That hijras have been labelled 'criminals' and 'thugs' is not surprising. Several middle-class acquaintances, familiar with my work, would at different times variously describe hijras to me as hermaphrodites, transsexual, disabled and abnormal. Some went to the extent of saying that hijras were basically muggers and a real source of public nuisance.

Ethnographic research has brought into view the centrality of class in the formation and abjection of gendered or sexed subjects. In her research on working-class women in the north of England, Skeggs (1997) has persuasively shown how imagery of class and respectability are inextricably intertwined in the derogatory representation of the working class. Skeggs shows how the notion of the middle class has been consolidated over time in relation to the discursive abjection of the working class. In a similar vein, in the popular imagination of the middle and upper classes in Dhaka, hijras are 'foul-smelling', 'dirty', 'violent' and 'shameless' people. It is the lower-class status, with its associated imagery of filth, foul smell, cheap and gaudy make-up and aggressiveness through which hijras are discursively produced as the abjected others in the dominant middle-class imaginary of Bangladeshi society. And it is precisely by constructing hijras as non-respectable that the middle classes consolidate their own notions of respectability and distinction. It is also instructive to note that the dominant middle-class imagination generally construes the working classes as not only non-respectable but also emasculate. Recent work on male domestic labour has also amply demonstrated the de-virilization and infantilization of working-class men in the middle-class imaginary on account of their association with putatively feminizing domestic settings (Bartolomei 2010; Chopra 2006; Sarti and Scrinzi 2010). It is therefore not only hijras but also the working-class populace in general that are conceived of as an undifferentiated whole characterized by a simultaneous lack and excess of sexual desire.

That working class people are often defined in terms of presumed genital lack or deficiency resonates with the wider history of sexuality in Europe. Johnson (2009), for instance, notes that the boundaries of the normative categories of gender and sexuality in the Western world have been distilled not only in relation to the 'deviant' within (lower classes), but also in relation to the racialized other without (primitive races). In a similar vein, the presumed genital lack or deficiency of hijra bodies metaphorically stands in for the lack of clearly defined gender of working-class populations evident not only in the generic class-specific demonization of hijras as demonstrated previously, but also in the way such understandings inform the distance that middle-class gay men seek to maintain from the working-class hijra populace, to which I briefly alluded in chapter 1. Such class-inflected constructions of hijras are further evident in the emergence of various kinds of medicalizing discourses among the middle classes in contemporary Bangladesh, where hijras are not only pathologized, but also to be potentially 'fixed'—issues which I explore in more depth in chapter 7.

While the interaction between the middle classes and hijras indicates some degree of hostility and class-cultural anxiety, the following section presents materials on the enforced location of the working class within which hijras are spatially located in Dhaka. Specifically, I present three different spatial arrangements within the working-class context where hijras are seen to interact with their normative working-class counterparts. Focusing on the neighbourhoods that hijras in Hridoypur inhabit, I demonstrate class-cultural solidarity between hijras and their normative working-class neighbours. Through a discussion of badhai, I demonstrate how conventions of neighbourliness that define space are transgressed by hijras in a bid to seek recognition as 'hijra'. Drawing on theories of gift exchange, I argue that hijras' exchange relations with their working-class counterparts can be partially explained in terms of the broader Islamically inspired cultural logics of gift exchange in Bangladesh. I also demonstrate that while badhai is a way for hijras to solicit recognition, badhai also serves as a site where masculinities are contested and transacted. Finally, I elaborate hijra presence within bazaar settings in Dhaka, where hijras solicit gifts from vendors as a way to further assert their hijra status and be recognized as hijra. I contend that hijras' presence and interaction with the normative crowd within the public bazaar settings, albeit often confrontational, takes on the appearance of carnivalesque conviviality.

Class-cultural solidarity and conventions of neighbourliness

Hijras in Hridoypur, I have already noted, are dispersed across the area rather than being concentrated into a colony-like neighbourhood. Like the majority mainstream, hijras in Hridoypur are also migrants from other parts of Bangladesh who have joined a hijra group in Dhaka not only to be away from their natal homes, but also for better income prospects. Hridoypur, as a relatively new settlement in Dhaka, is unique not only on account of its large number of working-class migrant workers, but also because of dense concentrations of mosques and Islamic seminaries.

Although hijras live alongside this mainstream population, the presence of hijras is also very marked in most of these neighbourhoods. For instance, every time I ventured into a new neighbourhood in Hridoypur, it was always the mainstream populace—whether someone gathered at or working on the tea stalls, or some casual passers-by—who directed me to the exact location where specific hijras could be found. Sometimes overenthusiastic children would go back inside to pass the word of my arrival to hijras. Despite a general tendency on the part of the mainstream to not rent out rooms to hijras (a grievance expressed by many of my interlocutors), hijras in Hridoypur were spatially in tune with their mainstream working-class counterparts.

Sathi lived in the middle of a dense bazaar on the rooftop of a ramshackle building next to an open space used as a mosque. Mona lived in a room belonging to an Islamic seminary. Mousumi lived within a constellation of households. Although they were all part of Jomuna's (the guru in Hridoypur) lineage, gathering at their house twice a week and publicly operating as hijras in that neighbourhood, they were looked upon by the locals not only as hijras, but also as neighbours. Mousumi had been living in their house for the previous two years and over this period had befriended their neighbours fairly well. Every time I visited Mousumi, I saw women and children of other households all crammed into their room watching cinema or a popular show on television. My arrival, however, always led to the disbanding of the gathering. As an aside, let me also mention that although Mousumi was the name given to them by their hijra guru, they were also known as Abul, a masculine-identified name, and like the majority of hijras, were known by both names in the neighbourhood. Unlike other hijras in Hridoypur, Mousumi lived with their mother, to whom Mousumi was Abul, despite their mother knowing full well about Abul's hijra vocation. Hijras in Hridoypur were also very close to Abul's mother.

Bristi, whose house I used to visit, would also draw a mainstream normative crowd in their house to watch television. On many occasions, I saw both Mousumi and Brishti help their female next-door neighbours with washing and cooking. For instance, during one of the marriage festivals of a neighbour's daughter, Brishti supervised the entire food preparation. Not only did Mousumi and Brishti and their neighbours share utensils on a regular basis, but they also would often share food. On occasion, hijra guru Jomuna would ask the children to bring some *dhupni* and *patli* (hijra words for cigarettes and tea, respectively) from the adjoining shops. As well as such good neighbourly sociality, hijras would also often be the first group of people to be approached by the neighbours in times of emergency. When a neighbour was undergoing an operation, hijras not only were there at the hospital throughout the process, but also lent money to help them. Neighbours reciprocated such favours. Abdul, an influential local vendor, once arranged a free space on the rooftop of a building for holding a hijra festival free of charge.

During one *baraiya* festival (the festival undertaken to celebrate emasculation) in Hridoypur, hijras danced to music in the open space around their makeshift tents. Dressed in gaudy make-up and bawdy female attire, hijras danced and sang while neighbours, mostly children, stood up close and watched. Suddenly at the sound of the call for prayer (*azan*), a senior hijra dramatically fluttered out from inside the tent and asked their hijra companions to suspend the 'ulu jhulu'. Hijras immediately stopped their dancing and singing spree and covered their heads with scarves. After the azan had finished and prayers commenced, they once again resumed the singing and dancing. On another occasion, a local *mullah* arrived at the scene and asked the hijras to behave since their dancing in the public was, according to the mullah, against propriety. The hijras stopped dancing immediately. They explained to me that they stopped not because they were scared of the mullah, but because they did not want to be in their neighbours' bad books.

In fact, several hijras in Hridoypur would not only say prayers regularly in the mosques, but also often take part in Islamic preaching. Sonia, also from Hridoypur, now in their late forties, had undergone emasculation some ten years previously. After being with a hijra group in Medinipur in India for about ten years, they had recently bought a house in Hridoypur and settled there. Sonia had latterly performed the *hajj* pilgrimage. Since returning from hajj, Sonia had been working with the local mosque as a volunteer in weekly Islamic preaching. Sonia, along with other Muslims, went from door to door preaching Islam. Sonia dressed like a man during their service for the mosque. They also worked as the branch manager of an NGO working on the sexual health of hijras in the same area. In the office and house, they stayed dressed like a female in line with hijra lifestyle. The mosque committee and the locals were aware that Sonia was a hijra. The fact that Sonia is a hijra has never been an issue for the mosque committee and the locals.

In Hridoypur, groups of devout Muslim men often went from door to door preaching Islam. On occasion, they accosted hijras, encouraging them to take up the path of Islam. The advice these groups meted out to hijras centred on the importance of saying prayers five times a day in the mosque and following the Islamic lifestyle. Hijras approached by them were never asked to give up their hijra identifications. Nor were they ever upbraided for their cross-dressing, as is often assumed to be the case in Muslim-majority societies.[1] In fact, a number of my hijra interlocutors in Hridoypur and elsewhere participated in *chilla*, a practice where groups of Muslims journey together for a certain period of time from one place to another to preach Islam. Although one of the hijras, after returning from chilla, reverted to their normative life as a man, they rejoined the hijra community about six months later.

What emerges is that hijras are spatially in tune with their mainstream working-class neighbours with whom they interact in a neighbourly capacity, and this tends to be reciprocated. While in quotidian settings, hijras share a lot with the females of the neighbourhoods, they not only join the menfolk at times to participate in public Islamic gatherings, but also often extend hands of cooperation during medical emergencies and social festivities. What these interactions underscore is that hijras live in keeping with the conventions of neighbourliness, like the rest of mainstream society in Dhaka, despite their being visibly marked as hijras within its working-class neighbourhoods.

In her paper on hijras in Pakistan, Pamment (2010, 30) contends that the elite class approves of greater gender bending and sexual norms in contrast to the lower and the middle classes, to whom gender and sexual transgression are unimaginable. In contrast, my fieldwork and experience of interacting with the hijras suggested, as evidenced in the vignettes presented above, that the working class populace are far more accepting of the hijras. This is, however, not to suggest that the general understanding of the working classes regarding gender and sexuality is different from that of their middle-class counterparts. Like the middle classes, the working-class populace too conceive the social universe in terms of tripartite categories of men, women and hijras. Yet working-class people, owing to their spatial proximity and everyday entanglement with hijras, tend to have greater understanding and acceptance of hijras in Bangladesh than the middle classes, including the gay-identified sections, for whom hijras are the working-class deviant 'other'

---

[1] The assumption derives from one of the oft-quoted *hadith*s, or sayings of the Prophet, according to which men who dress like women and women who dress like men are to be condemned. See also Murray and Roscoe (1997) and Rahman (2014) for historical and contemporary examples and discussion of varied practices of cross-dressing and sexual identifications in Muslim societies.

in opposition to which their own notions of respectable gender and sexual categories are negotiated and produced. The middle-class image of hijras is based largely on media reportage and various medicalizing discourses around gender ambiguity, which I elaborate in chapter 7.

Rethinking badhai, the quintessential hijra occupation

It was around 11:00 a.m. and hijras were gathered at the house of Meghna, the guru entrusted with the task of supervising the house of Jomuna. Jomuna, the nonagenarian hijra guru, had bought a small piece of land in Hridoypur some twenty years ago, and it was here that Meghna, Jomuna's favourite cela, conducted hijragiri. Hijras had started gathering at Meghna's house at 10:00 a.m. Later they broke into two groups. One group composed of three young hijras took a rickshaw to go to the sweeper colony in the old part of town. The other group, consisting of four young hijras, set out on foot as they would be conducting badhai in the adjacent areas. A point worth noting here is that each of these groups had one chibry (emasculated hijra) with them, while the rest were jananas, or hijras with penises. I joined the walking group but was told to stay at a safe remove so that the 'jodgman', the hijra word for regular members of society, would not suspect my being with them. Dressed in saris, four of them left the room with permission from Jomuna, who had come early that morning. One of them took a drum and slung it around their neck. With a small recorder in my pocket, I walked slowly behind them. Trawling through the narrow dust-filled alleys for about half an hour, they started looking for houses where newborn children might be found. One of the group went inside the houses, or peeped through the doors or windows, to see if there was any sign of a newborn child. I was told that one of the ways to find out was to see if there were *falia*s (small trappings) hanging from the clothesline to dry in the sun.

If a woman is *vabraj* ('pregnant' in the hijra argot), hijras count the months until the probable birth of the child and come back accordingly. After checking about a dozen houses, they chanced upon a house with a newborn. Unlike middle-class households, the gates of most of these houses were open. In poor neighbourhoods in Dhaka, gates are often left open during the day; however, there is commonly shared etiquette pertaining to how one enters through the gate into another's home. One of the hijras barged in to check first and then beckoned the others to move in. It was a single-storey building, within which there was a narrow, L-shaped passage with five rooms lined

Class-Cultural Politics and the Making of *Hijras*

Figure 2.1 *Hijras* performing *badhai* in a working-class neighbourhood in Dhaka
Source: Author.

up in a row. One hijra took the baby in their lap and started dancing and singing while the rest sat on the ground clapping and drumming. As they were performing, a group of curious bystanders elbowed through the narrow alley and encircled the hijras to watch the performance. After performing a few songs and dancing, one of them went inside the room and brought some mustard oil. They whispered some mantra-like words into the ear of the newborn and smeared oil on its head (Figure 2.1). When all this was over, they began to demand money for the badhai. The conversation that took place is given in translation below:

Mousumi: Give us money. ©[2]

(Hijras start to sing and dance.)

Mousumi: What is the matter? Where is the father of the child?

---

[2] I use the copyright sign (©) to indicate 'accompanied by clapping' throughout this chapter.

Mother: He is out on the road.

Three hijras in unison: Go and get him.

Liza: Go bring him here. © Go bring him. Or else we will insult you. ©

Neighbour: Sing another song.

Mousumi: Did you hire us with money to dance and sing? ©

Liza (pointing to the gathering crowd): Go away. What is wrong? Why are you here? Have you seen us before? Are you here to see new vaginas or what? Why don't you go? Give us something. We will go away. Don't just keep standing like this. Give something. Haven't you seen people like us in Bangladesh? ©

Neighbour (addressing the mother of the child): Go and get something. Or else they will attack and snatch away the child. Go, get 100 taka for them.

Hijras (suddenly conversing among themselves in Ulti): They have kept us waiting for long. Let us insult them. (One of them says to wait for a while.)

An old woman: Sing another song.

Mousumi: Go, you old whore. Go, sleep with the grandfather. You won't get pregnant, go and fuck him.

Hijras (talking among themselves in Ulti): We should insult them. Let us give them a serious bashing.

Me: What if they don't give anything?

Liza: No. We danced.

A male neighbour: If you don't sing a few more songs, they won't give anything.

Liza: Why don't you give? You are the uncle of the child.

Mousumi: We have been waiting for half an hour. We danced and sang so many times. What else do they want? We will have to go to other places.

Neighbours [addressing the mother]: Why don't you give?

Mousumi: Call the father. I will ask him to impregnate me the way he impregnated the child's mother. Let him marry me. I neither have a crack nor a hole. Let him marry one of us and then there will be no pregnancy. There will be no poverty. No hijra will come then. Both will earn. This is the first house we have come to demand badhai today.

Class-Cultural Politics and the Making of *Hijras*

The old woman: Sing another song.

Mousumi: You old whore. Why don't you sing? It hurts to sing. The householders are silent and you neighbours are so excited. Where is the mother of the child? Has the father fled away? Let me go out and bring the father inside.

Liza: I will insult like anything. I will curse. Give us our dues for the newborn.

Neighbour: You have been sitting. Why don't you sing? They will be happy if you sing and then they will give.

Mother: His father is calling someone outside for money. He has no money.

Mousumi: Your husband is involved in politics and has a regular flow of cash. You are not likely to be going short. He earns between 300–500 taka (US$4–6) daily. So you must give us 200 taka.

Mother: Take this one hundred. We are poor. I managed one hundred after a lot of requests from his father.

Mousumi (addressing the neighbours): How can they be poor? He earns cash every day. What does he do? Does he traffic in prostitutes? You must bring two hundred. And then we will leave.

Another woman: Don't you see they are poor?

Mother: This is all we have. Please leave.

Mousumi: If you don't bring two hundred, I will bang my head and bleed and tell everyone that you have hurt us.

Mother: This is not fair.

Mousumi: Only four of us have come. If you don't donate us something, we will bring ten more hijras. I will bang my head and bleed.

Liza: You can't fool hijras. ©

Neighbour: Just take whatever is given.

Mousumi: No way. Go, fuck and eat flattened rice.

Neighbour addressing the mother: Today you have been caught.

Mousumi (addressing the remaining crowd): Go and get us some betel leaves. We have neither cracks nor holes. So give to us. ©

Neighbour: Get the child. They will pray for the child.

Mother: Take these rice and potatoes.

Sonia: Put it in this red sack.

Mousumi: We would not have left without five hundred but we are leaving only because of you (addressed to the neighbour who insisted that the household was poor).

A number of themes emerge from the description above. Significantly, the household where the hijras performed was markedly lower class. This tallies with the assertion that hijras undertake badhai only in such working-class households in Dhaka. Crucially, hijras too hail from such a background, meaning that it is a milieu with which they are familiar. The fact that hijra performances are restricted to working-class backgrounds is significant, especially in view of the fact that in India the chief patrons of hijras are the middle and upper-middle classes (Jaffrey 1997; Nanda 1999). Here, what is worth pointing out is that unlike India where people commonly look upon hijras as cultural performers and ritual specialists, there is no corresponding recognition of hijras as such in urban Bangladesh. Ethnographers note that in the Indian context it is not only on the occasion of the birth of a male child, but also during marriage ceremonies that hijras make appearances to bless the newlyweds with fertility. Hijras in India are also said to gatecrash marriage ceremonies and make demands. In contrast, a similar sort of gatecrashing in the middle-class neighbourhoods of Dhaka would be inconceivable. As a middle-class Bangladeshi born and brought up in Dhaka, I never saw hijras making similar sorts of demands during marriage ceremonies. The very practice of hijras blessing newlyweds with fertility is culturally unrecognized in middle-class, urban Bangladesh.

Yet the badhai performance described here clearly indicates that hijras make some sort of a claim to being a special group of people with the ritual power to bless and curse. Does it mean that the working-class populace in Bangladesh conceptualize hijras differently from their middle- and upper-class counterparts? It is worth recalling that hijras, during their search for the houses, did not seek any permission to enter the houses. Moreover, when they found a house, they went straight into the room, took the child and started singing and dancing. What exactly is it that empowers hijras to barge into these households and perform? Why did the family finally pay the hijras? Does this practice of 'barging in' index local economies of belief wherein hijras are implicitly conceptualized as sacrosanct beings with the power to confer blessings? We can also note from the badhai performance here that the householder agreed to pay the hijras only in the face of irresistible demand and with the constant exhortations of the neighbours.

Class-Cultural Politics and the Making of *Hijras*   67

Although ethnographers of Indian hijras note a similar sort of bargaining, the very fact that hijras make claim to such status—and that people reciprocate—is explainable on account of the hijras' association with Hindu mother goddesses. Hijras, Nanda notes, invoke the name of the mother goddesses to confer blessings, whereas in Muslim-dominated Bangladesh there is no such popular conflation of hijras with a mother goddess, a reality hijras too acknowledge. Although hijras consider badhai to be their archetypal occupation prescribed by the goddess Maya Ji (see chapter 4 for a full unpacking of this myth), they also clearly acknowledge the lack of its cultural salience in Bangladesh, as evidenced by the following remarks from Jomuna:

> You know in India if you decline, hijras would beat you up and rebuke you badly. Do you know what hijras in Delhi, Bombay and Kolkata get? Twenty ounces of gold and twenty sacks of rice per household. And only then they leave.

In explaining to me the reason for the reluctance of the people to give, Jomuna pointed to the lack of skill on the part of the new generation of hijras, opining, 'You know those who you see these days are useless with no proper skill in either singing or dancing. All they know is sex. Why would people give to them?' She delivered this opinion with an air of despondence. Rina, another sadrali, told me that it is not easy to get money from the houses of the newborn. 'You know we have to talk them into paying us. Moreover, not every household we visit to conduct badhai pays us. Sometimes it is 100 taka and sometimes 150, and at times it is just 10 taka.' Many households in the face of hijras' persistent demand take them inside the house to show them their assets. Thus, it is only after prolonged bargaining, pleading and at times shaming and insulting that hijras manage to obtain 'alms' both in cash and kind.

It is important to note that hijras do not perform badhai in their immediate neighbourhood but in other working-class areas, where the same group of hijras are seen to take on a different persona, contrary to their image of being good neighbours. In other words, it is through transgressing the conventional norms of neighbourliness that hijras assert their identity. In her analysis of hijra use of abuse with the mainstream, Hall (1997) interprets such 'verbal insolence' as a subversive act whereby hijras pull the mainstream into conversations with them in order to challenge the discourses of respectability and heteronormativity that the mainstream deploys to marginalize them. Although hijras' conversation with members of the wider society serves as a site where notions of gender and class are transacted, what I intend to highlight here is that in terms of badhai and the encounter between the mainstream and hijras, what we see is a conventionalized form of exchange where transgression and haggling are part of the game rather than the exception. Hijra acts of barging into people's houses and making demands on the occasion of the birth of a child contravene the conventional rules of neighbourliness. Yet that hijras enter and make demands is not something that the households do not anticipate. It is, after all, a known fact that once hijras enter a household, haggling will follow. In that sense, badhai is a unique context where exchange of gift follows a pattern of conventionalized transgression, contrary to dominant anthropological perspectives on gift exchange. While anthropological accounts, as will be shown later, often underscore the centrality of gift exchange in the production of reciprocal sociality, rarely is haggling invoked as a part of the gift exchange convention.

My sadrali hijra interlocutors pointed out that they carry out badhai less for income generation and more for the sake of it being a central hijra occupation. Badhai, as many of my hijra interlocutors often highlighted, is an indispensable and defining feature of sadrali hijra identity. Unlike other activities like *birit manga* (see later) and sex work, badhai is considered sacrosanct. For instance, before setting out for badhai, hijras worship the *dhol* (drum) and seek permission from the guru. Hijras also carry a special red sack known as an *oli* to store foodstuffs like rice, potatoes, vegetables and lentils that they receive from the households that they visit. Upon returning to the house of the guru, hijras put the drum back and then hand the oli to the guru. Hijras maintain that the oli 'gets heated', so upon returning home their first duty is to 'cool down the oli'. 'Oli is the business of hijras. We hijras make our ends meet with the help of this oli,' stated Mousumi. The foodstuff and the money gained from badhai are given straight to the guru. The guru then distributes the money among the celas. The foodstuffs are either consumed by the hijras or sold out in the market.

What emerges is that although the wider society including the working class may not subscribe to the idea of hijra ritual and sacred power, hijras in Bangladesh do often claim to have such prowess, evidenced from their acts of paying respect towards the drum and the subsequent cooling down of the oli. More significantly, when hijras receive rice from households, they return a portion of it to their benefactors immediately. Hijras pointed out that if the rice is not returned, such acts of giving may in the long run bring bad luck for the household. 'You know it is bad for the household if everything they give is taken away by us. So we give a fist of rice back so that nothing bad happens to them,' explained Liza. How do we explain the hijra performance of badhai in a cultural context that does not explicitly recognize such performances as special or sacred? Perhaps one way to understand this is to look at the local systems of exchange relations within which badhai performances can be located. The importance of an exchange perspective lies in the fact that it helps us better understand the broader moral order across the class divides within which the very presence of hijras in Bangladesh is rendered intelligible. An exchange perspective also helps us come to grips with structural inequalities, class-cultural practices and the corresponding notions of respect, respectability and commensality.

Critiquing Dumont's postulation of purity–impurity as the structuring principle of Indian caste-based social structure, Raheja (1989) argues the case of (in)auspiciousness as a more nuanced way to re-conceptualize the exchange relations in the Indian context. Raheja's proposition centres on the idea that it is through acts of giving that the donor passes the inauspiciousness to the donee, which the donee then passes on to others or counteracts. Prestation, thus, is a form of exchange through which the giver gets rid of the evil, the 'poison in the gift', to expropriate Raheja. At first blush, hijra exchange relations during badhai may seem indicative of some embedded underlying structural logics of exchange in terms of which gifts are transacted between hijras and their non-hijra working-class counterparts. We see this in the way hijras return a portion of the 'gift' that they receive to ensure the welfare of the donating household. Although in Raheja's case such acts of prestation are redolent of a deep-seated reciprocal transaction wherein upper castes pass gifts to the lower castes, what is different in the context of badhai is that the donors and the donees are more or less of the same class backgrounds. While Raheja's disquisition on exchange relations in a casted society may not apply across the board in Bangladesh, her account offers insights into the Islamically inspired cultural logic within which prestational exchange takes place in Bangladesh.

In her paper on hierarchical gift economies among British Pakistanis, Werbner (1990) elaborates, among other things, systematics of gifting in Muslim-majority Pakistan, contending that while gifts are directed towards superiors, inferiors and equals in Pakistan with variable implications for social prestige and status, such acts of giving are intended in the name of Allah, whose blessings are sought through such giving. In a similar vein, in Bangladesh, gift giving, or *dan-khairat*, is predominantly understood as a form of exchange whereby the donor gives away to the poor in a bid to seek Allah's blessings. Here, the recipient is a mere medium to propitiate Allah, in whose hands the ultimate welfare of the people lies. For instance, the rich give to the poor on the occasion of Eid al-Fitr and Eid al-Adha, two important Islamic festivals marking the end of Ramadan and Hajj respectively. Furthermore, Muslims are required to give to the needy as part of their religious obligation. Such donations are not restricted to only Eid festivals. Muslims in Bangladesh make such offerings throughout the year, especially in times of *bipod-apod/bala-musibod* (bad times/danger). When people suffer from bala-musibod, there is a widespread practice of sacrificing animals and distributing their meat among the poor to get rid of the inauspiciousness inherent in such moments. People also often arrange a feast for the poor, called 'kangali voj', or make offerings to a shrine. Some also arrange *milad mahafil*, a special prayer after which the religious performers along with the guests are fed. In all these acts, the idea is to pre-emptively guard against the possibility of bala-musibod occurring.

Aside from such formalized acts of giving, people give away money to beggars on an almost daily basis. One of the striking features of Dhaka is a conspicuous presence of beggars almost everywhere. Those who give away a taka or two often do so to earn *sawab* (divine goodwill), or with the hope that this will bring some good in the long run. In that sense, people in Bangladesh through their acts of giving anticipate some celestial reciprocity. While literally it may seem like a transfer of evil to the poor, it is Allah who is expected to reciprocate rather than the poor. While the poor invoke the name of Allah during begging and remind people of Allah's bounty that they will be entitled to through such acts of prestation, what the donee offers is *dua* (prayer) to Allah for the donor. Here, both acts of giving and receiving are oriented towards Allah, who reserves the sole right to judge and reciprocate, while the donor becomes a mere medium.

Hijras categorically maintain that their acts of demanding are not in any sense akin to the acts of begging undertaken by the mainstream beggars (see also Saria 2019). For instance, hijras often justify such claims on the ground of their being born 'genitally disfigured'. On many occasions, I witnessed events that seemed to lend credence to the idea that this was a widespread notion. One of the houses where hijras found a newborn turned out to be the local imam's. I followed the hijras and went inside. While the hijras were waiting outside the gate of the room, a man suddenly appeared and inquired about what was going on. One hijra explained to him that they were there to get their dues for the newborn. In response, the man brought to the notice of hijras that the child of the imam was more than one year old. Mousumi immediately retorted by saying that they had a licence from the government that entitled them to badhai money for children up to the age of five. Mousumi sarcastically told the members in the house that the imam earned throughout the year and hence should pay them more than others did. In the meantime, the man sent a little boy to the imam, who was in the nearby mosque. The boy returned with a 100 taka note. The man immediately gave away the 100 taka note to the hijras. Later the hijras told me that because this was the house of an imam, they were not very harsh towards them and left peacefully without any bargaining. Later I spoke to the imam and was told that although 'disfigured', hijras were creatures of Allah and ought to be loved. On another occasion when a household questioned why they should pay, the hijras drew their attention to the fact that they were given a licence from the government to carry out badhai and that this was something they had been undertaking from time immemorial. 'This is our right. We are hijras. What can we do? We are not like men or women that we can take up a regular job. So you have to provide for us. Would you not have given some cash if any of your children were like us?' stated Mousumi.

What emerges is that hijras in Bangladesh, while demanding badhai, invoke the popular discourse of their being physically 'impaired' and 'disfigured' and it is on these grounds that they rationalize their demands. Although hijras in Bangladesh are not necessarily looked upon as sacrosanct with special religious power, they are still feared on account of their putative state of disfigurement, an image that hijras too routinely invoke in substantiating their demands. Yet the trope of disfigurement or handicap that hijras invoke is characteristically distinct from that of the normative 'handicapped' beggars in that while the 'disfigurement' in the latter case is visible, in the case of hijras it is not. That is, here disfigurement is conflated with a hijra's putative defective or missing genitals. In other words, it is not just as disfigured persons but as a specific sort of disfigured person that hijras make their demands. Key distinctions between hijra acts of demand and mainstream begging lie in the fact that while the mainstream disabled beggars do not generally force people to donate, hijras do. Furthermore, that hijras resort to coercive techniques to solicit their demands is anticipated, unlike in the case of normative begging. Moreover, hijras do not conceptualize their acts of demanding as begging. Rather, they draw a clear distinction between mainstream begging and their acts of demanding, which they try in various ways to ritually validate (see later for more on this). Another important distinction here is that while hijras carry out badhai in working-class neighbourhoods, the mainstream disabled beggars typically frequent middle-class neighbourhoods to beg. Also noteworthy is the fact that unlike the normative beggars, who remain at the mercy of the people, hijra presence activates masculine anxieties, thereby 'coercing' the householders into payment. Thus, while the broader cultural logics of gift and exchange elucidated in this section inform people's acts of gifting to hijras, what is at stake here is not just the supposed disfigurement of hijras, but more significantly masculine anxiety, to which I now turn.

Verbal slurs, masculine anxiety and badhai

While the broader cultural logics of prestation in Bangladesh partially explain working-class acts of donation to hijras, a closer look at badhai performance also reveals more interesting gender dynamics. Before I make my point, let me reproduce an excerpt from a heated conversation that hijras had with a reluctant mother that I recorded:

Hijra: If you don't pay us money, how will we live and eat? Call your husband and ask him to marry the four of us. Ask him to impregnate us all. We have been sent by the government to dance with the newborn. ©

Mother: In my village hijras work and earn. They don't do what you do.

Hijra: They are men. We are not. We are real hijras. ©

Mother: Leave my house at once. I will not pay you a penny.

Hijra: You fucking whore, give us money now.

Mother: This is why you have been born impotent. What Allah did to you is justified.

Hijra: Go and ask your man to pay us immediately. When he fucked and impregnated you, didn't he realize he would have to pay the price for this? ©

Householder (dramatically appearing from the house): Come back some other day and I will pay you.

Hijra: No we won't leave until you pay. You have been blessed with a male child. When he grows up he will earn and feed you. Now give something. ©

Householder: I have no money. Please come another day.

Class-Cultural Politics and the Making of *Hijras* 73

> Hijra: If you have no money then why did you fuck her and impregnate her? Why did you become a father? Would you not have given if your child was born a hijra? ©

There are a few things to be noted with respect to the excerpt above and badhai performance in general. First, hijras tend to perform badhai mostly on the occasion of the birth of a male child. Although hijras in Bangladesh also demand badhai money for the birth of a female child, when a male child is born the demand they make is much higher, mirroring hijra convention in India (Nanda 1999). During my several visits to working-class households where hijras demanded badhai, my interlocutors always demanded more when a male child was born. In that sense, my argument is that badhai can be read as a celebration of (male) masculinity.

Second, several households that hijras visited to demand badhai later argued that the reason they gave to hijras was not only because hijras were 'disfigured', but also because of the curses hijras hurled at them. For instance, one male householder specifically argued that the reason he gave what hijras demanded was to make sure that nothing bad could happen to his son. What he meant was that he would not want his child to become a hijra when he grew up. In other words, because a male child is desirable, someone who will 'light up the face of the father', a sense of fear that his child too might end up as a non-man/hijra is performatively instilled into the households via the presence of hijras; that is, hijra performance in the household setting instigates masculine anxieties whereby both the father and mother of the child are directly confronted with the possibility of their son being a hijra.

Third, in all the badhai conversations I reproduced here, hijras made the demand on the male householder and not the females. Hijras typically ask the women in the house to go and get the money from the men. Recall that in the first badhai I elaborated, Mousumi repeatedly asked the mother of the child to go and bring her husband back to the house and pay. Even in the case of the imam that I noted earlier, we see a similar pattern. Also noteworthy is the fact that in all these cases, the reason those householding men gave money to hijras was not only because of the fear that their male children might too become 'disfigured' like hijras, but also because they all wanted to protect the honour of the women in the house. That hijras invoke sexualized conversations brings dishonour to the householders, whose own masculine honour is jeopardized in the face of the hijra use of obscenities. For example, one of the householders categorically argued that the reason he met the demands of hijras was to get rid of them so that the women in the house were not shamed at the sight of them lifting up their saris. Also recall that the man in the last excerpt I presented dramatically appeared from out of the house immediately after the hijras started abusing his wife, highlighting his penetrating of her and making her pregnant. Also noteworthy in the first badhai is that while hijras shamed an old female neighbour, they refrained from abusing the mother. Rather, the main target of their vilification was the father who sired the child and therefore was expected to provide for the child. Hijras disgraced the householding men more than the women. In that sense, the use of verbal slurs by hijras poses a threat to the masculine honour of the household, which is dependent upon the protection of feminine virtue (see Osella, Osella and Chopra 2004 for more on masculine honour being dependent on feminine virtue in South Asia more broadly).

Fourth, aside from extensive use of profanities, one of the distinctive features of hijras is their clapping. While *thikri*, the hijra word for clapping, serves as a quintessential marker of hijra identity in public space in Bangladesh, hijras employ various forms of clapping depending on the context. While I elaborate other connotations and contextual variations of this semiotic practice in chapter 5, here I highlight only its deployment in the context of public settings, especially badhai. As I already noted and will further elaborate, hijras often let the wider society know of their presence through their distinctive clapping. My hijra interlocutors in Hridoypur and elsewhere in Dhaka often unambiguously stated that a true hijra could be separated from a false one from the sound of their clapping. In public, hijras employ clapping to make their bellicose imminence and presence felt. Accompanying demands, as in the context of badhai, such clapping also works to coerce the public to give in to hijra demands. Hijras claim sole ownership of this practice. Meghna once related, 'Every group has its symbol. We too have ours. For hijras, it is clapping.' One hijra once stated to me during a badhai practice that there was a time when hijras, by virtue of their special clapping, could exercise special magical power, including turning disabled children into able-bodied ones. While hijras publicly claim to possess the power to bless and curse on account of their disfigurement, internally, however, hijras often attribute their possession of such powers and clapping abilities to two hijra goddesses (I discuss this in more detail in chapter 4). Clapping works to assert one's authentic hijra identity not only in public, but also in private. Clapping is also a part of a generic practice known as 'borhani'—literally, frightening or shaming people. In the context of heated exchanges with the mainstream, a certain kind of clapping is a way of initiating borhani to communicate aggression and combat social hostility (Pamment 2019b). Hijras also argued that in times of emergency if a hijra is under attack, especially in a public setting, a single loud, flat-palmed clap is used to alert other hijras nearby.

Cholla manga: hijras in the bazaar

Cholla manga—literally, collecting money and foodstuff from the bazaar—is another ritually sanctioned source of income for the sadrali hijras. Typically, once or twice a week, hijras collect cholla both in cash and kind only within the birit, the ritual jurisdiction within which a hijra group is allowed to perform badhai and cholla. Collection from marketplaces is a major source of income for the hijra community in Bangladesh. Cholla is considered a legitimate source of income, unlike the monies earned through sex work, and is used for the conduct of hijragiri; collection from marketplaces is handed back to the guru who in turn distributes it among the celas, while money earned through sex work belongs solely to the hijras. Too often fights ensue over the trespassing of birit. To put the picture in perspective, I reproduce an excerpt from my diary:

> Jorina, Maya, Katha and Ishita, all dressed up in saris, gathered at Hira's house to set out for cholla. Paying respect to Hira, the guru, they started on foot for the bazaar. They had four big bazaars to cover while another group of hijras went to collect from the fruit market. Rahimpur being a birit full of bazaars of different sizes meant hijras not only had to do a lot of hard work but also that these groups on average had more income compared to hijras from other areas like Hridoypur. I followed the group led by Jorina. Jorina, now twenty-five years old, had been Hira's cela for the last five years. Maya and Katha were new initiates, while Ishita was recently initiated into the group via Jorina. After about twenty minutes of walking, as we neared the furniture market, they paused to buy some paan pata, or betel leaves. Beautifully folding a leaf and filling it with slices of areca nut and an iota of slaked lime, Jorina gleefully inserted the paan into their mouth. Crossing over to the other side of the road, they all started clapping and demanding cholla.
>
> The very presence of hijras in the bazaar, it seemed, was a breath of fresh air for the vendors otherwise tired of the din and bustle of the bazaar. As

hijras kept moving into the bazaar, vendors seemed overexcited. 'There they come,' cried out a few vendors at a remove. Many shopkeepers were acquainted with this group. Each shop they approached gave away one or two taka (equivalent to US$0.01–0.02). The hijras at times picked up fresh cucumbers or onions from the sitting vendors. While demanding cholla, Jorina and their gang flirted with almost all the shopkeepers with explicit sexual innuendos. 'How are you darling? I called you so many times last night. Why didn't you pick up? Don't you know I can't fall asleep without talking to you,' stated Jorina to one vendor. The vendor, seemingly in his late fifties, giggled and gave away a few potatoes. Another vendor refused to give any tomatoes. The hijras became angry and started threatening them. 'Give us tomatoes. Give us. Allah will give you in return,' said Jorina but the vendor stubbornly refused. Then hijras took a packet of tomatoes. The vendor tried taking it back and then a slight bargaining ensued. Finally, the hijras left with four tomatoes. While Jorina was collecting vegetables, Ishita was collecting monies on the other side. Maya and Katha, being new to this group and the area, were carrying the sacks and clapping off and on to back up Jorina and Ishita. As they went close to the row of rice shops, Jorina's group was greeted with laughter. Each vendor put a handful of rice into the sack as if they were all waiting to hand in the pre-agreed shares. One of the vendors wondered if they would like to have tea. Another vendor inquired about Maya and Katha: 'Who are they? I have not seen them before.' Introducing them as their celas, Jorina in an instructive voice stated, 'Hello uncle, look at their faces carefully. Next time when they come on their own, make sure you acknowledge them. These two are my new celas. They are real. Don't give to some fake hijras.'

There are a few things to be noted here. First, although there were middle-class customers all around, hijras demanded cholla only from the vendors and not from either the working-class or middle-class shoppers. It is also in such bazaar settings that hijras directly confront the middle classes, although there is hardly any interaction. Nowadays a new gated shopping complex is built in Dhaka every few months, to which hijras are not allowed entry. The new middle classes tend to shop increasingly in such shopping malls rather than the open markets where hijras traditionally make their demands. Second, unlike the middle classes who tend to be disgusted at the sight of hijras, the working-class vendors tend to be exuberant about hijra presence. As hijras promenade through the bazaar, they not only take control of the space by swaggering up and down but their very presence works to 'carnivalize' the lacklustre bazaar settings (cf. Gilmore 1993, Crichlow and

Armstrong 2010). The ludic eroticized playfulness and flamboyance mixed with belligerent recalcitrance often render the bazaar settings carnivalesque. Although very different from typical carnival settings, hijras speak licentiously and also lighten the minds of the people there. Nevertheless, such playfully sexualized repartee and ribald jokes that hijras deploy in a bid to demand their share often escalates into confrontations. Third, while hijras invoke their bodily defect as a rationale for their demanding vendors' goods, their aggressive and lecherous gestures, jokes and conversations push the envelope concerning the conventional rules of propriety that define public space in Bangladesh.

While I have more to say about hijra presence in public settings, I introduce another vignette to clarify the context. In Dhaka, as elsewhere, as already indicated previously, hijras often carry with them special 'identity papers' signed by the local law-enforcing agencies to justify their demands. I reproduce below excerpts from one such 'identity paper' in translation.

> Identity paper
>
> Subject: Permission to seek help from the inhabitants of Asulia area
>
> Sir,
>
> We (1. Rashida, 2. Putuli,) have been living in this area for 15/16 years as hijras with the help of the public. So far no harm has been done to the inhabitants of this area by us. There will never be any harm to anyone in the area in future as well. The markets we visit to seek help are as follows: 1) Amtola 2) Benipur 3) Shimulia 4) Gohayil 5) Jirani.... Once or twice a week and on special days like the two Eid festivals, we collect money from these aforesaid bazaars to make our ends meet. We, the members of the hijra community like to stay peacefully beside the brothers and sisters of the area. Under this circumstance we request you to endorse our application to work in the area.
>
> Sincerely yours,
>
> Rashida and Putuli.

This letter of appeal was approved, signed and stamped by the local police. The officer in charge of the police station also wrote a note requesting the inhabitants to extend their cooperation on humanitarian grounds. Although hijras do not necessarily carry such letters during cholla, they mention this letter of authorization as a way to justify their demands. I previously noted that hijras drew the attention of the households to their being given permission by the state to demand badhai. In a similar vein, hijras during cholla collection often invoke the government as empowering them to do so. While in the Indian context, hijras invoke the names of the mother goddess, hijras in Bangladesh invoke the state authority to press their demands, even though there is no such legal statute to grant hijras the right to carry out either badhai or cholla. That such letters are granted on humanitarian grounds is also indicative of the discourse of disfigurement and handicap in terms of which hijras are understood by the police and the wider society. One police officer later explained that because hijras are sexually handicapped, they need the support of the wider society to survive.

There are a few things to be noted here. First, in making the demand, hijras stress their being helpless people. Like the police authority, a number of rice and vegetable sellers drew my attention to the helpless situation of hijras as a reason for their patronage. 'Hijras are helpless. They don't have what we have. Allah made them that way. So we help,' stated one vendor. Hijras typically stress their being born with defective or missing genitals to justify their demands. While support for and approval of hijras from the working-class vendors in the bazaar settings is explainable in terms of the broader cultural logic of dan-khairat that I previously elucidated, here I want to highlight the discourse of disfigurement that both hijras and their patrons invoke in conceptualizing the hijras. In the context of south Indian beggars affected by leprosy, Staples (2011) draws our attention to gendered reading of disability, arguing that while disabled people, especially males, are popularly denied their masculinity on account of their disability-specific status, such stigmatized status also works to hyper-masculinize the disabled in their encounter with the non-disabled public. Drawing on Appadurai's (1990) concept of 'coercive subordination', Staples (2003) also highlights the contradictions of begging in the context of leprosy-affected persons' encounter with the mainstream. In a similar vein, while hijra acts of demanding position them as inferior to the wider public, their very invocation of embodied ambiguity works to produce a 'surfeit of masculinity', instilling a fear of curse by association. It is also through such encounters that hijras consolidate and become complicit with the wider societal conceptualization of their being 'disfigured'.

Second, such invocation of disfigurement and state power as part of their ritualized demand is a creative act of appropriating agency, not least because the traditional cultural role of hijra as performer is increasingly on the wane,

Class-Cultural Politics and the Making of *Hijras* 79

but also because the Bangladeshi state has taken strides to eradicate the hijra culture in a bid to mainstream them, issues I take up in chapter 7.[3]

Third, the socio-economic status of a hijra group largely depends on the birit; depending on the size and type of the ritual jurisdiction, income levels among hijra groups vary. While hijras in Hridoypur never really disclosed to me their monthly average income, they often drew my attention to other hijra birits and the relative income disparity. Speaking about Rahimpur, the birit that I already mentioned, hijras in Hridoypur argued that the average monthly income there was around 20,000 to 30,000 taka (roughly US$250–280) while during festivals like Eid, it could exceed US$1,000—a fact that, they argued, those hijra groups would never themselves disclose to outsiders. In speaking of cholla, hijras often drew my attention to 'birit bakhor', literally stealing of others' birit. Birit bakhor is considered a serious crime. Those found soliciting for money in unsanctioned territory are immediately penalized and at times special meetings are summoned to settle such disputes. If caught in the middle of a bazaar, hijras often expose the impostors to the jodgman as fake hijras. This is done by exposing the genitals of those hijras caught stealing, often followed by beating and chasing, and sometimes culminates in the instant cutting-off of the accused's hair. Here, the main purpose is to show to the wider society that those that pilfer are not real hijras but men in hijra guise. However, the irony of the matter is that those exposing are also often themselves jananas, or hijras with penises. Despite the fact that janana hijras are schooled in the art of magical disappearance of their penises, which I elaborate in chapter 5, under such circumstances, it is difficult to hide one's penis from public view, as a hijra once explained to me. The bazaar, therefore, serves as a site for intricate negotiation and contestation of authentic 'hijraness'.

Fourth, the encounter between hijras and the mainstream populace in the bazaar also serves as a site for gender transaction. In the bazaar settings, the exchange takes place between hijras and the male vendors. While people view hijras as non-men, the act of demanding in public space in Bangladesh is culturally understood as a form of masculine agency, such that the bazaar

---

[3] The recent initiatives of the government of Bangladesh to mainstream and 'rehabilitate' the hijras are reminiscent of the British colonial policy to ban such activities (Preston 1987). Hijra culture was also apparently banned in the 1960s in erstwhile East Pakistan (today's Bangladesh) (Pamment 2010). Also note that sadrali hijras often maintained that the police loved them more than others did. See also Nanda (1999, 7) for a similar observation.

is conceptualized predominantly as an all-male domain (see Osella 2012 for a similar kind of observation in south India). While hijras on account of their intrepid navigation of the bazaar environment and demanding cholla in the public space challenge the conventional stereotyping of them as non-masculine, it is precisely the paradoxical trope of their being non-masculine that both hijras and their patrons invoke to explicate those carnivalesque exchanges in the bazaar.

Conclusion

One of the key aims in this chapter was to foreground how class and gender and sexuality interact in the production of hijra subjectivities. I contend that the wider societal understandings about hijras are framed in class-specific terms as much as hijra senses of selfhood are inflected by the broader class-mediated notions of respectable gender and sexuality. Although people in Bangladesh, regardless of class background, conceive the social universe in terms of the tripartite divisions of men, women and hijras, the middle or intermediate category of hijras is often defined and described in class-specific terms. In other words, hijras are popularly invoked not only to describe gender nonconformity and failure, but also to describe specifically lower-class-style gender expressions. Hijras, in the popular imaginary, are therefore not just gender transgressive people, but class-specific gender 'deviants'. It is against the backdrop of such popular conceptualization that I described the enforced location of hijras in the working-class milieu in Bangladesh.

People generally conceive of hijras as not only working class gender 'deviant', but also as disfigured and disabled (Hossain 2017). While hijras are often complicit with the wider societal projection of their being so, the middle-class understanding of hijras is informed by media reportage. In contrast, the working-class people are directly entangled with hijras in their daily lives, with hijras living cheek by jowl with the mainstream working-class populace, not as some distant and ghettoized 'other', but as good neighbours to whom the mainstream working class can relate in terms of friendship and necessity. In contrast, I argued that there is no commensal interaction between hijras and the middle-class people in Bangladesh, for whom hijras often metaphorically stand in for the generic working-class people whom the middle classes imagine as simultaneously hyper-masculine and emasculate.

Finally, I demonstrated that unlike the stereotyped image of the working class as crude and unsophisticated and non-accepting of gender and sexual variance, it is the middle and upper classes who in Bangladeshi context fail to relate to hijras. Through ethnographically elucidating particular kinds of interaction between hijras and their working-class neighbours, I argued that not only are hijras spatially in tune with the working classes, but also that such interactions with their class counterparts serve as important sites for the production and reproduction of both the hijra subject position and the masculinities of the mainstream working-class men. Through appropriating various kinds of state machinery and establishment, hijras creatively exercise agency in pressing for their demands, acts that challenge the stereotypical image of hijras being 'effeminate'. Overall, this chapter foregrounded the politics of class in the positioning of hijras within the Bangladeshi social structure. Instead of taking class as a fixed category, this chapter complicated class as a process in the making that takes on critical valence in its encounter with other factors like desire and masculinities.

3 *Hijra* Erotic Subjectivities
Pleasure, Practice and Power

It was one of my regular visits to the house of Mousumi, one of the *cela*s of Meghna, the *hijra guru* in Hridoypur. Meghna was reclining on the bed while their celas were sitting on the floor. Hijras would often hole up at Mousumi's as their room was spacious and had a television. Nadira, a *gothia* of Mousumi, brought a 'dhurpiter chaya masi'—literally, 'film on fucking', or porn video, from a local CD shop. In one of the clips, a man was having sex with another man. Pointing to the penis and face of the penetrator, Mousumi started talking about a man they recently had sex with. 'The face and the penis of the person in the video take after my man,' they declared, while Mahi, Chottu and Hira, three celas of Meghna, were making erotic cries in a bid to taunt Mousumi. Within minutes the room was abuzz with laughter. Because the room was in the middle of a dense constellation of houses, the television sound was turned off. Although initially they had seemed extremely enthusiastic to watch this clip, the moment the actor who had been penetrated started penetrating, an utter sense of disgust was expressed, with profanities being yelled at not only the actor but also Nadira, who had brought this DVD. The television was switched off immediately and everyone in the room seemed extremely embarrassed.

The ethnographic vignette highlights a moment in the lives of my interlocutors and their exuberant engrossment in a porn video. It clearly shows that despite the popular perception of hijras being asexual, an image hijras themselves reinforce in their interaction with the mainstream, Mousumi spoke gleefully about their desire while the others revelled in playful sexual repartee. More importantly, it indexes a sense of disgust on the part of my hijra interlocutors towards certain types of male-to-male sexual acts. How do hijras negotiate *dhurpit*, the hijra word for sex and fucking? Why were my interlocutors in the above vignette disgusted? How does erotic desire shape hijra subjectivity? Would my interlocutors have reacted the way they did had I not been present in that room? In other words, did my presence as a normatively masculinized Bangladeshi subject work to prevent them from identifying with those sexual acts that they otherwise publicly denounce?

A closer inspection of extant ethnographic scholarship on hijras indicates a privileging of gender over desire as a critical analytical cipher. As already documented in the introductory chapter, Nanda's (1999) pioneering ethnography reads hijras as a third sex/gender while the overarching focus of later ethnographers (for example, Cohen 1995; Hall 1997; Reddy 2005a) was to develop a systematic critique of the inadequacies of the third sex/gender paradigm. While desire figured in their writings, it was framed mainly in terms of the trope of sexual renunciation and its (Hindu) scriptural valorization. Given the fact that the social standing of the hijras in India has historically been legitimized on the ground of putative asexuality, a view that hijras too reinforce on a daily basis, it perhaps makes sense that scholars amassed a wealth of scriptural evidence on the valorization of erotic asceticism as a way of coming to terms with hijras' lived erotic contradiction. Where this analytical move falters, however, is in its assumption that contemporary hijra erotic desires and practices are shaped by these scriptural standpoints. One outcome of this has been a sustained ethnographic inattention to erotic contradictions, ambivalences, meanings and practices that hijras, as will be shown later, deem central to their subjectivity. This dominant narrative of hijra asexuality has come under scrutiny with the advent of HIV/AIDS. In recent times, a growing body of scholarship, particularly in the field of public health, has documented a range of sexual practices through the lens of risk and disease (I. S. Khan et al. 2005; S. Khan, 1999). This slew of epidemiologically driven scholarship has had the (un)intended consequence of relegating the hijra subculture to a set of pathologies in dire need of intervention. While humanist and culturally sensitive ethnographies (Nanda 1999; Reddy 2005a) allude to hijra sexual practice, they rarely made any sustained attempt to adequately ethnographically illustrate the erotic practices and meanings that are central to the formation of hijra subjectivity. One of my central aims in this chapter, therefore, is to underscore the centrality of eroticism in the making of hijras.

There is, however, an obvious danger with any effort to map the sexual practices of hijras as disclosure of sexual practices may work to reinforce the orientalist proclivity to reduce them to positivist pathologies. From another slant, to bring into view hijra erotic desire and practice is to traffic in the obvious, that is, that hijras have sex is a common knowledge among social scientists who study them and is therefore analytically insignificant. For instance, Reddy (2005a) categorically contends that her project is to foreground how hijra subjectivities are not reducible to gender/sexual difference alone. Desire, in her analysis, is accorded critical valence in the context of intersectionality. It is on account of desire's imbrications with other vectors of social differentiation that it not only attains its critical significance but also is rendered sociologically intelligible. That sexuality or gender is constituted in a complex interplay with other modalities of differentiation like ethnicity, class, locality, and so on, is now common knowledge. The problem is that scholars concerned with exploring gender and sexual diversity are more interested in the intersectionality than they are in issues of desire. Put differently, critical sexuality scholarship often tends to be emptied of the actual erotic contents and sexual details of the lives of the people under study (Greenberg 1995). Against this backdrop, this chapter interrogates sexual practices and meanings not because they have been downplayed but because desire, as my hijra interlocutors pointed out, is central to their sense of selfhood. This incuriosity about hijra erotic lives is not just emblematic of scholarly indifference, but may very well be the corollary of a fundamental misunderstanding on the part of scholars as to what the occupation of a hijra subject position entails.

Dilemma, ambivalence and sexual conversation with hijras

Although hijras consciously refrain from talking about sex with outsiders and present an image of their being asexual, *dhurpiter khutni*, or 'sex talk', figured frequently in my interaction with hijras, not just because I was interested in their erotic lives, but also because of my long-term presence in the hijra universe in various capacities that I elaborate below. More often than not, I stood out as what hijras generically styled as a 'normative masculine man'. Yet my being there with them for such a long time led them to ignore my presence and go about their daily lives. For instance, among the *sadrali hijras*, who deem themselves and are deemed to be the embodiment of the ideal of asexuality, in keeping with the public understanding of what a hijra is, that is, persons born with defective or missing genitals and hence incapable of sexual intercourse and pleasure, talking about sex and desire was at times difficult. This was further compounded by the fact that by the time I became close with the sadrali group of Hridoypur, my presence as a friend of Meghna, the hijra guru in the community, was well established. Particularly among sadralis, a close male friend or a partner of a guru is a respectable figure whom the junior hijras are expected to treat respectfully. Junior hijras in Hridoypur would always address me as 'mama' (a term hijras often use to refer to the *parik*, the hijra word for partners of guru, though 'mama' in the mainstream means maternal uncle) and greet me with 'salamalaikum' (the standard Muslim greeting, literally 'peace be upon you', expressed when two people meet). Even Jomuna, Meghna's guru, would at times treat me as if I were their son-in-law. The fact that I was there to research and learn more about hijras made no sense to Jomuna or to the other hijras in Hridoypur. For instance, in response to my explanation for my frequent presence in Hridoypur, Jomuna once retorted, 'I know the game you men play. This is all nonsense. All you want is *butli* (buttocks). You can fool the whole world but not me. I am a hijra from the British era and I have seen this world more than you all have.' Because of the way I got adopted as Meghna's 'husband' by the members of the hijra group in Hridoypur, it was immensely difficult to talk to them openly about their sex lives. However, Meghna's gothias would often talk about sex explicitly. Ranu, a gothia of Meghna, would frequently tease me as if I were the husband of their sister. In addition, the *nati cela*s, or the grand disciples of Meghna, would often not only tease me but also behave in a coquettish manner. It is permissible for the nati celas and the gothias to flirt with the partners of a hijra, but anything verging on sex is to be strictly avoided in the interaction between the partner of a hijra and their immediate celas. Nevertheless, exceptions were made when at times some of my male friends accompanied me to Hridoypur. Celas of Meghna always inquired in Ulti not only about the intention of their visits, but also whether they were seeking sex. They often expressed their attraction and dislike towards my male friends by saying things like 'chis panthi' (literally 'a nice man') or 'bila panthi' (not a nice man) or 'aisi panthir khoma chis' (this man has a beautiful face) or 'oisi re takmu!' (I will eat him) or 'oisi ki hamsire dhurbo?' (would he like to fuck me?). On occasion, they struck up desirous poses or simply sat on their laps until a senior hijra scolded them to lay off.

While in Hridoypur, I could rarely speak to hijras about their sex lives, in other hijra houses I visited, initiating a discussion about sex was also difficult. For instance, when directly asked, hijras always inevitably denied that they were in any way sexual. It is, after all, the putative asexuality of hijras and its associated imagery of chastity that hijras highlight on a daily basis in their encounters with the mainstream. Yet sex sprang up as a topic in our interaction as soon as they realized that I was able to speak Ulti. Both the sadrali and 'dhurrani' (sex worker) hijras, having deciphered my ability to use Ulti, often remarked that I must have been a parik (a masculine-identified husband) of a hijra at some point in my life. My ability to speak Ulti indicated to them both my familiarity and closeness with hijras. Switching to a discussion on sex was also made easy by the fact that almost every hijra household had some members directly or indirectly linked with sexual health NGOs. In addition, sexual health materials—namely condoms, brochures, lubricants and posters—were to be found in (most) hijra households. Hence, a discussion on these NGO interventions always led to discussions on sex. Interestingly, it was mostly the junior hijras who seemed forthcoming in terms of sharing details about their sex lives, while the senior hijras often categorically denied any involvement with sex ever in their lives, although most of them had pariks. Senior hijras often argued that these NGO interventions were for the new hijras who did 'dhurpit turpit' (sex). Nevertheless, young hijras in the absence of their seniors drew my attention to the fact that their gurus were like them when they were young and as they grew old, they stopped doing 'night kam' (sex work) even though they all continued to have lovers.

The ambivalence registered by hijras towards sexual matters in public, as shown here, is contradicted by the hijras themselves. While the degree to which hijras share details with outsiders varies according to spatio-cultural locations, desire is internally deemed to be a central marker of the hijra subject position. And it is this constant tension between the public proclamation of asexuality and internal acknowledgement of desire that lies at the heart of hijra lives. I discuss this contradiction in terms of a mythic tale in chapter 4. I now go on to shed light on the way hijras navigate and negotiate these two contradictory universes of desire and asexuality respectively through the lens of Ulti.

Ulti universe of desire versus the Bangla world of hetero(a)sexuality

In the mainstream Bangla language, 'ulti' as a word means 'topsy-turvy', or simply 'reverse'. Ulti, or Ulti bhasa, also denotes language spoken in a reverse order, although in reality Ulti is not simply mainstream Bangla spoken in reverse order. Rather than considering Ulti to be a language, it is perhaps better understood as a dialect with a specialized set of words. Hijras, however, deploy this term to specifically denote a language of communication that they claim is spoken by hijras all over the world. Although the use of Ulti and its internal workings are not my focus here, suffice it to say that hijras use it not as a complete alternative to the mainstream Bangla. Rather, hijras tend to pepper their mainstream use of Bangla with Ulti idiolects to engender a parallel universe of signification that remains enmeshed in the mainstream yet makes an attempt to transcend it. While it is possible to use Ulti to have regular everyday conversations, hijras never really use it as an alternative to Bangla in that way. Rather, they routinely replace Bangla expressions with Ulti while registering erotic desire and practices.

That hijra or non-normative groups elsewhere often use special vocabularies is not a novel observation. Indeed, a lot has been written on the so-called secret or 'lavender' languages of sexual minorities in the Western context. In contrast, there is a dearth of scholarship on such semantic practices of non-Western sex/gender subjects (see Leap and Boellstorff 2004 for an exception). Several anthropologists, most notably Hall and O'Donovan (1996) and Reddy (2005a), have noted the presence of such vocabulary among hijras. Kira Hall was the first anthropologist to have paid sustained attention to hijra use of language, especially Hindi in India. Noting the use of this specialized vocabulary, or 'Farsi' as her interlocutors in Delhi styled it, she calls it 'hijralect'. More recently, linguists from Pakistan (Awan and Sheeraz 2011) also noted the presence of this special language among Pakistani hijras and contend that it is also known there as Farsi. While exact reasons why it is called Farsi and how it developed are unspecified in the existing literature, hijras in Delhi, according to Hall (2005), often traced it to the Mughal sultanate and its use of Farsi as the official language. Hijras in Bangladesh generally do not call it Farsi, although several Farsi words noted by others bear striking resemblance to hijra idiolects in Bangladesh.[1]

Although Hall (1997) critically interrogates the hijra use of Hindi, her prime concern is to foreground the ways hijra use of Hindi works to challenge the normative social codes through a system of semantic subversion. My approach differs from Hall's in that instead of focusing on the hijra use of language as a form of subversion, I examine the hijra language, or Ulti, through the lens of desire. My intention, thereby, is to foreground how hijras construct themselves as desiring subjects through Ulti and vice versa. According to my hijra interlocutors, Ulti is first and foremost a secret semiotic system. Hijras in Dhaka often contended that Ulti is not just a mere conglomeration of specialized vocabularies. Rather, Ulti is also about, in the words of one of

---

[1] See for example Mazumdar and Basu (1997) for a compilation of hijra Ulti words used in West Bengal, India and Bangladesh.

my interlocutors, 'facial expression, gesticulation and bodily comportments'. My observation is that while it can be read as a secret code, it also works to establish communitarian belonging and authentic membership (Boellstorff 2004a) within the broader universe of non-normatively gendered/sexed subjects in Bangladesh to which I alluded in chapter 1.

In their book *Language and Sexuality*, Cameron and Kulick (2003) bemoan the reduction of sexuality to sexual identity in much contemporary 'language and sexuality research'. They contend that while the dominant trend within this subfield is to foreground how language is used to forge and affirm identity, adopting the lenses of desire can nuance not only how we understand identity, but also how desire often exceeds both identity and language (see also Harvey and Shalom 1997 for a similar argument). Although they primarily propose psychoanalysis to examine desire, what I am interested in is how the very existence of Ulti allows hijras to navigate a different world of desire while being a part of the mainstream normative Bangla universe. Here, I follow Johnson (1997) to argue that hijras—much like his southern Filipino male-bodied, feminine-identified interlocutors—construe and conceive desire in terms of variously imagined worlds lying outside the geography of their origin. Yet I foreground that central to hijra erotic economy is a putative opposition between the Ulti world of desire and the Bangla world of hetero(a)sexuality.

Hijras explained to me that because sex and especially their desire for men are 'kacchi', that is, considered bad in the eye of the *jodgman*, the hijra word for the Bangla mainstream, Ulti had to be invented. In a way, understanding the Ulti universe, that is, the particular kinds of registers and conventions that hijras deploy to communicate desire, is tantamount to fathoming the internal workings of hijras. The fact that a different 'semiotic system of desire' (Cameron and Kulick 2003), or Ulti, is used underscores how hijras conceive eroticism and desire beyond and outside the mainstream Bangla world. Ulti, therefore, is not only a medium for secretive communication among members of the Ulti world alone, but, more importantly, a language of desire that cannot be articulated in mainstream Bangla. In other words, Ulti signifies and indexes a world of desire that is unsayable and unspoken in the mainstream Bangla idioms of desire. One of the widely used expressions among my hijra interlocutors was 'Bangla koti', an expression hijras use to refer to lower-class 'effeminate' males and middle-class gay men. The use of this pre-modifier 'Bangla' before 'koti' indexes a lack of formal affiliation with the alternative universe of desire. Every time my hijra interlocutors chanced upon non-Ulti speaking male-bodied, feminine-identified people in public gardens, they pejoratively labelled them as 'Bangla' or 'Bangla koti', highlighting the fact that they were yet to be schooled in the Ulti, or arcane, ways.

As previously noted, hijra ambivalence with regard to discussing sex derives from the contradiction between the Bangla societal understandings of hijra asexuality and the Ulti world of erotic desire and practice that hijras have to negotiate and navigate on a daily basis. Hijras both in Hridoypur and elsewhere always inevitably switched to Ulti while talking about sex. Ulti has a wide range of amorously loaded lexemes ranging from sexual organs to various kinds of erotic acts. Words related to erogenous body parts, sexual positions, and semen and sexual activities would always be described in Ulti, while the rest of the words in a sentence would be spoken in Bangla, the mainstream language.

What emerges is that, first, not only is the very existence of Ulti a manifestation of its being a secret argot for communication, but additionally, and more significantly, Ulti also works to affirm one's belonging to the hijra world or the wider universe of male-bodied, feminine-identified groups that are concatenated through a shared referent of Ulti desire. Second, it is through Ulti that hijras construct themselves as desiring subjects while being asexual in the Bangla mode, although their objects of desire, as I illustrate next and later in this book, are normative Bangla men, that is, men that are expected to be attracted to women. I elaborate the different articulations of hijra desire in relation to varied spatio-cultural contexts later in this chapter; I now turn to an elaboration of the structuring principles in terms of which hijras conceptualize desire and erotics.

Hijra erotic economy: engendering sexuality versus sexualizing gender

'We desire men (*hamsira panthi chis kori*). It is the desire for men that makes one a hijra,' explained Shefali, a sadrali hijra in Hridoypur. Like Shefali, hijras in Hridoypur and elsewhere often singled out their desire for men as opposed to women as the predominant reason why they are hijras. This sense of their not being men is causally linked with their desire for men. It is indeed difficult to pin down whether their identification as women is the direct result of their desire for men or whether their desire for men arises from their female identification (I elaborate hijra gender practices in chapters 4 and 5). What is, however, important to note is that it is not just desire for men but a shared expression of desire and one's conformity to it that makes one a hijra:

it is the desire to be anally penetrated by men that, hijras contend, makes one a hijra as opposed to the 'panthi', the hijra word for men who are by definition inserters. For instance, a hijra named Rakhi once narrated, 'I knew I was a hijra the moment I took a penis in my anus. Do you think a man can take such a thing in his back? Never. Only hijras can.' In hijra conceptualization, a man is, therefore, someone who penetrates, while those who receive are inevitably hijras. There is, however, in reality a discrepancy between sexual acts and identifications among the hijras which I will elaborate in due course.

Nanda (1999) argues that the very existence of hijras as a subculture is a proof of institutionalized homosexuality in South Asia. Descriptively charting the earlier scholarly debates about homosexual prostitution and hijras, she contends that hijras do engage in homosexual prostitution, although this very role of hijras as homosexual prostitutes should not debar us from recognizing the ritual role of hijras as specialist cultural performers in Indian society. While I agree with Nanda's suggestion that the institution of the hijras should not be reduced to prostitution, I take issue with her representation of hijra sexuality as homosexual prostitution. Hijras do not look upon their erotic/affective desire for men in homoerotic terms. Hijras neither identify themselves as homosexuals nor do they view their partners as such. Rather, hijras look upon their sexual desire for men in Bangla hetero-gendered terms. It is this very Bangla hetero-gendered model that hijras not only idealize, but also strictly police, and any digression from this normative model incites disgust as well as publicly jeopardizes the authenticity of one's hijra status. This is not to suggest that hijras talk publicly about their being sexual beings. Rather, my point is that even when they talk about desire, they always frame it in terms of the Bangla hetero-gendered protocols.

This tendency to frame desire in terms of hetero-eroticism is locatable within the wider Bangla societal hetero-normative idioms of gender and sexuality in Bangladesh, where sexuality is conceptualized within a penile frame of reference. For instance, in the popular imaginary, the very idea that two women can have sex makes no sense. The argument often given is that women, being without penis, are not in a position to have sex. More importantly, sexuality in the Bangladeshi context is not conceptualized in terms of a homo–hetero binary. It is instructive to note that although there is a word in Bangla for homosexual (*somo-kami*, a literal translation of the word 'homosexual'), the Bangla word for heterosexual (*bisomo-kami*) is far-fetched and is unmarked. In fact, heterosexuality and homosexuality are not culturally recognized as distinct ontological categories, nor are those popular linguistic currencies recognized culturally. While 'educated' middle classes may be aware of the existence of these lexemes, I have never heard any of my hijra interlocutors mention those words, although male and female same-sex desires are recognized and linguistically marked within the hijra erotic economy, which I discuss later. The expression hijras typically use to refer to sex is 'dhurpit'. To get fucked is 'dhur khawa' while to fuck is to 'dhur'. Like the majority Bangla universe, hijras too view sexuality through a penile frame of reference wherein acts of receptivity and insertivity are associated with femaleness and maleness respectively. I discuss and complicate hijra subscription to and appropriation of these Bangla models later in this chapter. I now present next various kinds of hijra erotic encounters and transactions in and within the Bangla world.

Erotic transaction and register in the public garden

'Dhurrani khol', the hijra expression for a cruising site or brothel, is a typical mainstream Bangla public space where hijras cruise mainstream normative Bangla men for sex. During my fieldwork, I routinely visited dhurrani khol. While some such sites are exclusively popular with feminine-identified hijras (that is, those who cruise those spaces always dressed like females), there were also sites that were popular with both hijras and other groups that I elaborated in chapter 2. Every time I told my close hijra interlocutors about my visits to one of these dhurrani khols, it always led to interesting conversations about some of their or others' experience in one of those public spaces. Jomuna, the hijra guru in Hridoypur, for instance, nostalgically stated that the original meeting point for hijras was the shrine premises of the high court, where hijras gathered freely until the 1980s; however, after lethal bombings took place in shrine premises elsewhere, the high court shrine was made off-limits to the hijras. Some of Jomuna's celas who had never cruised at that site contended that there was still no shortage of such cruising areas for them. Sundori, a sadrali hijra, argued that new areas often emerge as cruising sites as older ones become off-limits. Pointing to the crackdown on an area near the national parliament, they were very critical of an erstwhile government's coming to power and the subsequent intensification of security watch over that area. Sundori argued that in such difficult times, hijras often make cruising sites out of a new area. The expression used in relation to making a place suitable for cruising is 'pakki kora'. By *pakki kora*, hijras refer particularly to the managing of the locals and the police so that there is no disruption. Once a place is made suitable for cruising, my hijra interlocutors would undertake 'panthi thekano'. Here, *panthi thekano* refers to what I understand to be cruising in English. A rough translation of it would be 'to capture or hold a man'. Aside from the cruising sites, this expression is used to refer to a hijra's 'capturing' a man anywhere.

In some of the cruising sites—namely the shrine premises and the public garden that I frequented regularly—hijras typically start cruising from 7:00 p.m. onwards. Every time I went to a dhurrani khol alone, I was approached by the cruising hijras. In most cases, they either struck up an inviting pose by acting in an excessively feminine manner or simply slowed the pace of their walk while making some gestures with their eyes. The act of checking out a Bangla man, or panthi, either for sex or otherwise, is known as 'lohori'. For instance, when a man checks out a hijra or when a hijra checks out a man, the exchange of gestures and glances is called 'lohori khawa'. In contrast, when I was accompanied by my hijra interlocutors, cruising hijras would often direct me to certain spaces inside the gardens or at times just ask me to sit on one of the benches. On occasion, I would also be asked to walk slowly behind them as if I was not known to them. Let me reproduce below one entry on a 'dhurrani' khol straight from my field notes.

Lakeside sex

Gulshan Lake is one of the popular cruising sites with hijras in Dhaka. Although the area boasting this lake is marked out as a diplomatic zone with all the embassies located in its vicinity, there are huge pockets of shantytowns. Trawling through the lakeside passage I saw tall walls and gates with mounted grilles to demarcate the rear boundaries of continuous rows of apartments. Security guards peeped through the netted grilles and the hedgerows off and on with prurient curiosity. Peripatetic tea sellers appeared every few minutes. After minutes of walking, I crossed over to the other side of the lake. My plan was to stroll through the total length of this cruising route. People walked past me every now and then. As I kept moving, I found a few hijras standing scattered across the space. In the space between the lake and the passage was dense coppice with broken bricks, discarded garbage and open sewers. Hijras spoke a word or two to the passing men. Tina, a hijra who accompanied me, was walking in front of me as if I was not known to them. Tina had been cruising in this lake area for the last five years and was well known to the hijra frequenters there. As I walked past a few hijras, one of them asked if I would like to have sex with them. Dressed in saris, they wondered, 'Amar sate kam korba (will you do me)?' I ignored the call and kept moving. I saw a man walking up and down the road with a sense of panic. After a while I saw him vanish with a hijra only to reappear pretty soon. I realized that they went into the bush to have sex. Working-class men coming from their places of work were walking quickly through the lane. Two men slowed the pace of their walk and stole up behind a tree while another man stood a bit away from a hijra as if he were waiting for someone. One hijra moved towards one of the men under the tree and spoke for a while, then they vanished into the tunnel-like structure underneath the lakeside passage; the other man with another hijra did likewise after a brief conversation. As I was loitering around that road, another band of working-class men were passing through. They suddenly stopped. After a few moments three of them went to the cave down below in response to the gesture of the hijras while the rest left. I followed those three men slowly. It was a rather narrow, bumpy, muddy path running along the lake. On the left side was a big cement-built tunnel where two men entered with two hijras. I walked along pretending nonchalance and took a furtive glance at the hole. A man was standing right in front of the tunnel as if he was deployed to guard the surreptitious play going on inside. Later I realized he was waiting for one of them to come out so that he could take his turn. He seemed undisturbed by my movement. Later as those hijras came out onto the lakeside passage, Tina inquired whether they ate grass or counted the stars. In response, one of them said, 'Sister, I only eat grass. The space inside the cave is uneven.' 'Eating grass', as was later explained to me by Tina, refers to hijras crouching on all fours while the men penetrate from behind, while 'counting the stars' is to lie on one's back with the man on top, which in the above case was not an option because of the uneven surface on the ground.

The response of the hijras to Tina's question about whether they ate grass or counted the stars indicates the way hijras talk about assuming sexual positions in a coded manner.

Typically, when hijras have sex with men in public space, they first take the *jholki*, the hijra word for money. Although rates vary depending on the socio-economic background of the clients and the situational interaction, Bangla men who typically buy sex from hijras in the aforesaid lakeside park are markedly lower class. Tina later told me that the charge ranges between one and two hundred (less than US$2) if the men are poor. Ruposhi, another hijra cruising there, once stated that hijras generally charged more than the female sex workers, although I was not able to confirm this with the latter.

Hijra sexual encounters with the lower-class Bangla men in such cruising sites is a form of commoditized sexual relations where hijras receive money

Figure 3.1 Sex-worker *hijras* at a public garden in Dhaka
Source: Author.

from the Bangla men for sexually servicing them. Although men who bought sex in the aforementioned case were markedly from the lower class, middle- and upper-class men too frequented such cruising sites. In the same lake area, I once saw a middle-class man stopping by to solicit sex. Although he was jogging, he suddenly stopped and stole up behind a tree with Rina. Later Rina told me that all that he wanted was a quick release, for which they were paid 500 taka (roughly US$3). Given the lack of space and convenient erotic hideouts, middle- and upper-class men were relatively less visible in this lake area, although men from the middle and upper classes would often cruise for hijras in other big and spacious public gardens (Figure 3.1).

We went for 'party' last night: erotic encounters with middle-/upper-class Bangla men

In the previous section, I elaborated not only the coded manner in which hijras speak about cruising sites, but also more specifically their commoditized

Hijra Erotic Subjectivities

sexual transactions with working class Bangla men. Here I present materials on how hijras interpret their erotic encounters with middle- and upper-class Bangla men. The common expression used by the hijras to refer to their sex with men from the middle and upper classes is 'party', a fitting term given the popular and public association of parties with affluence and the upper class in Bangladesh. While hijras generally use 'party', as I suggest later, in relation to their being picked up by men in vehicles, hijra erotic transactions with middle- and upper-class men in public gardens are not linguistically marked as 'party'. Furthermore, men who pick hijras up by car are not always affluent: on many occasions, hijras drew my attention to their customers being drivers rather than owners of the vehicles.

As already stated, to be hired by a man or men with cars is to go for a 'party'. For instance, my interlocutors would often say things like 'long time no party' or 'I went for a party yesterday'. Although I could never speak to any of the men taking my hijra interlocutors for 'party', there were stories galore about 'party'. I copy below one such entry from my journal.

> I got picked up from [the] Dhanmondi area. I was in the lake area close to the *dingi* (a food shop). It was around 11:30 p.m. I was dressed in salwar kameez (female-identified attire). I never cruised in this area until then but one of my gothias told me about this place and I was strapped for cash that week. So I asked my guru to grant me leave as I was supposed to stay at the house of my grand guru that night. I'd always heard about 'party' but never went to one. I was taking a stroll on the right side of the bridge while other 'dhurrani' hijras were scattered on the other side. Suddenly a running jeep pulled up and the man inside asked if I would like to go with him. After a bit of confusion, I jumped in the car. I didn't realize that he would be taking me to his home. It was Baridhara, [on] the other side of the town. He was very nice to me. He didn't speak a lot in the car as he was constantly receiving calls. I barely understood what he talked about as he conversed in English. When we reached his house, he took me inside. It was an empty duplex flat. He took me upstairs and asked me to take a shower. After I came out of the bathroom, I saw him wearing nothing but underwear. He took me to the bathroom again and asked me to use the soap and clean myself up again. I did accordingly. He also took [a] shower. We spent the night together. He fucked me very slowly. He put some spray into my anus before inserting his penis. During the night he fucked me three times but he proceeded very slowly. Later at around six in the morning, he gave me 5,000 taka (roughly US$40) and then I left.

Hijras who get picked up in this fashion are not always taken to the houses of their clients. More often than not, they either have sex inside the car or are taken to an office premises or a hotel. A few hijras also told me about their being taken abroad for sex. Rupali, an ex-sex worker and now an NGO worker, once proudly related that she had gone abroad twice for 'party'. Rupali stated,

> I went to Dubai with the help of one of my gothias who used to work there. People in that country prefer hijras to women. I went and stayed for a week and made a lot of money. The receptionist in the hotel as well as the bell boys fucked me. The boss of my gothia who sponsored my trip took me to other hotels and houses where I had sex with other men. Then after a week I came back. The trip to Singapore was arranged by a Nigerian football player who once picked me up from Gulshan in Dhaka. He was playing for a Bangladeshi football team. We became so close that he would meet me two or three times a week. Later I went to Singapore with him and stayed there for three days.

While such stories of hijras being taken abroad are rare, hijras on occasion shared their sexual experiences with foreigners in some of the most expensive hotels in Dhaka. Notwithstanding their boasting about sex abroad and with foreigners at times, hijras generally displayed a dislike for 'party', as such work often involved risks. In 2004, a university teacher was murdered by a hijra who went on a 'party'. Although it received insufficient attention in the media, it led to an outrage among some of the hijra groups in Dhaka not because, as Meghna contended, they got implicated in a murder case, but because it exposed the Ulti practices to the Bangla public.

Anus versus vagina: hijras as providers of 'English sex'

One of the themes that my hijra interlocutors repeatedly revisited was their ability to pleasure men in ways that they contended women were traditionally incapable of. And it is precisely because of these erotic skills that the Bangla men, regardless of their class affiliations, preferred hijras to women. Jomuna, the nonagenarian hijra guru, once nostalgically recounted, 'I am now old and incapable but there was a time when I was a real beauty. Men the world over would approach me. Now they approach my disciples for *English kam* [literally, sex] that women cannot give.' Crouching on the bed and inserting the forefinger of their left hand between the thumb and index finger of their right hand, Jomuna cried out, 'Tight ah pleasure ah; you can fuck a hijra in whatever way you want. Women's vagina is slippery but ours is tighter.' Later, upon inquiry about what exactly Jomuna meant by 'English' sex, I was told by their cela that Jomuna was referring to receiving the penis in the anus and sucking it. Jomuna later explained,

> Men seek pleasure. Women can't give what men really want. Suppose you have married a woman and then for one or two years you may enjoy sex with her but then you will see that your penis is just sliding in and out without much friction and pleasure and regardless of how much you fuck her you will not be able to ejaculate easily.

Sweety, another sadrali hijra guru in Dhaka, once remarked, 'The vagina is for reproduction while the anus is for pleasure.' Arguing the case for hijras' superior ability as pleasure-givers relative to women, Sweety drew my attention to the fact that they had been married to a man for about ten years and had they not been skilful in satisfying their man, he would have relinquished them by now. 'I have international sex with my husband. You know what that is? I take his penis in my anus and that is international sex,' related Sweety.

On occasion, hijras outside of Hridoypur wondered whether I would like to have sex with them. When I declined, they argued that I was unlucky not to have had the pleasure hijras could offer. Payel, a sadrali hijra who also worked with me during my fieldwork, shared their regret at my erstwhile heterosexual marriage, arguing, 'If you had known me before you met your woman, you would never have settled for her.' Dipali, now a sadrali, was previously involved in the film industry as a dancer. In speaking of how hijras can pleasure men better than women, Dipali recalled one of their experiences from the past:

> When I used to work as a dancer, my female colleagues and friends would often bring men to my place for sex. One day a female friend brought a man to my house. While she was kissing him, I started touching his penis. Later I put it in my mouth and sucked it. That man had never had sex with a hijra. But that day afterwards he fucked me instead of my female friend. In the end, he was compelled to say hijras really were better than females in terms of giving satisfaction.

Dipali also argued that while they were very adept in artful sucking of the penis, they knew hijras who were more capable than them. Dipali once commented,

> you know there are hijras who can take both the penis and the scrotum simultaneously inside their mouths. Hijras also eat *sudrani* [the hijra word for semen] which no Bangladeshi woman would do. Why do you think men of wealth would come and throw themselves at our feet despite their having wives? Is there any shortage of *dhurrani neharun* [female prostitutes]? Those who had tasted us would never *chis* [like] women.

Echoing this sentiment, Asma, a gothia of Dipali who had previously worked in a hijra group in Medinipur, India, but was now living in Dhaka, described the superiority of the anus over the vagina in the following metaphorical terms: 'A *butli khol* [anus] is made with a thousand molten *chippu*s [vaginas]. If the vagina of a neharun [woman] is a pond, the butli khol of a hijra is an ocean. Men can swim endlessly in the butli.'

What these ethnographic vignettes underscore is that hijras present their erotic practices as non-Bangla, evident not only in the way they consign these erotic practices to the realm of Ulti, but also in their use of words like 'English' and 'International' to reference anal sex and fellatio. Additionally, hijras not only construe their sexual practices as foreign to the Bangla world, but also project themselves as the only medium through which Bangla men can access those 'forbidden' pleasures. The switch to either Ulti or English expressions to index erotic desire and practices underscores a central tension that lies at the heart of hijra lives. While on the one hand they solicit recognition as hijras in the wider Bangla society on the ground of their being asexual and above desire, on the other hand they inhabit a parallel universe of pleasure and desire wherein they not only assert their sexual desire but also take exaggerated pride in their Ulti and putatively English/international erotic skills. Away from the Bangla world that entwines sex with reproduction, hijras open the floodgates of pleasure for Bangla men that they contend women with vaginas are unable to offer. Presumably many Bangla men are aware of that parallel universe. In that sense, the Ulti world is something of a shared secret between hijras and their Bangla partners, a theme I explore in detail in chapter 6.

Anal power and the politics of pleasure

While my hijra interlocutors often boasted about their abilities to pleasure men, they rarely spoke about how they derived pleasure. Every time I tried to

Hijra Erotic Subjectivities

initiate a conversation on how they were pleasured, my interlocutors always blushed and covered their faces with their palms or a patch of clothing or just giggled. Jomuna once reluctantly pointed to 'butli khol', the hijra word for anus. 'You know our pleasure is in the backside. When we take a *ligam* [penis] in our butli, we experience pleasure,' related Meghna. Overhearing our conversation, Shima, a gothia of Meghna, burst out into a guffaw and blurted out: 'We hijras get this *khujli* [itching] in the anus every now and then, and when we get this itching we need a ligam to curb this itching and that is how we get pleasure.'

Aside from highlighting anal receptivity as the apogee of sexual pleasure, my interlocutors often emphasized the size of the penis as a critical factor in receiving pleasure. In speaking of panthi in the context of sex, my interlocutors often talked about how big or small the penis of a man was. If the penis of a man one had had sex with was small, hijras typically expressed dissatisfaction by saying 'lutki ligam' (literally, 'small penis'), while the expression 'arial/akkhar ligam' (literally, huge penis) was used to signal greater satisfaction.

One of the recurrent themes that emerged in my conversation with hijras on erotic delight was what I can roughly translate as 'roughing up'. Tahmina, a sex-worker hijra, once related in Ulti, 'I desire men with a huge penis who will fuck me real hard' (*Hamsi arial ligam ala panthi chis kori, ar jeisi hamsire akkhar koira dhurbo*). Dipu, also known as Dipali, a sadrali hijra, once related one of their sexual fantasies. Although Dipu had had a stable partner for the previous two years, and occasional sex on the side with other panthis, they had a recurrent dream in which they were 'roughed up' by a man and then fucked from behind. Dipu argued that the reason they had this dream every now and then was because their partner went 'soft' on them. Moina, another sadrali, once related that it was through their being 'roughed up' that they not only felt pleasured but also felt more like a 'real' woman. Although my interlocutors often valorized the 'rough and tumble' sort of man, it seemed like an exaggeration, as the pariks I spoke to did not fit those descriptions. This is not to suggest that the pariks were not that way in bed with my hijra interlocutors. While it was not possible for me to empirically verify these claims, partners of most of my hijra acquaintances seemed to me to be rather soft spoken and mild, at least in terms of demeanour.

One very popular perception among my hijra interlocutors was that the men they had sex with were not in a position to find out about their genital status. The *janana hijra*s, or those with penises, with permanent pariks categorically maintained that their men were not clued up about their having penises. When pressed on the topic, hijras often told me that they simply did not let the men find out about their penises (*panthi go ligam chamai na*). Zhinuk, previously a dancer in the film industry and now a part-time sadrali janana, had been involved with Rasel for about two years and during this period they had shared the same house. Zhinuk argued that Rasel, their boyfriend, did not know about them having a penis. I wondered how this could be possible when both of them had not only lived together but also had sex on a regular basis. Insistent on this view, Zhinuk showed me some pictures of their sexual acts with Rasel, stored on their cell phone: 'Look, we are having sex,' said Zhinuk. 'Can you see that I have a penis?' I was told Rasel had taken the photos while they were having sex. Interestingly, Mala, another hijra present during this conversation, volunteered to demonstrate how a hijra could hide their penis while having sex. Mala went on all fours and hid their penis between the 'jung', or thighs. I wondered if they always had sex in that style. Zhinuk then argued that they could hide it even when they had sex with the men on top. Zhinuk said when they had sex with a man on top, they would never undress completely but would rather cover their penis under their t-shirt. Like Zhinuk, Dilara, another non-emasculated hijra, had been involved with a man for the last seven years. Although Dilara was evasive in their response to whether their partner knew about their penis, Dilara claimed that they never let Raihan, their parik, touch their penis. 'Once Raihan laid his hand on my penis,' they confided; 'I instantly jumped up and slapped him!'

In a similar vein, sex-worker hijras maintained that the men who bought sex from them in the cruising sites always took them as women and not as hijras. The same view was expressed by the *chibry*, or emasculated hijras. Chibry hijras with partners argued that their partners never realized that they were emasculated. Rather, their partners always took them to be women. 'You know when my panthi looks at my genitals, what he sees is my chippu [the urethral hole remaining after the emasculation]. So he thinks it is my vagina,' related Julekha. Sweety, an emasculated sadrali hijra, had been married to a man for the last ten years. Sweety argued that their husband in all these years had never realized that they were a hijra. Sweety maintained that because they had large breasts which they said were naturally developed, their partner always thought they were a woman.

While the contention that the partners of the hijras were not able to find out about their genital status seems like an exaggeration to me, what is noteworthy is that this sense of embarrassment and discomfort associated with the disclosure of their genital status was always expressed in relation to partners (both casual and permanent). What my janana interlocutors found disgusting was not just the fact of their having a penis but, more importantly, its erectness in the presence of their partners. 'Ligam forkano', the hijra expression for erection, was a recurrent theme when hijras spoke among themselves about sex. Time and again, janana hijras taunted other jananas, particularly pointing to their inability to control their erections in the presence of panthis. Although my janana interlocutors experienced erections while being anally penetrated, they took every possible measure to hide it from the view of the men. In addition, hijras always expressed not just an irritation, but an utter sense of repulsion at the thought of their genital area being touched by men.

In his study of Brazilian transgender prostitutes, Kulick (1998) argues that while his *travesti* interlocutors were comfortable penetrating the male clients who bought sex from them, it was never acceptable for the same group of travestis to penetrate their male partners at home. Noting this, he contended that while the travestis derived their gender from their partners, they derived sexuality or pleasure from their clients whom they penetrated. In contrast, my hijra interlocutors in Bangladesh always dismissed any possibility of their being in the penetrative position either with their partners or with male clients. Although it was acceptable for hijras to penetrate women as evident from the fact that there are heterosexually married hijras (on which I elaborate in chapter 5), it was totally unacceptable for hijras to penetrate men under any circumstance. This is not to suggest that hijras never penetrated men. There were in fact stories galore about situations where hijras had to endure the embarrassment of being asked to penetrate. I reproduce below a few such stories that my interlocutors narrated to me.

Rupali met a man at a bus stop. One day while Rupali, a sex-worker hijra and a sadrali janana, was waiting for the bus to come, a man approached them after minutes of exchanging glances. Later Rupali went with the man and had sex. The experience in Rupali's words was as follows:

> I could not believe myself. He was such an *akkhar panthi* [a real masculine man]. He asked my name and where I was going. I was coming back from the house of one of my gothias in Uttara. Later he asked if I would like to go with him to his house. He was so handsome. I felt so delighted and nervous. We went to his house and then started making out. We undressed completely and then when I was ready to take his penis, he refused to enter me. Instead

he asked me to enter him. Can you believe that? I felt the sky was about to crash and fall on my head. I was speechless. I refused to enter him but he was insistent and begged me and said he would pay three times the amount but I still refused. I was so disgusted that I put my clothes back on and left immediately without taking any money.

Jhorna, previously a full-time sadrali hijra and currently working in an NGO as a peer leader, was involved with a 'dengu', or policeman. Recently Jhorna broke up with their parik. The story they narrated to me is as follows:

I met him [at] a cruising site. I didn't know he was a dengu. We had sex in the park. He said he would come again to meet me and then the next day he came and I went with him to his house. Afterwards we exchanged telephone numbers. We used to have sex regularly. One day at his place he asked me to penetrate him. I thought he was joking with me. But later I realized he was serious. I was very embarrassed. Later I penetrated him. After that every time we had sex he was more interested in being penetrated than penetrating me. You know what the problem is. It is not that I am incapable of penetrating but it is just that I don't want to penetrate him. The very thought puts me off and I lose erotic interest in a man who yearns to be penetrated. This is the reason I don't want to penetrate men. Once one experiences the pleasure of being penetrated, it becomes an addiction. Being fucked (dhur khawa) is more pleasurable than fucking (*dhurano*).

Trisna, a sadrali who previously worked as a hijra in Hridoypur but later joined another hijra group after a row with their guru, once related the following:

I am just not attracted to men who like to get penetrated, but the truth is many hijras penetrate men, though they rarely talk about it publicly or even with other hijras. I once met a very handsome panthi. We used to have sex. One day out of curiosity I put some lubricants in his buttock hole and stirred and then penetrated him. I laughed during the entire period of sex and later that night I kept laughing. But I don't blame that panthi. Once a person gets the pleasure of being anally penetrated, it is difficult to resist the temptation to get it through the anus.

The vignettes above reiterate my previous contention about the hijra sense of discomfort and disgust associated with the disclosure of their genital status, especially in the presence of their partners. The reason for this sense of disgust derives not only from the fact that disclosure of genital status publicly jeopardizes the authenticity of one's hijra status, but more significantly because this very disclosure was an erotic turn-off for my interlocutors. While it was acceptable, although not encouraged, for my hijra interlocutors to penetrate women, penetrating men was not. It was through their being anally receptive in intercourse with men that they derived utmost pleasure. Thus, it is not just due to a sense of disgust that they refrain from penetrating men, but because the acts and thoughts of their penetrating men foreclose receptive anal erotic pleasures, which my interlocutors considered central to maximizing erotic delight.

That hijras assert anal receptivity as more pleasurable than penile insertivity runs counter to conventional accounts of male-to-male sexual encounters. For instance, too often such receptivity is dismissed as a form of repression where only those who penetrate are pleasured at the cost of the penetrated. Typically in cultural frameworks structured around the inserter/insertee model, it is assumed the insertees often find other ways to derive pleasure via either being masturbated or being allowed to penetrate their partners. In Western contexts, such models have often been vehemently critiqued on the ground of repressive traditionalism, where versatility or instances of both penetrating and being penetrated are posited as more egalitarian and democratic alternatives to those erotic frameworks that idealize inserter/insertee models (Kippax and Smith 2001). In contrast, the hijra conceptualization of erotic desire can be read as an appropriation of the hetero-patriarchal and phallocratic model of Bangla sexuality that resonates with the dominant Western conceptualization of erotics and pleasure through the cipher of the penis (Potts 2000). While power differentials inevitably structure sexual practices and most especially penetrator–penetrated relations, in the case of hijras such ready-made assumptions would be analytically short-sighted, not only because underlying such a conceptualization of power inequality is an essentialist proclivity to conflate the penis with pleasurability, but also because acts of receptivity by my hijra interlocutors do not render them either powerless or inferior.

In the hijra conceptualization, as already noted, only those who are anally receptive qualify to be hijras, as opposed to the panthis, who are penetrators. In recent times, this very koti–panthi (penetrated–penetrator) model of male-to-male sexuality has been critiqued in the context of HIV/AIDS prevention work in India. Particularly critiquing the NGO interventions framed in such terms, scholars like Boyce (2006, 2007) and Cohen (2005) contend that the indigeneity ascribed to this koti–panthi framework is questionable. They contend that the very ossification of this koti–panthi framework is the by-product of HIV/AIDS activism. While both Boyce and Cohen make a valid point about the problematic reification of this model, what needs mentioning here is the ready assumption about insertees being in a position of inferiority. S. Khan (1999), for instance, argues that in this indigenous model of penetrator–penetrated sexuality, it is only the kotis (and hijras) who get censured, while those who penetrate always escape condemnation. While I do not contest the wider societal denigration associated with the receptive status and the production of gender in such erotic encounters, it would be reductive to assume that this disproportionate power dynamic structures the lived erotic practices between hijras and their panthis. In other words, despite the wider societal valorization of penetration, penetrators do not necessarily exercise greater dominance in the actual erotic play. Rather, based on my interaction with hijras, I would argue that the power dynamics in actual sexual practice is often if not always reversed, with hijras taking the style and position of a stereotypical masculine man. The ethnographic episodes mentioned earlier about the hijra sense of discomfort and embarrassment about genital status expressed in relation to their partners indicate that my interlocutors often dominated the actual play in terms of determining what could and could not be done during sex. Given that, the assumption that receptivity is tantamount to submissiveness is analytically naive. Nor is the pleasure of penetration illustrative of a superior dominant position at all times.

There are a few things to be noted here. First, hijras tend to frame their desire in hetero-gendered terms where one's hijraness and manliness are produced on account of the assumption of penetrative and penetrated styles respectively. Hijras, I already noted, strictly police this inserter–insertee model, and any deviation from this triggers strong reactions (see also Boellstorff [2004b] and Johnson [1998] for similar accounts in Indonesia and the Philippines respectively). That hijras consider this model to be inviolable indicates a structuring principle of pleasure in terms of which hijra erotic economy is organized. Yet such a spatio-hierarchical paradigm of sexual intercourse gets complicated when the principle of pleasure enters the picture, that is, hijras valorize anal receptivity as central to authentic hijraness, as for them being anally penetrated is more pleasurable than penetrating. Second, the positing of the anus as the apogee of erotic gratification by hijras not only challenges the conventional Bangla and Euro-American hegemonic privileging of the penis as the fount of erotic delight but also calls our attention to the possibilities of non-penile bodily and erotic pleasures and their desublimation (Hocquenghem 1978). Third, the reason for hijra objection to a man's being receptive, I would submit, may also be explained in terms of an entitlement principle, that is, only those who are hijras are exclusively entitled to this realm of pleasure. Put simply, in order for one to be eligible for anal erotic delight, which according to hijras is the *supreme* delight, one has to take up a hijra subject position. In other words, hijra as a space for actualizing nonconventional erotic possibilities are off-limits to normatively masculinized subjects. In order for one to explore and enjoy those bodily pleasures, one therefore has to jettison the normative masculine pleasure and privilege. In other words, one's entitlement to those (*ulti*) erotic anal pleasures, in principle, hinges upon the extent to which one is ready to eschew the conventional (Bangla) penetrative pleasures.

Beyond grammar: erotic transgression and taboo in hijra sexuality

I was sitting under the shed in Hridoypur with Ruma and Tahmina, two sadrali hijras. We were talking about NGO intervention in the hijra community. Suddenly Tahmina started castigating one of the leaders of an MSM (men who have sex with men)-focused NGO. Tahmina angrily pointed out that even a few years ago that NGO leader had been a 'dhurrani' and now by throwing dust into the eyes of the wider society, he was impersonating a panthi. Pointing to the fact that the person in question recently got married to a woman from a village, which according to Tahmina was another instance of how cunning he was, Tahmina continued, 'It does not matter how many times he gets married, he will always be a *gandu* to me.' Suddenly Rupali, another hijra, chipped in, 'He used to cruise in the Gulisthan area with me. In those days he would often come to me and tell me his stories of plight, I still recall. One day, you know what he did? He even had sex with another koti and later with the parik of that koti.' Tahmina immediately burst out, 'Spit on him. Such a *kudenga, Khai khowara.*' 'Kudenga' and 'khai khowara' are two derogatory expressions synonymous with 'gandu' often used in relation to those male-bodied people who fuck men and also get fucked by men. When I inquired about why they were so mad at that person, they seemed perplexed by my inability to understand the reason and Tahmina disdainfully opined, 'You know hijra to hijra sex is like eating the meat of crow while being a crow yourself. It is incest.'

The vignette above resonates with the opening contention of this chapter where hijras expressed a strong sense of repulsion at the thought of a penetrated male being in a penetrative position. More specifically, while the issue of hijras fucking men indispensably triggered a strong sense of disgust, any suggestion about hijra-to-hijra eroticism was an absolute taboo. In a way, the hijra normative protocols defining acceptable and unacceptable sexual practices bear resemblance to Rubin's (1992) idea of sexual stratification, a system of erotic economy that differentially valorizes sexual practices in a hierarchical gradation. That hijras too subscribe to and strictly police (at least publicly) those normative protocols is also informed by the broader Bangla societal ideologies around sexual values. Yet I came across incidents during my fieldwork that verged on what my interlocutor here termed as 'incest'. In this section, I explore whether this apparent sense of opprobrium associated with hijra acts of penetrating men or 'their own kind' is a mere public proclamation, much like the way hijras in general deny any involvement with erotics and desire in public. In other words, I try to shed light on how my interlocutors would have reacted had I not been present in that room, as described in the opening vignette. Could it be that they would have refrained from expressing any sense of disgust and kept on watching or even engaged in sexual play among themselves? While definite answers to these questions are difficult to generate without further investigation, I encountered several incidents during my fieldwork that led me to reflect on such possibilities. My intention therefore is not to assert but to gesture towards erotic possibilities within the Ulti universe other than those publicly proclaimed by my interlocutors.

One of my closest interlocutors during my fieldwork was Choyonika. Choyonika was a sex worker until they became an NGO worker. Recently, Choyonika had heard news about some of their old sadralis with whom they used to cruise in the airport area. Sokuntala, one of their oldest sadralis, had recently undergone emasculation and was working as a full-time hijra in Faidabad, on the outskirts of Dhaka. As planned, we set out for Sokuntala's house without informing them, to give them a surprise. After reaching the area and wading through dark alleys for about twenty minutes, we arrived at Sokuntala's house. In the house were Sokuntala and their cela. Both Sokuntala and their disciple were emasculated. Sokuntala was heterosexually married with two children and was still not officially divorced. Pictures of their daughter and son were hanging on the wall. Not realizing I was conversant in Ulti, Sokuntala started talking to Choyonika about the times they had spent together at their cruising site. After briefing each other about some of their common hijra acquaintances, Sokuntala started teasing Choyonika for their activities in the airport area. Sokuntala continued,

'I would never forget what you used to do to the new hijras. I was new in that dhurrani khol and you were the queen there, always dressed like an air hostess. Do you still recall that night when I went with you to your room and you fucked me?' Utterly embarrassed, Choyonika said to me, 'Brother, please don't tell this to anyone. I will lose face if people find out about this.' Later as the ice was broken, Choyonika explained that every time a new hijra started cruising in the airport area, they had to pay compensation to the old hijras, and being fucked by senior hijras was the way this compensation would be paid. 'I too was fucked by Mithila hijra who was the leader before me. Mithila introduced this rule. So if you want to castigate (*kacchi kora*), castigate Mithila, not me,' quipped Choyonika. Later in the conversation, Choyonika acceded to Sokuntala's allegation that they were very base but then they argued that Sokuntala was even worse. 'Remember what you did. I may have fucked you and other hijras, but you used to demand compensation even from the new female sex workers. Remember Dalia, that girl from Naya Bazaar? You used to fuck her regularly.'

The vignette above is not intended to suggest that hijra-to-hijra sex is rampant. Like fucking men, hijra-to-hijra sex is also strongly frowned upon and taboo in the community but is not uncommon, although hijras may not generally talk about it. When I asked Sokuntala about why they had sex with women, they related by saying that they did that as they were blessed with a penis by Allah and so they put it to use but now they were no longer comfortable with it, so they had got rid of it. In addition, both Choyonika and Sokuntala pointed out that those were playful acts or sisterly banter and not really erotically charged. As to the issue of sex-worker hijras being fucked by senior hijras, both argued that it was more like an initiation into the world of dhurpit, and a kind of parallel to the manner in which sadrali gurus initiate new celas (see also my discussion on initiation of new celas by gurus into the art of phallic dissimulation in chapter 5).

The above assertions and confessions of both Choyonika and Sokuntala about their previous erotic entanglements run counter to the conventional narratives of not only the ideals of hijra asexuality but also the normative erotic systems in terms of which hijra desire is performed: the fact that anal receptivity is the single most defining feature of the hijra subject position as opposed to the practice of insertivity that hijras ascribe to men. Previously I complicated this erotic model and the principle of pleasure underwriting it. Here I intend to push this conventionalized erotic protocol to suggest that the picture may be far more complex than hijra narratives of sexual practices indicate.

In Hridoypur, on occasion, I saw junior hijras grab the breasts of their gothias. Once I was sitting in the room of Jomuna waiting for them to come back from the mosque. Seated on the floor, Tarana, a cela of Jomuna, was applying henna to Sraboni's hair. After a while, I went out to fetch myself a glass of water outside. In the meantime, Tarana squeezed the breast of Sraboni and commented, 'Ki akkhar lilki!'—literally, 'How beautiful your breasts are!' In response, Sraboni cried out, 'Where did you learn this *chiputbazi*?' When I inquired what 'chiputbazi' was, Sraboni explained that it is like 'neharun neharun dhurpit', literally 'female female sex'. On another occasion, on the shrine premises of Shah Ali in Dhaka, a popular cruising site among both hijras and female sex workers, Choyonika introduced me to two tea-selling women whom Choyonika described as 'Neharun dhurrani neharun'—literally, women fucking women. Choyonika knew both these women from one of the cruising sites. In recent times both of them had left sex work and started selling tea to eke out a living. Both these women, fluent in Ulti, agreed to Choyonika's suggestion about 'neharun neharun dhurpit' and stated, 'Hamsira lesbian kori'—literally, 'We do lesbian'.

Later in Hridoypur when I was sharing this experience with Jomuna, they were taken aback at my being surprised and contended that it was a common practice among the female sex workers and that emasculated hijras too practised something similar, known as 'chiputbazi or *chipti bazi*'. Chiputbazi comes from the word 'chippu' or 'chipti', the hijra word for vagina, as well as the urethral opening remaining after emasculation. Jomuna explained to me that chiputbazi is one kind of 'neharun neharun dhurpit'.

> You know those who are chibry can't release but like women they too have to menstruate every month. While women release blood, chibry hijras release a kind of liquid which is lighter than sudrani (semen). Without releasing that, their bodies heat up. So they do it to cool their bodies down. Chibry hijras use the sticky substances of eggs and then smear it over each other's chippu and that is how they release the heat.

Jomuna also told me that this practice is not widespread and even when it takes place it is never between an emasculated guru and their cela but always between hijras of equal rank. When hijra-to-hijra eroticism either between jananas (hijras with penises) or chibrys (emasculated hijras) occurs, it is conceptualized as a form of 'neharun neharun dhurpit' (female-to-female sex), or a form of sisterly banter or frivolous playfulness devoid of any erotic charge. The practice of chiputbazi, on the other hand, is not considered as a form of eroticism at all but as a way to release the bodily heats akin to female menstruation. In addition, while female-to-female eroticism or sex is linguistically unmarked and culturally unrecognized in the Bangla mainstream, these practices are recognized in the hijra erotic economy.

While in the context of my fieldwork hijras rarely spoke of hijra-to-hijra eroticism and always condemned such possibilities point-blank, it would perhaps be analytically naive to rule out such a possibility based merely on their public presentation of what is and what is not sexually appropriate. Noteworthy here is the fact that despite Choyonika's being one of my closest interlocutors, they never really disclosed to me the way hijras in the cruising sites not only had sex with each other, but, more significantly, how new entrants into that cruising site had to pay the guru sexually in order to be given the rights to cruise. What exactly happens when a guru tries to teach a cela the art of phallic dissimulation that I discuss in chapter 5? Is there an erotic charge in such initiations? While I am not in a position to offer definite answers to these questions at this point, I take a cue from a Bangla novel written by a gender-nonconforming author in West Bengal, India. In her 2002 novel *Antohin Antorin Proshitovortika*, Somnath Bandopadhay, a scholar working on the concept of 'third sex' in Bangla literature, sheds light on the hijra world through a fictional character, Subir, who has left his family and travelled all the way to Kolkata to be initiated into a hijra group. Bandopadhay provocatively illustrates Subir's sexual rites of passage at the hands of Shamoly Ma, the hijra guru. Shamoly not only touches the erogenous zones of Subir's body but also licks, sucks and bites Subir's nipples. What comes across is that Shamoly was not only teaching Subir the art of pleasuring men but also arguably seeking pleasure themself.

Conclusion

This chapter has disclosed ethnographically the Ulti universe that not only enables varied forms of publicly forbidden pleasures but also complicates recognizable (hetero) sexualities and male-bodied erotic possibilities. While the Bangla world of normative men and women deem the hijras to be asexual, the Ulti universe in contrast acknowledges both the Bangla conventions of heterosexual desire and parallel possibilities of erotic entanglements and desire between hijras and men. Yet the Ulti world of desire is in many ways similar, though not identical, to the Bangla world in that it strictly follows the Bangla cultural logics in which insertivity and receptivity are equated with masculinity and femininity respectively. Any attempt to move away from this convention inevitably results in both internal and public disparagement. Gandus, or male-bodied people who are both inserters and insertees in sexual intercourse with men, are, according to the Ulti view, the worst objects of derision as they contravene both the Ulti and Bangla protocols of desire whereby men are stringently defined in terms of exclusive penetrative capabilities and pleasures. In other words, Ulti protocols are as much about protecting hijras' exclusive access to anal pleasure as they are about the imposition of Bangla norms. That hijras take great pains at least in public to maintain these boundaries between Banglaness and hijraness, understood and associated primarily with pleasures of penetration and pleasures of the anus respectively, underscores a 'this or that' sort of communitarian principle in which only those ready to forgo the Bangla pleasures of penetration are entitled to the anal pleasures of receptivity. Yet such tightly drawn demarcations also tend to collapse with hijras penetrating not only Bangla men but also other hijra-identified people. What is significant here is that such practices, although generally clandestine, are described within the Ulti universe of hijras in terms of female-to-female same-sex desire, whereas in the Bangla worldview such non-phallic erotic possibilities are culturally and conventionally unrecognized.

Another key contribution of this chapter was to foreground male-bodied erotic possibilities outside the essentialist locus of the penis. While the Ulti universe recognizes penile pleasures in terms of which hijras define Bangla men, the Ulti system expands the Bangla horizon of pleasure by eroticizing other bodily and, most notably, anal possibilities of pleasure. In that sense, while the Ulti universe serves as a site for Bangla men to partake of conventionally unavailable tastes of forbidden pleasure by positing the putative superiority of anus over vagina, the Ulti system also nullifies the penis by locating supreme pleasure in the anus. The significance of shifting the focus from penis to anus in the Ulti world lies in the fact that it foregrounds the possibility of cultural recognition within Ulti that erotic and sexual pleasures are possible outside the grammar of the phallus. While in this chapter I interrogated the non-phallic possibilities of erotic delight, chapter 4 extends on this theme and sheds light on the hijra practice of getting rid of the penis altogether.

4 The Paradox of Emasculation

Sathi, a *janana hijra* whom I had known from the very first day I set foot in Hridoypur, used to live on the rooftop of a building next to a mosque. Because of the location of Sathi's house, I would often drop by at Sathi's before heading off to the house of Meghna, the guru in Hridoypur. Sathi was not only one of the oldest members of the hijra group in Hridoypur, but also one of Meghna's favourites. One morning I turned up at Meghna's as planned in order to travel with their *cela*s to a part of town known as Sweepers Colony to observe a *badhai*. However, on arrival, I realized that Mousumi, one of Meghna's celas with whom I was supposed to be going, had already set off to the other side of the river to distribute cloves. *Long bata*, or distribution of cloves, is what hijras do to invite other hijras to their homes, especially when arbitration is to take place. While Mousumi went to invite Alo, a veteran emasculated hijra, another cela of Meghna went to the house of Jomuna, the guru of Meghna, to bring them to the house. After a while, I found out that Sathi, who was to be one of my guides to Sweepers Colony, had been excommunicated from the hijra group in Hridoypur because of their undergoing emasculation the night before and a sudden arbitration had been called to settle the matter. When I asked Meghna, they angrily told me that although they had asked Sathi to become *murad* (to take the vow to undergo emasculation) when another cela of Meghna was emasculated two months ago, Sathi had declined—only to later spontaneously have it done without Meghna's consent.[1] While Meghna was exceedingly angry at Sathi's sudden infraction of this communitarian rule, they also expressed anxiety about what could have happened to Sathi in the absence of the support and care of other hijras during the process. Although Sathi, the arbitrators later decided, would be kicked out of the hijra group, the injunction was later lifted after Sathi paid a massive don of

---

[1] While I acknowledge the psychoanalytic connotations of 'emasculation', I do not use it to refer to the theories of Oedipus complex. Rather, I use emasculation to refer to ritualized removal of the male genitals by the hijras.

20,000 taka (roughly US$235). What exactly is it that Sathi did that drew the wrath of the guru and led to their initial excommunication? Why is it that a hijra has to get the consent of the guru to opt for emasculation? What is it that hijras mean when they talk about emasculation and how important is it for one's sense of being a hijra? It is this related set of questions surrounding *chibrano* or *nirban*, the hijra expressions for ritual excision of the scrotum and the penis, that I will elaborate in this chapter.

I revisit the classical trope of emasculation in the construction of hijra identity, highlighting various meanings, rituals, cosmologies, processes and practices in terms of the broader cultural logics and politics of masculinity and renunciation in South Asia. In organizing this chapter, I first introduce the mythic story of two archetypes to which hijras in Bangladesh trace their lineage. I demonstrate that this mythic tale operates as a cultural resource in terms of which hijras make sense of emasculation as embodied practice. Consequently, I draw attention to practical and functional reasons in terms of which hijras read emasculation. Here, the point I highlight is that while this mythic story works as a creative resource, hijra decisions and practices around emasculation are not to be read as the outcome of some overdeterminate mythic structure. Rather, a complex set of factors, ranging from bodily urge to partners' volition, also directly contribute to their decision to undergo emasculation. I also underscore the cultural risks associated with this practice, particularly in terms of the conduct of the operation. I then present some ethnographic materials on the ritualized celebration of *baraiya*, a practice conducted on the twelfth day after emasculation to mark the rebirth of a newly emasculated hijra. Underscoring contradictions and conflicts around the supposed attainment of special spiritual power through the cipher of desire, I highlight paradoxes of ritual emasculation. Although a hijra is supposed through emasculation to be cleansed of masculine blood and normative masculine comportments, I argue that emasculation paradoxically renders hijra bodies hyper-masculine both in cultural and somatic terms. Finally, I critically interrogate the South Asian cultural politics and logics of masculinity, renunciation and Islam to challenge the dominant orientalizing proclivity to read hijras through the lens of Islam and emasculation.

Hijra cosmologies and ritual practice: Maya Ji and Tara Moni

In the majority of the hijra households I visited in Dhaka, drums called 'dhol' frequently hung on public display when they were not being used in ritual performance. Hijras consider the dhol sacred. Every time hijras go out to perform badhai, the traditional occupation of dancing the newborn, they honour the dhol. On one occasion, after a day's hard work of badhai and *birit manga*, a group of celas gathered at Meghna's house where the latter was entertaining Jomuna, the senior hijra guru. On entering Meghna's house, Moina, the hijra who played the dhol during badhai, slung it onto its hook and wearily sat down on the ground. Jomuna immediately took them to task for not paying respect to the dhol. Before setting out and after returning from badhai, hijras, they angrily stated, are to pay respect to the dhol. If respect is not paid to the dhol, I was told, the *oli* that hijras carry during badhai to keep the alms both in cash and kind does not cool down. After a shared meal, we drank locally made alcohol (*khilwar*) and relaxed. Suddenly Jomuna burst into tears and cried out: 'Now that I am old you people are least respectful of me. You don't care about me. Remember when I was young I was a beauty. People always marvelled at my ability to sing and dance. And you are all so unskilful and good for nothing!' They continued to curse their celas, invoking the name of Maya Ji and Tara Moni: 'Maya Ji will punish you all for your misdeeds and negligence towards me. Don't forget you too will become infirm one day!'

Maya Ji and Tara Moni, whom Jomuna invoked to solicit their celas' deference and berate them for being inattentive, are the two hijra goddesses most associated with (and in whose name hijras commonly undertake) *hijragiri*, the hijra occupations of badhai and birit manga. The story of these two hijra goddesses and their association with the defining occupations of hijras are recounted in origin myths that were narrated to me by a few older hijras; however, the majority of my hijra interlocutors had little knowledge of these origin myths. Generally, when I asked about how the subculture of the hijras emerged, I was simply told that it was bequeathed to them by previous generations of hijras, and that hijras the world over followed the same practices as devotees of the goddess.

In what follows, I reproduce the origin myths as they were narrated to me by the most senior hijras who presided over three influential hijra groups in Dhaka. The myths I reproduce here are not verbatim accounts but constructed from the different accounts given by those three hijras. More or less the contents of the myths described to me were structurally isomorphic, but the style and the context of their narrations differed.

> It was the age of truth. In the first place, there was only one hijra called Maya Ji and they were alone. They were a true ascetic without any worldly

lusts. They devoted their life to the service of Allah. Temples/shrines were their abode. They were a janana; that is, a hijra with a penis. Yet they were neither a male nor a female, as despite their having male genitalia they were never a male at heart. They had the preternatural power to vanish their penis with three claps. They could also bring it back with the same. They lived alone for years, serving at the temples and shrines, and then one day they implored Allah to send them a companion. In response, Allah sent Tara Moni as a disciple to them. Tara too was a janana and was blessed with magical powers. They would use roosters to traverse the length and breadth of the earth and entertain people.[2] Roosters were their divine vehicle. Maya would lead the rooster while Tara would sit on its back. They would don saris and put on ornaments made of clay. Every day while setting out for their destination, they would ask the clay to turn into ornaments and put them on. Upon return at dusk, they would break the bangles and the bracelets. They were purely asexual and it was their asexuality that gave them the power to perform miracles.

Once during their visit to a king's house, Tara Moni fell in love with the prince. Tara Moni was so enamoured of the prince that they by virtue of their magical power turned the prince into a garland and left. Later upon reaching home, as they sat to have food, Maya Ji found that though two plates were put in place whenever Tara served food, two plates magically broke into three plates. When it first happened Maya put the food back and re-served the food, but this made no difference and then they realized what their disciple had done.

Having deciphered the sin Tara had committed, Maya convulsed with anger and asked the earth to split. Immediately the earth cracked open and Maya entered into the hole to vanish from this earth [the place where they slipped into is now apparently the site of a temple somewhere in India—though an exact location was not specified]. While she was falling, Tara grabbed their hair and implored Maya to tell them about how they (Tara) should lead their life in their absence. Maya Ji then told her, 'Since you have become debauched you have lost all your powers and from now on you will lead a cursed and despised life. Now you are no longer asexual and pure. From now on, you have to get rid of your genitalia artificially, beg from door to door, dance for the newborn and entertain the people for your livelihood.'

---

[2] On one occasion, the disciples of Luna hijra came back from the bazaar with alms while I was sitting on a bed with Luna, the hijra guru. Among the cash and foodstuff was also a rooster. Luna was enraged that their celas brought with them a rooster and considered slaughtering it for consumption. This was another occasion when the myth of Maya Ji and Tara Moni was narrated to the celas.

In the Indian context, Nanda (1999) notes that hijras worship a mother goddess called Bahuchara Mata, whereas Reddy (2005a) notes a similar goddess called Bedraj Mata. During my fieldwork, unsure as to whether Maya Ji was also the same goddess named differently, I once showed some hijras a poster of Bahuchara Mata perched on a rooster. They immediately identified the goddess seated on the rooster as Maya Ji. Yet what is striking is not only the difference in the plot of these origin myths—of Maya Ji and Bahuchara Mata, the mother goddess whose temple is in Gujarat—but also the fact that both Maya and Tara were jananas who devoted themselves to temples and shrines and prayed to Allah, an eclectic religious frame of reference that I will enlarge upon below.

Myriad tales about androgynous gods and goddesses circulate at the popular level in India. While Hindu scriptures contain references to numerous instances of sex/gender subversion (Pattanaik 2002), hijras also often invoke such gender-transient gods and goddesses to authenticate their position in Indian society (Nanda 1999; Reddy 2005a; Ung Loh 2014). In Bangladesh, however, although hijras routinely invoke the name of Maya Ji in the company of fellow hijras and understand hijra occupations to be in some sense acts of devotion proscribed by those founding figures, they do not generally refer to these origin myths as a way to legitimize their position in wider society, as has already been elaborated in chapter 2.

One of the central themes that emerge from the numerous tales that scholars of Indian hijra culture reproduce is the lack or loss of genitalia in the origin stories of hijra selfhood and sacredness. For both Reddy and Nanda, the two well-known ethnographers of the hijras, hijras are a group of religious 'men' who sacrifice their genitals to the mother goddess in return for the power to confer blessings. In contrast, both Maya Ji and Tara Moni were jananas (hijras with penises) who could make their manhood disappear with their magical claps. That mythical status corresponds to the real-life context of many of the sadrali hijras in Bangladesh who are not only non-emasculated, but also often heterosexually married, simultaneously living the lives of hijras and of masculine householding men (I unpack this in chapter 5). One of the misfortunes that fell on subsequent generations of hijras as a result of Tara Moni's deceit was that they lost the magical ability to make their penises disappear on command. Today, janana hijras must learn the physical arts of 'ligam potano'—the art of vanishing the phallus. At the same time, the myth explains why at least some of the subsequent generations of hijras undergo a more radical form of vanishing via emasculation.

Functional factors and stories of emasculation

Although the mythic tale described here explains the ritual commandments for undergoing emasculation, very few emasculated hijras actually pointed out this mythic prescription as a reason for their undergoing emasculation. In fact, hijras in Dhaka in general had very little knowledge of these origin tales although they all knew the names of the goddesses. While the ritual context in which senior hijras pass down the knowledge of these cosmologies will be discussed later in this chapter, here I want to highlight a few cases about how hijras in real-life situations ended up going through this process.

There are periodic reports in the media about the forceful abduction and castration of individuals to strengthen the member base of the hijra community. Contrary to this popular belief, I did not see or hear of a single case where any of my chibry interlocutors had been coerced into emasculation; rather, they always opted for it voluntarily. Cohen (1995) calls the act of emasculation a 'bloodied violence' at the cost of which the status of third gender/sex is sealed in the Indian context. In a similar vein, Agrawal (1997) draws our attention to the fact that even when Indian society grants the hijra a special status, it happens at the cost of castration. While their arguments are made in opposition to Nanda's celebration of Indian society as accommodating, my contention is that hijras in Dhaka do not view emasculation as a form of violence.

Sweety, a hijra guru now in their forties, was widely known among the hijras in Bangladesh for their dauntlessness. Rumour has it they cut off their own penis long before they became a formalized sadrali. The very first time I visited Sweety, they generously shared their story. Sweety used to live with their parents in the old part of Dhaka. Although they were attracted to men from an early stage and came into contact with the local hijra groups, because of their family they were not allowed to associate with hijras. At the age of seventeen, they cut off their own penis. They did it with a razor that they borrowed from a hair salon near to their house. Sweety took some tablets and was in a state of trance for three consecutive days. On the third day, there was a calling (*sot*) from within and then they chopped off their penis with three diagonal cuts. They tried to stem the flow of blood but nothing was working. Then they blacked out and later discovered themself in hospital. Sweety's family and their lover spent a lot of money to save their life. Since they had lost a lot of blood, they needed to be given eight bags of blood. On the very first day, their parik had to spend one lac taka (almost US$1250). In the hospital, they were speaking in English with the doctors. Being in a state of trance, they spoke in a language in which they were not adept. Sweety had severe complications afterwards. Initially, they were having trouble urinating and the doctors said they would not be able to urinate through the chippu, or urethral hole. The doctors wanted to insert a pipe on the left side of their waist for urination. Then they cried before Allah and asked Him to take their life. They asked Allah to keep them alive only if they could urinate through the chippu.

One of the things worth noting here is that although Sweety single-handedly cut off their penis long before being a part of a hijra group, the language they used to describe their experience was in keeping with the typical hijra description. For instance, they argued that they experienced 'sot', the hijra word for an internal calling, which eventually led them to cut it off (I discuss *sot* in detail later in this chapter). When I asked why they described it in the way they did, they contended that while they might have learnt the word 'sot' later, the feelings they experienced were actually akin to 'sot'. In other words, it was because of the call of Maya Ji that they could summon up the courage to cut it off on their own.

While I spoke to many senior-level chibry hijra gurus, no others spoke in such candid terms as Sweety. While senior hijras always spoke of being born that way, it was mostly their celas who spoke unreservedly about emasculation. In speaking of senior chibry hijras, celas contended that most *nayak*, or senior hijra leaders, had not undergone emasculation until very recently. Meghna, the guru in Hridoypur, once related that it was only in the recent past that Jomuna, the nonagenarian hijra guru, had undergone emasculation.

The reason why Jomuna underwent emasculation so late in their life, according to Meghna, was *birit*, the ritual jurisdiction to which a hijra group is entitled in terms of collecting money and ritual performance. When Jomuna's guru was ill, they wanted to hand over the control to Jomuna—but because Jomuna was not emasculated, other celas of Pushpo (Jomuna's guru) had vetoed and demanded a greater share of the birit. So to ensure their fair share of the birit, Jomuna had to become a chibry. On numerous occasions, hijras invoked birit as the single most important factor in explaining chibrano, or emasculation. Although I note in chapter 5 that in reality one's being a chibry does not necessarily correlate with higher status in the community, evident in the way jananas not only control birit but also have emasculated hijras as their disciples. Undergoing chibrano, explained a janana, does not guarantee birit, although it is often easier for chibry hijras to secure birit. This is so not because emasculation automatically confers superior status on one, but because emasculation makes one conform to the public understanding of what a hijra is, that is, the idea that hijras are born with defective or missing genitals. Hijras outside of Hridoypur also spoke of birit as an important reason for becoming chibry. Josna, a hijra who had undergone emasculation two years previously, related, 'Suppose I am in the bazaar collecting money. If suddenly a vendor challenges my hijra status, I will have no option but to show them that I have no ligam (penis). If they find out I have a ligam, then they will beat me up as a fake hijra.' Although I rarely heard of any such incident actually taking place, hijras in Hridoypur and elsewhere often told me of instances from the past when hijras with penises were caught red-handed in broad daylight and were eventually beaten and kicked out of the birit. In reality, the non-hijra populace exposing hijras is rare. Rather, it is often the hijra members who 'out' other hijras in the event of birit *bakhor*, the trespassing of a jurisdiction.

In speaking of chibrano, hijras also singled out 'bodily urge' as a driving force. Meghna, for instance, stressed what they called 'the uselessness of a pen without ink'. Although hijras in public tend to talk of their being born without any ligam, those who do so often present themselves as being devoid of any functional ligam, that is, either the size of their ligam is very small or they are impotent. It is worth recalling here that notwithstanding this rhetoric in public, many hijras undergo this operation not because of any genital defect or lack of prowess but because of the sense of shame and embarrassment caused by the very functionality of their genitals in their sexual interaction with partners, as already discussed in chapter 3. Recall the opening vignette of this chapter where I introduced Sathi, a hijra who became a chibry without the consent of the guru. Later Sathi told me that they had to do it on that night as their partner was upset about Sathi's having male genitals (I discuss partners of hijras in detail later in this book).

There are a few things to be drawn out here. First, although hijras present a variety of reasons for their decisions to become chibry, these reasons are not necessarily mutually exclusive. Those who single out a partner's discontent as a reason may also link it to birit and vice versa. Second, very few hijras pointed to 'sot', or the calling from those mythic figures, as the primary reasons for their becoming chibry, even though, as will be suggested later, it is also in terms of this mythic significance that many hijras seek to sacralize emasculation. Finally, I want to note that in the life-historical trajectory of a hijra, economics, partnership, affect, bodily urge and cosmology may variously contribute to one's decision to become a chibry.

Fear, secrecy and the operation

Chibrano, the hijra word for emasculation, literally means the excision of the scrotum and the penis. During my fieldwork, I directly observed two such operations. Hridoypur, the main location of my fieldwork in Dhaka, is a vast expanse of marshland situated on the banks of the Buriganga, the river that runs along the city of Dhaka. While one can enter Hridoypur from the main city of Dhaka, the other side of Hridoypur is directly connected to the Buriganga. More often than not, I along with my hijra interlocutors in Hridoypur crossed the river by boat. The area on the other side, often referred to as 'o par', was home to another hijra group with whom the hijras in Hridoypur were closely associated. That area is an important location as it is there that several of Meghna's celas became chibry.

In 'o par' lived Joynal, widely known across the community for his special cutting skills. Those who operate are called 'katial'. Joynal, once a long-term parik of a hijra, had learnt these skills from his hijra partner who had died some five years previously. A katial can be either a hijra or their partner. As planned, we set out from Meghna's house, with Jorina, one of Meghna's celas, at just after midnight. The reason we set out after midnight was to ensure that the neighbours did not see any of us leaving. Although I was not sure why they were so surreptitious, Meghna later told me that this was to maintain secrecy in case anything went wrong. Here, what Meghna meant was that if in the process of becoming a chibry Jorina died, and if the cause of their death was subsequently leaked, then they would not only be in the bad books of the jodgman, but they might also become embroiled with the courts and the police. Hijras generally maintain that hijra affairs are totally a matter of their own discretion and even in the case of a hijra being murdered by another hijra, that it is the hijras themselves who have the sole right to adjudicate. However, of the thirteen chibrano operations I directly knew of, none of the initiands had died. As we crossed the river by boat and reached the other side, Joynal, the katial, was already waiting for us. We took a three-wheeled vehicle known as a 'tempo' to our destination, which took about half an hour to reach.

Walking through what seemed like a paddy field for about twenty minutes, I saw a tin shed standing in the middle of a field. Although I could see lights from a row of tea stalls on the other side of the field, there was total silence in that area. Unsettled, I followed my companions into the room. There we met Alo, the hijra guru in that area, along with one of their celas. Contrary to my expectations, the operation did not take place there. Later I found out that the katial had been collecting the instruments that he had left there earlier that morning. I was told that we would have to go deeper into a village to avoid any possible danger of being seen. Because I was told it would be risky to be visible around the *karkhana*, or the place of operation, we stopped by that house so that Jorina could finish seeking sot—the power and blessing of Maya Ji to undergo the process. While we waited inside, Jorina went out near a tree, stark naked, whereupon she sat down and began to pray. Before the operation, an initiand has to seek sot from a tree.[3] I was told that it was on account of the sot received during this crucial moment of meditative prayer that the initiand would receive the power and courage to undergo the process, and that once one receives this power, then the operation must take place regardless of how bad circumstances may get. The very tree in front of which the initiand seeks sot remains the perpetual witness to one's becoming a chibry. If sot is not sought in the presence of a tree, then on doomsday the cut genitals are believed to turn into a snake and bite the initiand.

As soon as Jorina returned, we set off for the karkhana. The katial took a spacious pot with a sharp knife and stitches stored inside it. After walking about for another half an hour, we finally reached the karkhana. The karkhana, which seemed like a typical house from outside, was dilapidated inside with used newspapers draped over the walls on all sides. A wooden bed, a table and two chairs were all there was in that room. On one side was an earthen stove. Leaving torn pieces of cloth on the table, Joynal put a bowl of water on the stove to heat while Jorina, Meghna and their other celas sat on the bed. Finally, after some deliberation, I decided not to observe the operation and stayed outside while Meghna and their other celas were inside along with the katial and Jorina. Extremely worried and panicky, I anxiously waited outside, anticipating some groans of pain; however, to my utter surprise the whole procedure was completed in about ten minutes without any noise from inside. The katial came out with a *bodna*, a pot where he kept the excised genitals. Joynal dug some earth near a tree and buried the genitals underneath. As promised, I left the karkhana before sunrise.

Before the surgery, I was told, Jorina was made to drink alcohol to be anaesthetized. Jorina was placed upon a chair while Meghna and others

---

[3] Hijras did not specify whether this was a particular sort of tree or any tree, although some hijras contended that sot could be sought only from a special tree whose name they did not disclose.

held them from behind. Joynal tied up Jorina's penis and scrotum with a long string. Then, with the knife, Joynal severed the penis and the scrotum with three diagonal cuts. Burnt clothes and flour mixed with hot water were applied to the scar to cauterize the wound. Jorina stayed at Joynal's for the next three days and as they recovered, they were transferred to the house of Alo hijra where they stayed for another seven days to recover. Later another day Joynal told me that the blood that gushes out after the cut is 'impure' and should therefore be allowed to drain out to cleanse the body. The thorn of a tree known as 'bel', whose juice is also ingested by the hijras to undermine erectile potency, is inserted into the urethra so that the hole does not close up. At times, a silver stick is also used for the same purpose. The time immediately after the surgery is considered the most crucial and those undergoing the operation are not allowed to sleep until the danger period of twenty-four hours has passed. Joynal also told me that only those without the sot would make a sound, but because Jorina had the blessing of Maya Ji, they were able to endure the operation without any difficulty. Joynal also related that once someone gets the call, they would follow it irrespective of whether a guru approves or not.

While in a moment I will go on to an elaborate discussion of the next stages of chibrano that the hijras in Hridoypur held to celebrate this rebirth, I want to stress the point of secrecy. Time and again, hijras in Hridoypur explained that chibrano is always conducted clandestinely. Payeli, another cela of Meghna, once told me that in the case of death of a hijra resulting from chibrano, the body of the deceased is cut into pieces and then thrown into the river to be eaten by the fish so that no evidence is left. Echoing Payeli, hijras in other areas also articulated a similar line of argument. While these pronouncements seemed a bit exaggerated to me, hijras stressed that the two famous karkhanas outside Dhaka are situated close to rivers precisely for that reason.

Baraiya festival: welcoming 'newborn' hijras

Baraiya—literally, the festival observed on the twelfth day after the operation—is the most ceremonious and formally ritualized practice among hijras in Bangladesh. Baraiya marks the completion of the twelve-day liminal period during which the initiand is segregated from the outside world and prepared for their reincorporation into the community as a reborn chibry. The rituals are generally performed in private without the presence of outsiders.

However, hijras from other areas are frequently invited to attend the celebrations. Thus, while baraiya rituals are conducted in secret and closed to non-hijra outsiders, the wider public is frequently aware of the festivities surrounding the ritual process.

From the night before the baraiya, Jorina was swathed in a yellow sari, which was changed only after the ritual cleansing, or bath. Before the bath, which was conducted by senior hijras, turmeric was smeared over Jorina's body. After the bath, Jorina was brought back to the room and dressed in a new yellow sari given by their guru. A thick dab of vermillion was applied to the forehead. Jorina was then brought to the room where the ritual was conducted. A senior chibry hijra drew the figures of Maya Ji and Tara Moni with red colour on the wall. Five different types of fruit, five betel leaves, sweets, five candles and five small, earthen bowls were placed on the altar (Figure 4.1). After ritually cleansing the space through mopping with wet clothes, Jorina was made to sit before the altar. Coconut husks were burnt to create smoke while special mantras were chanted invoking the names of Maya ji and Tara Moni. Fruits were exchanged between Jorina and a janana. It is believed that the janana that receives fruits from a chibry on the occasion

Figure 4.1 A senior *hijra* preparing the altar to pay respect to Maya Ji and Tara Moni on the occasion of the *baraiya* ritual
Source: Author.

of baraiya would hear a call from Maya Ji in their dream, at which point this janana must themself undergo emasculation. After the exchange, Jorina genuflected before Maya Ji and Tara Moni. Immediately after the submission, Jorina became possessed and blacked out. Water was poured into their mouth to bring them back to consciousness. Instantaneously, a coconut was thrown on the ground. All the participants in the ritual then frenziedly scrambled to get hold of the broken pieces of the coconut. During this worship, Jorina was believed to directly communicate with Maya Ji. Later, when Jorina gained consciousness, a senior hijra fed them a piece of meat, marking the end of twelve days of abstinence.

While the ritual bath and worship took place in the afternoon, elaborate preparations were underway for another round of celebration in the evening. The celebration was to be held on the top floor of a three-storey house belonging to Lokman, a non-sadrali gothia of Meghna, the hijra guru. An ornate canopy known as a 'pandal' covering all sides of the rooftop was erected. Glittering electrical lights were hung from the roof down to the ground. A stage decorated with rows of yellow and red flowers was created in one corner of the rooftop. In front of the house, massive culinary preparation was underway. Madhu, a hijra who worked as a cook outside Hridoypur, was busy cooking rice, beef and chicken curry. From 7:00 p.m. onwards, guests started arriving. Hijras from ten different *ghor*s (symbolic lineages in terms of which hijra groups are identified) were invited along with some local neighbours.

It bears noting that the non-hijra locals I had spoken to in Hridoypur told me that they were invited to what they were given to believe was Jorina's birthday celebration. Jorina, along with Jomuna and other hijras, sat on the stage. Jorina was dressed in an elegant yellow sari with their hair decorated with yellow garlands. With vibrant red lipstick and thick layers of make-up, Jorina stood out from the crowd. All the hijras were dressed in yellow except Jomuna, who wore green. Alo, another hijra guru, came in yellow *salwar kameez*, loose pyjama-like trousers. The two rows of chairs placed in front of the stage were occupied by hijras and some locals. One hijra started singing songs while playing the dhol; meanwhile the guests made their way to the stage to liberally apply turmeric to Jorina's face. Different kinds of fruits and sweets were placed in front of the stage for people to pick up and feed Jorina. The first person to apply turmeric to Jorina's face was Jomuna, the nonagenarian hijra guru. Celebrants who applied turmeric to Jorina's face also smeared turmeric paste onto their own faces. In the meantime, a few hijras started dancing in front of the stage. Once the round of turmeric-applying ended, popular music was played from a cassette player with a loud speaker to which younger hijras started to dance.

Each of the hijra houses gave money to Jorina's guru as gifts. At Meghna's request, sitting in a corner with a small writing pad, I took down the names of each of the hijras and neighbours who gave money. Later, after the celebration, as everyone made their way to eat, I was asked to calculate the total amount received in gifts. Meghna, the guru of Jorina, spent about 11,000 taka, while the total amount received in gifts was 10,071 taka. Typically, the kind of celebrations that hijras arrange depends on the socio-economic status of the hijra group. The hijras in Hridoypur are poorer, relatively speaking, than most other hijra groups in Dhaka. For this reason, the celebration was not, according to Meghna, as grand as they had wanted it to be.

There are a few things to be noted here. First, many hijras, including some newly initiated ones of the very hijra group conducting the baraiya, had little prior knowledge of the origin myths behind the rituals: that synoptic knowledge is held by senior hijra gurus and partly underpins their ritual power. Rather, for the majority of hijras, it is only through their participation in specific ritual contexts that they acquire knowledge of those origin myths, whether it be in the performance of badhai, or in undergoing emasculation. Second, hijras often consider their occupation of hijragiri to be Hindu in origin. The ritual aspects—namely the genuflection before Maya Ji and Tara Moni, the drawing of vermillion on the forehead and the chanting of mantras invoking the name of these two goddesses—are markedly Hindu aspects with which hijras in Bangladesh, despite being born into the Islamic faith, wholeheartedly identify. This, however, does not make the hijras Hindu (see below for more on the problematic communalization of hijras in South Asia). My hijra interlocutors do not see any contradiction between their Islamic identification and the observance of these rituals. Utter consternation was expressed by hijras when I raised the question as to whether they identified themselves as Hindus or Muslims. Jorina, whose baraiya I described, adamantly told me that they were no less a Muslim after the baraiya than they were before. Neither they nor any other hijra I spoke to saw any contradiction between their allegiance to Maya Ji and their Islamic identification. Third, the ritual of baraiya corresponds to one of the most popular marriage rituals in Bangladesh. Known as 'gaye holud', it is a ritual in which relatives and friends smear turmeric on the face and hands of the bride and the groom, just as hijra initiands are marked with turmeric in baraiya. While the ritual of baraiya marks the reincorporation of the initiand into the house of the guru, gaye holud in the mainstream is a pre-marriage ritual through which the bride and the groom are purified and beautified for their imminent heterosexual union. What strikes me as significant is the symbolic similarity between this heterosexual marriage and the reincorporation of the cela into the house of the guru. While I do clearly acknowledge the significant difference between these two events, the guru–cela relationship in many important ways resonates with the husband–wife relationship (Reddy 2005a), a possibility I hinted at in chapter 3.

Contradiction, authenticity and ritual power

Laila, a chibry hijra, once related, 'Once emasculated, one becomes *sati*, or chaste, and one is no longer prone to sexual sin.' In other words, one becomes a real hijra only after undergoing emasculation. I challenge the easy transposition of hijra status onto emasculated bodies in chapter 5; here, I highlight some of the conflicts and contradictions between janana and chibry hijras. Although anthropologists writing on hijras in India have often reported such contestations centred on genital status, this trope of realness actually means different things in different contexts. The invocation of authenticity by hijras in Dhaka is intended to facilitate a claim of realness based on some inborn genital status. It is instructive here to recall my discussion on 'vabrajer chibry' that I elaborated in chapter 1. As noted there, those born with missing or ambiguous genitals are neither part of the hijra group nor are they welcome. In other words, while hijras both of the janana and chibry type often contest each other's status, internally it is common knowledge that none are 'real'. Chibry hijras often berate the janana hijras not only on account of their having male genitals but also because of their failure to live up to Maya Ji's ideal of asexuality. Chibry hijras also invoke the emasculated hijras who reportedly serve at the shrine of the prophet to validate their status.[4] It is also instructive to note that hijras tend to perform *hajj* only after emasculation.

Paradoxically, emasculated hijras undertake hajj as men and not as hijras; as one of the emasculated hijras once related, 'You can deceive the whole world but not Allah, who created us as men and not as hijras.' Jananas, however, contend that chibrys undertake hajj to atone for the sin of emasculation. Janana hijras castigate the chibrys for contravening Allah's will by altering

---

[4] See, for instance, Marmon (1995) for a fascinating history of eunuchs and their association with the Prophet's grave.

their God-given male genitals. Janana hijras argue that the severed organs turn into a snake and bite the chibry on the day of judgement. Janana hijras also talk about the decision taken by chibrys to undergo emasculation as driven by their desire to have a greater say in birit, as being emasculated makes one conform to the public understanding of what a hijra is, that is, people born with missing or defective genitals. In reality, however, there are several birits controlled and supervised by janana hijras under whose aegis chibry hijras operate. While contestations and conflicts around genital status typically emerge surrounding the trespassing of birit, allegations of fakery are always hurled at the trespassing group, regardless of whether the trespassing hijras are jananas or chibrys.

In fact, each hijra group in Dhaka has both jananas and chibrys as members. Internally, however, chibry celas of janana hijras in Dhaka never challenged their guru on account of genital status. Rather, emasculated hijras are often disparaged by jananas as being less real on account of the artificiality of emasculation. Furthermore, in Hridoypur and elsewhere, chibry status does not entail either a greater share of the monies or a lesser workload. Furthermore, both janana and chibry hijras have special ritual powers in the hijra community. For instance, it is only the chibry hijras who are entitled to draw the pictures of Maya Ji and Tara Moni before the initiand's genuflection during baraiya. On the other hand, jananas are the only group of hijras with the exclusive privilege of worshipping the dhol, one of the most sacrosanct objects of the hijras.

There are a few things to be noted here. First, my contention is that there is neither any consensus nor any clear status differentiation based on genital status. This can be explained in terms of the cultural resources that hijras draw on to consolidate their position. On the one hand, both janana and chibry hijras creatively appropriate Islam to contest and affirm each other's position, as suggested earlier. On the other, ambiguity and ambivalence contained within the mythic tale of Maya Ji and Tara Moni are productive of such contestations. While the myth clearly marks out jananas as 'real' hijras in that both Maya and Tara were hijras with penises, it also denies them realness on account of their reluctance to abide by Maya's instruction to undergo emasculation.

Second, the main bone of contention over authenticity is not centred on genital status alone but more significantly linked with erotic desire. After all, hijragiri from the perspective of that mythic tale can be read as a form of atonement for the original sins of Tara Moni; had Tara been chaste, there would have been no need for them to resort to artificial means of emasculation. The problem, however, was not that Tara Moni desired, but the fact that they acted on it. While this was the explanation several chibry hijras offered, in reality all the chibry hijras I knew had lovers, although they generally denied this in public. When I raised this issue with a close acquaintance who was a chibry hijra, they argued that it is not just the removal of the genitals that guarantees the power and blessing of Maya Ji; rather, it is through abstention from desire that one can receive the power of Maya Ji. After all, the difference between Maya Ji and Tara Moni is not that Maya Ji had no desire while Tara did. Rather, the difference lies in the fact that despite their having erotic desire, Maya could exercise restraint while Tara succumbed.

Third, from the perspective of desire that I teased out previously in chapter 3, emasculation does not render one asexual, not least because emasculation in the Bangladeshi context is not culturally valorized, unlike in Hindu-dominated India (Nanda 1999; Reddy 2005a), but, more significantly (and as already indicated in chapter 3), erotic desire is deemed by hijras to be located in the anus and not in the penis. What this underscores is that while emasculation renders the penis redundant, it does not signal asexuality in the Ulti universe, where the possibility of supreme pleasurability can only be obtained through the anus.

Paradoxes of bodily metamorphosis and the hyper-masculinity of emasculation

Emasculation, I have already noted, entails the attainment of sot, or special ritual power, as expounded in the mythic tale of Maya Ji and Tara Moni. More importantly, through emasculation, a hijra becomes the ritual embodiment of Tara Moni, the goddess who lost their magical powers due to their sexual lust. I also noted that one of the purposes of undergoing chibrano is to get rid of all forms of vestigial somatic masculinity, evident in the way the initiand's masculine blood is allowed to drain out. What does chibrano entail in terms of bodily alterations? Hijras generally maintain that once emasculated, they lose the masculine bodily compartments—namely roughness, body hair, and so on. Yet hijras likewise maintain that emasculated hijras, despite these bodily changes, become the repository of masculine prowess unbecoming of even the toughest of men. In other words, chibry hijras attain a degree of intrepidness and aggressiveness that the wider society—including hijras—culturally read as 'hyper-masculine'.

Hijras in Dhaka often maintained that the chibry hijras are not only 'aggressive' but also 'dangerous'. Once I asked a few hijras in Hridoypur to introduce me to Hamida, an emasculated guru in another area in Dhaka. Mousumi and Payeli, with whom I first discussed this, immediately cringed, saying, 'Don't even think of it. Even the very sight of Hamida makes our hearts beat faster. Even the police are scared to talk to Hamida. They are one of a kind and they are also extremely feared by hijras in Bangladesh.' The reason for this fear, I was told, was not only the way they looked, walked and talked (Hamida was tall, dark and stout with heavy shoulders, attributes which, when present in combination, are equated with someone's being diabolical in the Bangladeshi context) but more importantly because they underwent emasculation.

Echoing the same sentiment, hijras in other areas spoke in similar tones about some of the well-known chibry hijras. In speaking of Roksana, an emasculated *hajji* hijra, hijras drew my attention to one incident. In the words of Hira, a hijra in the Mirpur area of Dhaka,

> Roksana was once walking alone in the middle of the night in the Dhanmondi area. As a car zoomed past, some miscreants from that car cat-called. Roksana turned back and started shouting at them. In response, a widely known terrorist came out of the car with an AK47. Roksana not only seized the gun but also held the scrotum of the terrorist until they all apologized.

Another similar event I recall unfolded thus: once at around 2:30 a.m. when I was about to leave a hijra house, I expressed concern about hijackings, which had become quite common in that area. Noticing my anxiety, Ranu, an emasculated hijra guru, volunteered to walk me through the notorious bazaar road. When I wondered how they would return, they laughed and said that hijackers or whoever they were would all be scared to see them at this time of the night. Once, in the house of Roksana when I raised this issue about their image, they proudly related, 'In this town there is none like me. Be it police or thugs, they all bow down before me. I am that hijra. Not like those who put their buttocks on sale in the market these days.' It is instructive to note that although the very sight of the hijra often incites laughter and mirth on the part of the wider society, it also sparks fear among the mainstream. This sense of fear is not just rooted in pollution (Douglas [1966] 2002) that their inauspicious presence occasions; more specifically, it is hijras being 'violent', 'shameless' and 'hyper-masculine' that the wider public are scared of. As a middle-class Bangladeshi, I had often heard my friends and acquaintances speak about the hijras not only in terms of jocularity and a sense of disgust, but also in terms of a genuine sense of fear.

What emerges is that although emasculation is intended to permanently erase masculine prowess, paradoxically it confers on the chibrys a special aura of courage and belligerence bordering on what would—in both normative Bangla and Ulti imagination—be classed as 'hyper-masculinity'. In speaking of these special traits of the chibrys, it is important to note that this attainment of hyper-masculinity is not actually the contradiction it may seem in the first place to be. Several chibry hijras I had spoken to maintained that chibry hijras manage to become fearless as they have transcended that which society valorizes the most: the penis as the embodied truth about masculinity. That male genitals are considered culturally precious and valuable is evident in the mainstream labels used to variously describe the penis. For instance, two very common Bangla expressions used are *sona* and *dhon*, meaning gold and wealth, respectively. Furthermore, the very excision of the male genitals, in the accounts of my interlocutors, engenders an incremental build up—and therefore intensification—of sudrani, the hijra word for semen, that makes the chibry hijras more masculine than normative Bangla men.

Here it is instructive to note that while the middle classes ascribe hyper-masculinity to hijras based on representation of hijras as dangerous thugs in the media, the working-class understanding about hijras being 'hyper-masculine' derives from their direct encounter with the hijras in daily settings. One roundabout example of this can be found in the sermons of the *hakim*s, or religious doctors, who are often seen to canvass in the evening in busy marketplaces in urban Bangladesh. Dressed in Islamic outfits, such bearded canvassers typically draw a large number of working-class male crowds to whom they sell various kinds of special medicine related to premature ejaculation and semen discharge. During my fieldwork in Dhaka, I attended several such gatherings and discovered that one of the issues explicitly spoken about in such public space by such hakims is not only hijras as a special kind of people but also men's sexual relations with hijras and the resultant loss of penile virility and the shape and size of the penis. For instance, one hakim once contended that the lack of 'staying power' of the penis and inability to satisfy women is directly linked with men's sexual involvement with hijras. The circulation of such footpath discourses exemplifies working-class men's anxiety over the retention of semen (Rashid, Akram and Anam 2012).

Furthermore, there is a widespread belief both among sections of the working class and hijras that chibry hijras tend to live longer than the janana hijras. Pointing to nonagenarian Jomuna, Meghna once related that the reason Jomuna was still so healthy and free from disease was because they were above the vices of lust and release. In a similar manner, Roksana, the aforementioned chibry hijra, once argued, 'Hijras are above decadence and destruction. Women menstruate while men release—but we hijras don't discharge. So we are not decadent like the men and women.' That hijras in Bangladesh view emasculation as a route to attaining masculine vigour on account of semen retention is not surprising as semen and its retention are often linked with vigour and prowess at the popular level (see Das 1992 on semen retention among the Bauls of Bengal). A vast body of ethnographic scholarship on South Asia has expounded on the theme of semen retention and anxiety as central to the construction of masculinity (Alter 1995, 1997; Srivastava 2004). Although often juxtaposed with Hindu India, the value of semen as precious 'interior matter' in the context of Muslim-majority Bangladesh has rarely been interrogated.

Revisiting the cultural politics of emasculation in South Asia

So far I have discussed the bodily, ritual and gender practices of emasculation in the context of the hijras of Bangladesh. In the vast literature available on this subject in South Asia, ethnographers have often posited emasculation as the foundational truth about hijras. In other words, the extant scholarship reads hijra identity as inhering in and emanating from emasculation.

Nanda (1999) argues that the practice of emasculation is a religiously inspired ritual sacrifice in return for which hijras in India become spiritually powerful beings with the capacity to bless and curse. It is on account of this sacrifice of male genitals that hijras in India become the practical embodiment of one of the mother goddesses and receive the power to paradoxically confer fertility. Particularly highlighting the fact that no government until that date had been able to erase this institution, Nanda problematically sees in the widespread practice of emasculation a manifestation of Indian men's generalized inability to reconcile their Oedipal anxieties. In addition, Nanda maintains that though the tolerance of hijras in India emanates from the predominance of Hinduism with its valorization of sex–gender variance, hijras in India paradoxically display a special bias towards Islam. For instance, Nanda (1999) notes that the seven hijra houses—that is, the symbolic descent lines to which hijras in India trace their lineage—were all founded by Muslim hijras. In addition, drawing attention to the Mughal patronage of eunuchs in the royal regalia as harem guards, Nanda (ibid.) argues that Islam in the Indian context provides a practical/historical model of accommodating hijras.

Noting Nanda's observation about Islam being a 'positive influence', Jaffrey (1997) in her quasi-historical account of hijras in India takes Nanda to task for not sufficiently acknowledging the link between hijras and Islam. Jaffrey argues that the link between hijras and Islam is not merely casual; rather, hijras are the direct descendent of the Islamic institution of eunuchdom, a proposition she then corroborates by quoting at length from a report produced for the Indian government according to which it was only after the Muslim invasion that the practice of castration became widespread in India. Although non-academic in style, Jaffrey's account resonates well with the popular perception in India about hijras being not only Muslim, but also Islamic in origin (Reddy 2003). In a similar vein, Taparia (2011) argues that while emasculation is Islamic, *nirban* (rebirth), the hijra word for genital excisions in contemporary India, is Hindu in origin. Taparia's argument is that hijras today adopted Hindu practices as a consequence of the loss of their courtly prestige under the Mughal sultanate. From being a cruelly enslaved commodity under the Mughal, hijras actively exercised agency to transform the practice of emasculation into a culturally acceptable trope of idealized renunciation in Hindu-dominated India.

Reddy (2005a, 99), drawing on her ethnography in south India, argued that hijras demonstrate a heavy bias towards Islam. Despite being born as Hindus and their recourse to Hinduism to justify their position in Indian society, Reddy's hijra subjects generically identify themselves as Muslims. Reddy maintains that her hijra interlocutors understand Islam through the lens of practice. In other words, hijra claims that 'we are all Musalmans now' (ibid., 99) are facilitated by their ritualistic observance of practices marked as Islamic. Thus, once initiated into the hijra community, one becomes a Muslim by default. Reddy reads hijra self-identification as Muslim in Hindu-dominated India as a manifestation of a minority coalitional politics where hijras reputedly claim a special sense of affinity with Muslims on account of their respective subaltern identifications (ibid., 113–114). Reddy contends that hijra identification with minoritarian Islam makes the hijra a true supra-local/national subject in the Indian context.

Reddy's projection of hijras as supra-local/national subjects opens up novel ways to re-conceptualize hijras. The problem is that the automatic conflation of hijras with Islam on account of hijra practices of circumcision and castration in fact works to reinforce rather than subvert the Hindu cultural politics of virile masculinity. Reddy argues that her hijra subjects identify themselves as Muslims on the ground that they undergo circumcision and castration, both of which are considered indispensable rites of passage to becoming a hijra. That Muslim men undergo circumcision is often invoked in popular and political discourse in contemporary India to demonize Muslims (Ramaswami, 2007). Thus, the observation that hijras in India look at castration as an exaggerated form of circumcision by virtue of which their self-identification as Muslims is expedited gels well with the stereotypical representation of Muslims as 'incomplete men'. Instead of challenging Hindu masculinist nationalism, the link between castration and circumcision further reinforces and consolidates the dominant Hindu projection of the Muslims as simultaneously 'emasculate' and 'hypersexual' (Bhaskaran 2004; Hossain 2012; Hansen 1996; Moodie 2010, 539) on other ways that Islam has been repeatedly and variously linked in cultural politics to either perceived sexual deviancy or its inverse, sexual repression.

While in Hindu-dominated India hijras' self-identification as Muslims on account of their observance of Muslim-marked rituals may emerge as extraordinary, the ritualistic observance of Islamic-identified beliefs and practices by hijras of Bangladesh, most of whom emanate from Muslim families, are rather ordinary features of what Muslims in Bangladesh generally do. In the Bangladeshi context, hijras concurrently observe both Hindu-identified and Islamic beliefs and practices. Yet unlike Hindu-born hijras in India, Muslim-born hijras in Bangladesh do not come to identify themselves as Hindus on account of their ritualistic observance of Hindu-marked practices and beliefs that I previously discussed. Similarly, though there are also Hindu-born hijras in Bangladesh, they generally adhere to and identify with their religion of birth and there is no communitarian pressure on the Hindu-born hijra, 'chaiton' as hijras call them, to become 'surki', the hijra term for Muslims. Nor do the Hindu hijras talk about becoming Muslims on account of their initiation into the hijra community, as Reddy suggests. Muslim hijras in Bangladesh often situate their Hindu-marked cosmology and practices within the framework of an open and transcendent Islam. Though they argue that their asexuality and gender liminality transcend all religious and geographical borders, evidenced both in their accommodation of Hindu-identified beliefs and practices as well as Hindu-born people, they nonetheless cling to their Islamic identity.

Conclusion

In summary, this chapter challenges the master narrative of hijra identity as inhering in and deriving from emasculation. First, as my ethnography suggests, hijras in Bangladesh do not necessarily become less masculine on account of their undergoing emasculation. In fact, hijras recognize the chibry hijras as an embodiment of hyper-masculinity on account of their presumed retention of semen. Second, hijras do not view emasculation as an exaggerated form of Islamization as some scholars suggest. Nor do the hijras in Bangladesh identify themselves as Hindu on account of their becoming chibry, which they read as Hindu in origin. Emasculation is highly ritualized and confers on the operated special ritual power, but that position is not uncontested within the hijra universe. Third, emasculation is best understood as part of a wider set of bodily and cultural practices, a processual approach to the gendering and experience of becoming a hijra that I develop further in chapter 5.

5 Practices and Processes of Gendering

A: I heard them calling you guru. Are you a *sadrali hijra*?

S: Yes I am.

A: But you are not dressed in female attire.

S: Do women today put on sari?

A: I see. What is your name?

S: Which name do you want? The male one or the female one?

A: Whichever you want.

S: I am Sobuj but when I put on female clothes I call myself Sushmita Sen.

A: Are you new in this shrine?

S: Nope. I live close by.

The excerpt presented above is gleaned from a conversation that I had with a hijra called Suki who my sari-clad hijra interlocutors addressed as 'guru' on the premises of a shrine in Dhaka. This normatively attired, hijra-identified person was, I later found out, not only heterosexually married, but also an influential sadrali hijra guru in that area. During my fieldwork one of the things that fascinated me was the way several hijras I had known continuously oscillated between a hijra subject position and that of a masculine householding man. What does such movement across and between heterosexual masculinities and the hijra subject position entail in terms of bodily and sartorial practices? How do hijras interpret these various practices through which they transform their gender?

This chapter explores hijra notions and practices of gender. It challenges the stereotypical notion that a hijra subject position inheres in and flows from emasculation. While hijras do often talk about their being an intermediate gender, a closer attention to the actual practices and processes through which hijras gender themselves brings into view a picture far more complex and nuanced than the extant trope of 'third sex' allows for. Rather than view the hijras as a static and ahistorical third gender category, I elaborate how hijras not only understand and explain normative categories of gender, but also practice those categories in quotidian settings. The guiding principle in this chapter is that gender ideologies are not to be understood as discontinuous with the practices in real-life situations. Rather, the ideals that hijras publicly proclaim and the practices they enact are mutually co-constitutive, and it is through an interrogation of this mutual interplay that we may be able to understand not only the limits of a third sex framework, but also the concept and praxis of gender.

Following a brief discussion on the hijra notion of gender, I take on board various 'male femaling' practices through which hijras seek bodily and sartorial metamorphosis. I then illustrate practices through which hijras come to understand femininity. In explaining and expanding on the hijra notion and practice of gender, I demonstrate how hijra gender ideologies are appropriations and extensions of broader hetero-patriarchal Bangla cultural logics. Moving on from there, I examine the constant shift between heterosexual masculinities and the hijra subject position that my interlocutors practised on a daily basis. Attending to the way such movements transpire between and across Bangla masculine subjectivities and that of the hijra subject position brings into view the processual nature of hijra identity. Focusing on the art of phallic dissimulation that hijras perform, I further expound not only the making of hijraness, but also the limits of a third-sex framework. Rather than read hijraness as an intermediate and 'failed' subject position, I argue that hijras in Dhaka disavow Bangla masculinity to be able to explore varied gender and erotic possibilities that are otherwise unavailable to normatively masculinized subjects in Bangladesh.

Notion of gender among hijras

There is no widely used word for 'gender' in Bangla, the predominantly spoken language among the mainstream majority. The common translation in the wake of NGO-driven activism that certain sections of the middle classes employ these days is 'samajik lingo'—literally, social genitalia, a phrase that is more confounding than clarifying. There is no word for it in the hijra clandestine argot, Ulti, either. Yet 'gender' as is commonly understood in the

Anglo-American world is central to the way hijras view the world.[1] When asked about what a hijra is, responses typically ranged from 'we are neither men nor women', to 'we are two in one' and 'we are people above sex/gender', to 'we have a woman's mind but a man's body' and 'we are an admixture of masculinity and femininity'. More than any other factor, hijras emphasize the gendered aspect of their selves when asked to speak about themselves. I elaborated briefly the hijra view on the gendered social universe in chapter 1; here, I expand on those themes to situate the hijras not only in relation to the wider societal understandings of gender, but also in relation to their own gendered cosmology.

According to hijras, the gender categories are as follows: (*a*) *panthi/parik* (man), (*b*) *neharun* (woman) and (*c*) *koti*/hijra. So what is a man according to hijras? During my fieldwork, I asked this question every now and then. More often than not, my interlocutors laughingly said 'apni', an honorific address in Bangla meaning 'you'. In speaking of what a man is, my interlocutors typically argued that those who are possessed of a *jhumka* (scrotum) and *ligam* (penis) are men. Upon further prodding, some said men are those who have a deeper voice. Some pointed to walking styles, while others focused on moustaches and facial hair in general. Some also said men are those who marry heterosexually and father children while others argued that a man is someone who dresses like a man. What emerges is that my hijra interlocutors look at manhood first and foremost through the lens of anatomical features, namely the penis and its reproductive capabilities. Second, they conceptualize men through the lens of certain societal norms of masculinity, such as bodily comportment and sartoriality.

The hijra understanding of manhood is reflected in the way they define a panthi or a parik. 'Panthi' is the hijra argot for 'men', while 'parik' is the word for an intimate partner, or husband. Both panthi and parik are used to refer to grown-up men as opposed to a 'tonna', the hijra word for boy. I examine the role of pariks in the life of hijras in chapter 6; here, I highlight some preliminary features as a way to understand the hijra notion of manhood. Hijras define a panthi as someone who is 'manly' in the way he deals with the world. An ideal panthi has to be endowed with a large penis and should be capable of fucking hard or what the hijras call 'akkhar dhur'. More

---

[1] See Cornwall and Lindisfarne (1994, 11) for a similar observation on how categories including gender are imprisoned in the strictures of the language in which we are describing.

importantly, a panthi is someone who is indisputably a penetrator and never a receptor. Though my hijra interlocutors stress the possession of a penis as a defining feature of manhood, it is not the possession per se, but rather the use to which the penis is put that defines the hijra conception of manhood.

In response to my question as to what a woman is, hijras in Hridoypur always pointed towards a vagina and breasts as essential features of femininity. Additionally, they also often spoke about softness, shyness, lack of facial hair and sartoriality as traits defining women. Josna, a hijra in Hridoypur, argued that women are those who stay inside the house, cook and take care of the domestic chores, while Payeli contended that women are those who give birth to children. In fact, the ability to give birth to children was often pointed out as a very important factor in the way hijras defined women in general.

Hijras look at both men and women through the lens both of physiological properties—namely genitalia—and normative societal attributes. Yet hijras complicate their own narratives by challenging such essentialism by categorically rejecting the manhood of those men who receive the penis in sexual intercourse with men. It is thus not just the somatic traits and reproductive capabilities but more specifically the uses to which they are put through which hijras conceptualize man, and hijras. For instance, hijras differentiate themselves from panthis in terms of sexual receptivity. A hijra or a koti is someone who is by definition receptive as opposed to a panthi, who is penetrative, regardless of how manly or effeminate a person is, although it is commonly assumed that those who receive are always necessarily feminine. It is on account of this receptivity that hijras think of themselves as being akin to female. The most common response to my question as to why they identify themselves as female was their desire for normative masculine men. For my hijra interlocutors, desire for men and feminine identification are isomorphic: men who desire men are not men but hijras, and 'men' who identify themselves as women inevitably desire men. In that sense, gender and sexuality are not two distinct ontological domains for hijras. I have already examined the entanglement of desire with gender in chapter 3; here, let me simply reiterate that this trope of receptivity as the defining factor of hijra subjectivity is so pervasive that any digression from this model jeopardizes one's status as an authentic hijra. Those found to violate this norm, that is, those who both penetrate and get penetrated, are often denounced in a derogatory fashion as *gandu/gaira/do-porotha* (double-decker).

Several anthropologists have also made similar observations in their respective fields. Johnson (1997), for instance, in his study of the male-bodied, feminine-identified *bantut bantut* of southern Philippines, contends that his interlocutors not only talked about their having a 'women's heart stuck in a man's body', but also operated within a strict gender regime that draws a clear distinction between the penetrated and the penetrator. Johnson contends that any suggestion that his interlocutors might be insertive in sexual intercourse with men was not only met with opposition, but also provoked a deep sense of disgust. In a similar vein, Boellstorff (2004b) argues that the *waria*, the Indonesian 'transvestites', often spoke pejoratively about those who penetrate and get penetrated. Further afield, Kulick (1998), in his study of Brazilian transgendered prostitutes, maintains that his *travesti* interlocutors categorically drew on a system of gender configuration whereby those who penetrate are unambiguously accorded the status of men, while the penetrated 'travesti' are culturally grouped together with the females.

The brief discussion of the studies above highlights that notwithstanding the contextual differences and complexities of the respective cultural fields, gender and sexuality are not understood to be distinct conceptual domains in many non-Western contexts (see also Jackson 2000 and Peletz 2009). However, what is distinct about the hijra notion of gender is that while penetration defines men and masculinity, derogatory labels are used to disparage male-bodied, feminine-identified people who penetrate men and not women. In other words, while penetrating women is acceptable, although not desirable, penetrating men is not.

Male femaling and the practices of bodily and sartorial transformation

One of the persistent themes that sprang up in my conversations with hijras was a generalized flair from an early age for feminine bodily comportment and sartorial practices. My hijra interlocutors maintained that it was because of this proclivity that they were often taken to task not only in their families, but also in the wider societal settings—namely the school, the playground and the neighbourhood at large. In explaining this flair for feminine deportment and lifestyles, hijras often invoked some essentialist narratives of their being born with such tendencies. But while those 'innate proclivities' may qualify one to be part of the hijra group, becoming a member of a hijra group entails systematic acquisition of and conformity to certain prescribed bodily and sartorial practices. Nevertheless, hijras contend that only those with such inborn tendencies will be able to master these rules and rituals.

Practices and Processes of Gendering

In speaking of hijras, my interlocutors always highlighted their distinction in bodily and sartorial terms from men. For instance, Jomuna categorically drew a distinction between hijras and men by pointing at 'sadra', the hijra word for female-marked sartoriality. Although in the hijra argot, 'sadra' simply means 'sari', an unstitched length of cloth wrapped around the waist, with the loose end of the drape to be worn over the shoulder, baring the midriff, worn by women across South Asia, hijra use of the word extends beyond simply wearing the sari, to embracing the sense of adopting a way of life. Although not all members of the community wear a sari at all times, wearing a sari is a must especially when hijras perform their two ritually validated hijra occupations of *badhai* and *cholla*.

Munira, now in their early thirties, once recounted the initial days when they were still struggling to learn the hijra ways. They pointed out that although they were feminine from an early age and experimented with their mother's clothes surreptitiously, they had to perfect the way they wore the sari after joining the community. They vividly recalled the way they used to be upbraided by their guru for not being able to wear the sari properly. Because they were not adept at wearing the sari in a proper manner, they were debarred from participating in badhai and cholla. But later, with practice, Munira perfected their sari-wearing skills. With time, Munira has refined their skills so much that these days whenever a new member is initiated, Munira is the first one to be given the task of instructing the novice. Rumana, a gothia of Munira, once argued that if they were men they would have worn pants and shirts, although in reality many hijra-identified persons do in fact wear normative masculine attire.

In addition to 'sadra', hijras also often stress their bodily comportment as intrinsic to hijraness. Monalisa, a hijra guru, once argued, 'If we were men would we have our ear and nose pierced? Did you ever see a man with such piercings?' Another hijra called Babli once commented, 'Don't you understand that we walk differently from men? Do men sway their hips the way we do? Are their hands unhinged at the wrist like ours?' Most hijras I spoke to in Dhaka wore a bra and blouse while wearing a sari. Typically, my hijra interlocutors filled their bras with cotton, coconut husk, pads of cloth or tennis balls. Although very few hijras developed breasts, younger hijras often experimented with various breast enlargement techniques. One very popular practice is the regular ingestion of contraceptive pills, or 'maya bori', widely available in the market. Although widely used as birth control pills, hijras call them 'lilki/nilki bori', literally pills for the enlargement of breasts.

On many occasions, my hijra interlocutors longingly spoke of growing breasts, although to their utter dismay only a few could actually develop breasts. One of the popular brands that I saw in many hijra households was Renshen, a Chinese breast-enhancement cream. Hijras who used it argued that three tubes of Renshen would do the trick, and if there was no improvement then they would try some other methods. A popular perception among hijras is that regular ingestion of contraceptive pills undermines penile potency and consequently the sperm gets congealed in the breast, leading to its enlargement. While they could not explain the exact origin point of sperm, the idea that sperm travels through the body resonates with heterodox biological understandings of sperm in Bangladesh.[2] Initially, after about two to three weeks, some sort of a lump is formed in the breasts and one finds out that the breast is forming when one starts to experience pain in those lumps. Nevertheless, very few of my interlocutors had been successful in enlarging their breasts either by ingesting these pills or applying breast-enhancing creams. One very popular alternative technique to make breasts was to pad out a bra with water-filled condoms—a practice known as 'ilu ilu'. However, I had only seen this to be prevalent among the sex-worker hijras in the public gardens. Many hijras also drink the juice of the leaves of a tree known as 'bel' (wood apple) to weaken penile prowess. It is believed that regular intake of this juice causes erectile dysfunction, leading to an enlargement of the breast. My hijra interlocutors also drew my attention to medical techniques of breast enlargement, as this was a recent trend that had been gaining some traction within hijra communities. It was as yet not widespread, however, and only a handful of hijras I had ever come across had had such an implant or surgery.

Hijras with a prominent bust are often envied by other hijras who jealously remark about their large breasts (*akkhar lilki*). In Dhaka, hijras told me only a few were successful in developing large breasts with the help of pills. Although breast enlargement is a preferred practice among the sadrali group, one of the hijras famous for their natural breasts in Dhaka was not a sadrali but a sex-worker hijra who, despite having big breasts, always dressed like a man. Once during my visit to a cruising site, Chadni volunteered to show me their breasts to prove the point of my other hijra interlocutors. Chadni, then twenty-one years old, had started consuming pills when they were seventeen,

---

[2] See Das (1992), for instance, for an account of translocation of semen within the body in Baul (a group of mystic singers) thought and practice in Bengal.

and within a few months had ended up developing breasts, unlike others who despite painstaking efforts at enlargement had failed. While most hijras I had known had to pad out their bras to make breasts, Chadni, being a *kari koti* (a koti in the guise of a male), always tied their breasts with a length of cloth to hide them from the public.

Hijras typically pluck their facial hair out with a *chimpti* (tweezers) instead of shaving them, a practice they call 'darsan potano'. 'Darsan', also known as 'dargarani', refers to beards while 'potano' is to get rid of, or erase. Munira once explained to me that while men shave, hijras pluck their *darsan*. Senior hijras typically carry a chimpti tied to a thread worn around their waist. The very first time I saw it was when Jomuna, the guru in Hridoypur, perched on a bed, was stretching out their body and the chimpti was dangling from the thread around their waist. When I asked what it was, they tried changing the topic but later, as I grew close to Jomuna, they told me that it was a secret and precious possession that very few hijras these days have. They maintained that a proper chimpti is made with either silver or gold and the one they had was an inheritance from their guru. Because Jomuna was the most liked of all the celas of their guru, the latter had passed it down to them. Although sadrali hijras generally use chimptis to erase facial hair, a few of Jomuna's celas shaved. Mousumi, a junior hijra, once related, 'My facial hair grows too fast and too thick and it is almost impossible to pull them all out. It is not only painful but also very time-consuming. So I thread[3] it. Plus I always put on thick layers of make-up on my face when in public so as to hide the blackness of my face.' Sundori, another hijra in Hridoypur, always wore thick make-up. While hijras generally put on thick layers of pancake[4] make-up, a full coverage foundation intended to cover scars, discolouration and facial hair on the face, Sundori would always have a few extra layers on their face. So dense and blatant was their make-up that I struggled to make out the features beneath it. While the hijras in Hridoypur would not normally put

---

[3] Threading is a traditional method of hair removal done with the help of a single thread. While with a tweezer each hair has to be singly plucked, with threading an entire row of hair can be erased in one go.

[4] A brand of cosmetic face powder popular with the hijras in Bangladesh. Upon researching, I found this to be an expensive product, although the pancake make-up boxes hijras used were locally made and relatively cheaper. Hijras often begrudged its high price and spoke about this brand and style of make-up being used by heroines in Bangladeshi cinema.

on make-up during cholla and badhai, Sundori always did. When curious, I asked the reason, Sundori told me that this was how they could avoid being seen by their family members to be with the hijras. Mousumi and others, however, contested this, saying that they wore thick make-up to hide acne scars.

Jok, literally hair, was another important dimension of hijra bodily metamorphosis. Sadrali hijras typically keep their hair long and those who fail to grow long hair wear false hair known as 'velki jok'. Hijras believe that because of the curse of Maya Ji, the hijra goddess that I discussed in chapter 4, all hijras lose their hair and grow bald as they age. Mousumi once contended that when Maya Ji was falling between the cracks of the earth, Tara Moni held them by the hair and because of this, all hijras lose their hair as they grow old. For this reason, hijras tend to take very special care of their hair by applying henna dye and other herbal products.

Assuming femininity

Hijras, I already noted, seek bodily and sartorial transformations by resorting to various techniques. What do these transformative practices entail? After all, my interlocutors often maintained that they were male-bodied persons with feminine minds. It was clear to all my interlocutors that despite their attempts at bodily and sartorial transformation, they never became 'real' women. Nor did they aspire to be so. Rather, for most of my interlocutors, acting like or passing oneself off as a female was tantamount to actually being female. This was so not only with the chibry hijras, but also with the janana hijras. However, it is important to recall here that, as discussed earlier in this chapter, the hijra-defined notion of normative femininity does not necessarily refer to the actual lives of women. While in reality normative female femininities vary considerably in keeping with class, status and position in the life course, my hijra interlocutors always indicated certain stereotypical traits in describing normative femininity.

Hijras, I have already noted, put on thick layers of make-up and don various female attire. But those who could wear it more like a woman, that is, in such a way that others would mistake them for 'real' women, always took pride in such imitations. Dipu, a hijra, took pride in their ability to change their voice and speak like a female. Dipu could comfortably switch between both masculine and feminine voices. Once it so happened that Dipu spoke to a man in his forties for some time on the phone and then that man came to visit Dipu. When that man came, Simmi, a female friend of Dipu, was in the house. That man mistook Simmi for Dipu. Romana, another hijra, liked talking to men on the phone. Romana had dated several men through such telephone conversations. Romana said that most of the panthis mistook them for a woman over the phone, but since Romana was somewhat masculine in their looks, men could easily recognize them as 'velki' (fake) as soon as they met them in real life. This trope of passing oneself off as a woman also resonates with my interlocutors' claim about men being unable to distinguish hijras from women at the time of intercourse that I already touched upon in chapter 3. While the veracity of such claims may be questioned, what is noteworthy is the way hijras take pride in such acts of dissimulation.

In explaining to me what it means to be a female, my interlocutors often referred to their adoption of feminine bodily deportment—namely walking with swaying hips, plucking their eyebrows, wearing make-up, bras and long hair, emasculation and breast enlargement. My interlocutors also stressed 'wifely duties' as central to being a female—namely taking care of the household chores, cooking for husbands and attending to the husband's emotional and physical needs. Hijras also often contended that they were capable of outperforming neharuns not only in terms of erotically satiating the men, but also in terms of wifely duties (I elaborate the discrepancy between this claim and the real-life wifely duties that hijras perform in chapter 6). While hijras take on putatively feminine comportment and mannerisms, it is via continual practice that such gender-switching skills are acquired and perfected. More importantly, hijra enactment of femininity is context-specific and subject to alterations in keeping with the demand of their changing surroundings. For instance, hijras often take on exaggerated feminine trappings at the cruising sites to attract normatively masculinized or Bangla men, as previously discussed. Echoing many of my interlocutors, Nili, a hijra, once related, 'I masquerade as a female to attract men. If I don't act like a *neharun-pona* (female), will panthis come to me? So I do all these subterfuges.'

When new members are initiated into the community, they are always given a new female-identified name; however, the previous male-identified names are not relinquished. Both the names are used within the community as well as in the neighbourhood. In Hridoypur I heard many hijras being called by the male-identified name in the wider community, even when they were dressed like females. Gurus too at times call their celas by their masculine-identified names. As Mousumi once explained, 'You know

Abdul, my next-door neighbour. I am very close to him and his wife. Sometimes when Abdul visits his friends and relatives I dress like a man and accompany him. Or else how can I go with him? What would his relatives or friends think about Abdul?' Typically, the female names hijras take are names of the famous film actresses of Bangladesh and India, as in southern Philippines (Johnson 1997). At first meeting, almost every hijra introduced themself by the name of a famous heroine. Also noteworthy is the fact that celas address their gurus as 'guru ma', or mother, while hijras of similar rank address each other as 'gothia', literally sister. However, this female identification is not rigid. Words like guru and cela are male-identified in Bangla. Moreover, senior gurus are also often referred to as *nayak*, literally 'leader', which is also a male-identified moniker. In the mundane settings within the hijra households, I had often seen gurus calling their disciples 'maigga', a pejorative Bangla colloquialism denoting effeminate males, and never as 'magi', the widely used swear word to refer to 'loose' women.

Although hijras are required to wear a sari during cholla, they are taught to be tough in the face of any likely danger in bazaar settings, as they have to constantly haggle with the Bangla vendors to get money. As already suggested in chapter 2, hijras typically swagger up and down the bazaar and approach any potential vendor in an aggressive vein. Often accompanied by boisterous clapping and excessively nasalized speech, the hijra act of demanding is anything but docile femininity. The very act of demanding from the wider society requires masculine vigour unbecoming of normative women. When refused, hijras often lift up their saris in public and typically throw erotically loaded comments at the vendors; such behaviour would not be associated with women in general.

At the level of household domesticity, the picture is also far more complex than the hijras might have one believe in the first place. Despite the rhetoric of demurral and docility that the hijra definition of femininity often lionizes, in their interaction with their partners within the domestic sphere hijras are anything but docile. For instance, there is a widespread practice among hijras known as 'parik pala'—literally, 'making a pet of a husband'. All my hijra interlocutors with husbands tended to dominate their relationship with their husbands. While I discuss at length this dynamic in chapter 6, suffice it to say that the main decision makers in those households were the hijras and not their husbands.

Once, in a cruising site, I was with Nili, a janana hijra. There we met two of Nili's regular clients who over the last few months had grown close to Nili.

Just five minutes' walk from the shrine premises where Nili was cruising was a dark bridge over a road. We climbed up one side of the bridge to have a conversation. Since I was interested in talking to Nili's clients, Nili asked them to go there. In the course of conversation, one of the clients started praising Nili's wife, saying *vabi* (the Bangla word for wives of brothers and friends) was very nice and had a respectable character. Nili, a heterosexually married hijra, lived in the same vicinity with their female wife. Every night Nili would go to a friend's house to change into female attire before cruising. In response to their client's praise for their wife, Nili nodded in total agreement. Because this client was a close friend of Nili, he had often visited Nili's heterosexual home. Nili, however, was known as Nil at home, a male-identified name. In the course of this conversation, I asked Nili if their wife knew about their being in this profession. Nili said their wife had no clue but she had known all along that Nil was a bit 'like a female'. More importantly, when I asked what would be Nili's attitude towards their wife's being in a similar occupation and making money that way, Nili along with their clients vehemently opposed such an idea, saying, 'Chi chi chi!', the Bengali expression used to articulate a strong sense of disgust and disapproval. On another occasion in Hridoypur, a female friend of mine came to visit the hijras. That friend had short hair and was an insatiable smoker. During her visit, we all smoked and drank alcohol and talked about hijras in general. Later one day, the hijras in Hridoypur wondered if that female friend of mine was a prostitute. When I asked why they thought so, they argued that a respectable woman would not keep her hair short as she did. Nor would she smoke and drink alcohol in public.

There are a few things to be drawn out here. First, hijras not only publicly articulate a particular stereotype of what they deem desirable and appropriate femininity, but also never really adhere to those self- and other-ascribed stereotypical feminine trappings. That is evident not only in their interaction with their husbands, where they reputedly exercise greater dominance over their masculine partners, but also in real-life settings, where hijras often take on masculine comportment despite their feminized status. Second, the hijra idealization of certain feminine traits and their publicly professed desire to live up to these ideals run counter to the way normatively gendered women behave in real-life situations in Bangladesh. For instance, women in general do not wear such thick layers of make-up as the hijras do, and nor do they walk with such an exaggerated swaying of the hips (Figure 5.1). Third, hijra approximation and adoption of feminine traits are not an expression of generalized hijra desire to be normatively female, although in public they

Figure 5.1 *Hijra*s in Hridoypur dressed up and posing with the author for a photo
Source: Author.

may proclaim so. Rather, the taking on of aspects of femininity for hijras is a relational practice, that is, they adopt and idealize these practices in relation to their desire for and construction of equally idealized and stereotypical normatively masculinized men. Finally, I would contend that the assumption of a hijra status requires simultaneous disavowal of masculinity and espousal of certain traits of female femininity. Attending to these processes of negotiation and practices foregrounds how hijras are gendered and gendering subjects.

Heterosexual masculinity and hijras

Ethnographers of hijras (Nanda 1999; Reddy 2005a) have located the institutionalized presence of hijras in India within the broader Hindu cultural logics of renunciation. While hijras do not represent the life stages of the Hindu life cycle in the strictest sense, the reported practice of renunciation of reproductive heteronormativity makes them true renouncers. If Hinduism, as Kakar (1990) notes, is a theory of de-sublimating sexuality into spirituality, hijras, by virtue of their genital excision, transform themselves into true ascetics. The dichotomy between renunciation and householding status in Hindu thought is inherently fraught with tension, which hijras purportedly transcend through their ritualized sacrifice of the male genitals, which in turn exemplifies an abstention from desire. I complicate this trope of conflating emasculation with lack of desire in chapter 4; here, I intend to challenge the assumption about hijras being located outside the domain of heterosexual householding masculinity. There is, indeed, some sort of a scholarly consensus about hijras being outside the domain of heterosexual sociality. It is, after all, on account of one's severance of natal familial ties that one becomes an authentic hijra. However, what I demonstrate in the following section is that the assumption of a hijra subject position does not necessarily entail a renunciation of the householding status (see Osella and Osella 2006, 159–165 for a discussion on the overlap between the renouncer and householder status). To illustrate my point, I reproduce here a few ethnographic episodes from my fieldwork.

Meghna, the hijra guru in Hridoypur, the first guru that helped me navigate the hijra universe, is not only heterosexually married but also a full-time sadrali hijra. Around fifty hijras that they supervise are all aware of Meghna's heterosexual marriage and children. Although I had known Meghna for a decade, they never brought it to my attention. It was only by chance that I came to learn about their having a heterosexual family with children. Once, one of Meghna's celas told me about their dropping off some chicken and vegetables at Meghna's non-hijra household, assuming that I had already known about this side of Meghna's life. Perceiving my sense of shock, they asked me to never mention this to Meghna or any other hijra in Hridoypur. On another occasion, Jomuna, the nonagenarian guru of Meghna, suddenly started talking about some domestic problems their daughter was facing. Jomuna, an emasculated hijra, was previously heterosexually married. Later in the conversation, Jomuna mentioned Meghna's children while talking about the distribution of *birit*, the ritual jurisdiction. Noting Meghna's discomfort, I pretended not to have heard and started talking to the others. Later one day, Anwar, a heterosexually married man living in the vicinity of Meghna's hijra house in Hridoypur, invited me to his house. During our conversations, Anwar started talking about how hospitable Meghna's wife was every time he visited Meghna's non-hijra house. In fact, the very fact of Meghna's being heterosexually married was known not only to all the hijras in Hridoypur, but also to some of the close non-hijra neighbours.

Purnima, another cela of Meghna, was about ten years older than their guru. Although I had visited most of the hijra households in Hridoypur, I never had the opportunity to visit Purnima's house. One day, I was told that some kind of a gathering would take place at their abode. Having arrived at the appointed hour, I started interacting with my usual acquaintances.

Big owls of rice, chicken curry and beef were being cooked close to the main entrance of this tin-shed, three-roomed house. The rooms were abuzz with people that included not only the hijras in Hridoypur, but also some non-hijra people. In one of the rooms I was asked not to enter a girl was sitting next to a young man. With them were a few older women from the neighbourhood and Jomuna, the hijra guru. Usually when Jomuna is present in any of the houses of their cela in Hridoypur, I am asked to sit in the same room, but that day Meghna categorically asked me not to sit there, as women from the neighbourhood would be joining them. Later, after having delicious meals, and while the hijras were leaving, I saw some of them handing money to Purnima, who along with Jomuna had been sitting next to that girl and the young man. The event I described here was actually the marriage ceremony of Purnima's daughter; at a later date, the whole episode was related to me by one of the hijras in Hridoypur. Purnima, a heterosexually married hijra, lived a kind of split existence, spending six months in their village as a normative male and being a hijra in Hridoypur for the rest of the year.

Abdul, another influential guru, is a heterosexually married hijra. Abdul has two houses. In the area where they conduct hijragiri, they have a small room from which they supervise the hijra group, while their heterosexual household is located close by. Abdul's celas, many of whom are emasculated, as well as Abdul's wife, are aware of Abdul's dual existence. Abdul, unlike Meghna, was quite open about it from the onset of our interaction. Abdul does not really keep these two households separate. Abdul says their wife is 'pakki', the hijra expression connoting knowledge about the hijra ways. When I visited Abdul's wife, she not only spoke to me in Ulti, but also left me with the impression of her being totally accepting of Abdul's hijra vocation.

Rahim, a hijra in their late forties, works as a sex worker in a public garden. Every day in the afternoon, they come to the other side of the town where they have a small room, which they share with other hijras. Once on this side of the town, Rahim is known as Rahima. Rahim in Bangladesh is a male-identified name, while Rahima is marked as a female one. Rahima uses this room to dress up like a female every evening before going to the cruising areas. Generally at about 3:00 a.m. they return to this room, change into masculine attire and then head back to their heterosexual household. Rahima is also a cela of Shima, the hijra guru in the area where they cruise. As Shima's cela, Rahima also takes part in hijragiri. Once I went to Rahima's non-hijra household. On our way, Rahima categorically asked me to refrain from referring to anything about their hijra life.

As we entered Rahima's tin-shed house in a poor neighbourhood, I met Rahima's wife and two children. Although I barely spoke due to the fear that I might unintentionally allude to the hijras, I was intrigued by the way Rahima transformed themself into Rahim. After an hour, we left and took a rickshaw to get back. On our way back, Rahim once again evolved into Rahima and started to speak Ulti and act like a hijra.

Tanaka, a national-level hijra leader, has risen to prominence in recent times for their health activism. More often than not, Tanaka is seen to be flanked by two children in public. Once on the occasion of a hijra fashion show organized by an NGO, Tanaka turned up with these two children. Dressed in sari, Tanaka was ushered by junior hijras to a row near the stage where three seats were booked for them. Seated in the row behind Tanaka, I heard the children calling Tanaka 'abba', the Bangla expression for father. When I asked Tanaka about who they were, they said they were the children of their sister. However, other hijras present at the show later told me that they were actually Tanaka's own children and Tanaka was still heterosexually married. Due to the sensitivity of the issue, I did not try and confirm this with Tanaka, but the same story was repeated to me by Tanaka's celas.

It is not only the janana hijras who commonly lead such dual lives; the chibry hijras, too, are often seen to be in touch with their children from previous or existing heterosexual marriages. Jomuna, the guru I mentioned earlier, has ministered to the financial needs of their daughter throughout her life. Joynal, another hijra who recently underwent emasculation, regularly sends money to their heterosexual family and pays for their children's education. Joynal's wife works in the Middle East as a cleaner and is aware of their having undergone this operation but, according to Joynal, their wife is not keen on divorcing them.

Among the *gamchali* hijra group I discussed in chapter 1, the majority were not only janana hijras but also heterosexually married. Coming from outside Dhaka, gamchali hijras work as cooks in the burgeoning construction sites in Dhaka. Like many sadrali hijras, gamchali hijras regularly send home money earned through their cooking. Gamchali hijras claim that their families and children back home are unaware of their being hijras, although they all have male lovers. Rabeya has been a gamchali hijra for about ten years now. Prior to coming to Dhaka, they also worked in other areas of Bangladesh as a cook. Rabeya says that when they go back to visit their family, they assume a masculine householding attitude that they referred to as 'akkhar panthi-pon'—literally akin to 'the manners of a masculine man'. Lokman has three daughters, all of whom have been married off, and interestingly a relative of the husband one of their daughters was once his sexual partner, but both Lokman and that relative of their son-in-law act as if they had never met. Like Lokman, when gamchali hijras go and visit their families back in the villages, they try not to walk in the way they walk here in Dhaka. Nor do they dress or talk in a fashion I often heard being referred to as 'maigga', a derogatory expression which, as mentioned previously, is used to refer to effeminate males. Moufuli, another gamchali hijra, opined that their family back in the village had always been aware of their being a bit 'soft' (*norom sorom*) but were aware neither about their sexual relations with men nor their association with hijra groups.

In a society where heterosexual marriage is the norm, the idea that male-bodied people (including hijras and kotis) might marry heterosexually is not unacceptable. Many of my hijra interlocutors wished to marry heterosexually at some point in their lives. While some do so due to familial and societal pressure, others opt for it voluntarily to prove their masculine potency. Babita, who has been a hijra for the last ten years, recently got married. Before getting married, they left the hijra group. They used to live with their mother in the same area. Babita says they got married as their mother was alone. When I asked about it, Babita stated, 'Do you think just because I wear sari like a female and do hijragiri I can't father a child?' Leaving their newlywed wife and mother in the village, Babita joined the hijra group once again. Soma, another sadrali hijra, divides their time between hijragiri and their heterosexual family. Soma, which is a feminine-identified name, is known as Sumon, a masculine name, in their heterosexual household. Soma's wife works in a garment factory in Dhaka. During the day, Soma does hijragiri while at night they work as a sex worker. Since Soma is recognizably 'effeminate', their parents thought marrying 'him' to a female would cure them of effeminacy. Soma contends that they were known for their 'maiggagiri' in the village. Owing to this image, their parents had a lot of difficulty finding them a bride. Nevertheless, when the family of Soma's present wife came to visit, their current brother-in-law took them aside to inquire if they had any problem. Soma showed him their penis and then the marriage was finalized.

There are a few things to be drawn out here. First, there are not only hijras with penises but more significantly many of these hijras are heterosexually married. There are, as shown here, instances where the heterosexual households of these janana hijras are located adjacent to areas where they conduct hijragiri. While the gamchali hijras work as cooks far away from their heterosexual families, sadrali jananas often operate in locations near their heterosexual households, and at times their spouses are aware of this. There is also one hijra guru with an (inter)national reputation in health activism who, contrary to public perception, is heterosexually married. Second, the presence and preponderance of janana hijras is not an exception but very much the dominant pattern whose legitimacy derives from the hijra origin myths that I discussed in chapter 4. Third, while these frequent movements between their normative heterosexual households and hijra status may be seen to echo the classical South Asian dichotomy between renunciation and householding status (Osella and Osella 2006, 159–163; Reddy 2005a, 35–40; Taparia, 2011, 175), these literal and symbolic movements in the case of Muslim-majority Bangladesh do not exemplify such tensions. Rather, what these shifts between and across various gender, ritual and sexual statuses exemplify is the simultaneous habitation of an Ulti universe—where these male-bodied, feminine-identified people are practitioners of alternative desires—and the Bangla world of hetero-erotic masculinity in which they practice normative reproductive heterosexuality. In other words, many of these hijras are simultaneously masculine householding Bangla men and Ulti, or hijra, nationals. This apparent incommensurability can be explained, as I demonstrated in chapter 3, in terms of my interlocutors' desire to explore varied gender, ritual and erotic (ulti) possibilities that are otherwise foreclosed to normatively masculinized Bangla subjects.

The art of 'gender-(dis)appearing'

One of the questions that intrigued me throughout my fieldwork was the way my interlocutors simultaneously lived the lives of masculine householding men and those of hijras. More often than not, heterosexually married hijras, as I previously noted, operated as hijras in a location away from their heterosexual households. It was not thus a case of their being both at the same time in a literal sense, although in the case of Abdul as noted earlier, this distinction was blurred. Every time I raised this issue, hijras burst out into giggles and contended that it was only hijras who were capable of being so many things at the same time. In the words of Mousumi, hijras are polymorphic beings (*bohurupi*), while Sathi styled it as a special art that only hijras are capable of mastering. It is precisely these mystique-making capabilities (*chola kola*) and their systematic mastery on account of which one can become a successful hijra. Yet hijras asserted that this art comes naturally to them, that is, regardless of the amount of training one receives, only the 'real' hijras are able to acquire this art.

One particular art that hijras generally spoke about in relation to polymorphism is that of 'ligam potano': 'ligam' in hijra vocabulary denotes the penis; 'potano', as previously mentioned, is to erase or make disappear. In other words, *ligam potano* is the art of 'vanishing the phallus' in the twinkle of an eye. Although hijras refer to 'potano' in the specific context of hiding the penis behind and between their legs, the very symbolism of this art of phallic dissimulation extends beyond the physical art of stretching the penis backward behind the thighs. I would contend that this art of 'vanishing' can serve as a powerful metaphor to capture the enactment of the multiple and fluid gender practices of hijras. Following Lacan, I therefore translate ligam as 'phallus' rather than just 'penis'. For Lacan, the phallus is not reducible to the physical penis but is rather the symbolic embodiment of the unconscious, and the realm of representation. The phallus is therefore the symbolic sublimation of the penis (cited in Garber 2008, 119–120). The Lacanian take on the phallus resonates well with the way hijras vanish not only the penis, but also its cultural manifestation in the form of heterosexual household and masculinity.

Hijras trace this art of 'vanishing' back to Maya Ji and Tara Moni, the two primordial archetypes that I discussed in chapter 4. According to my hijra interlocutors, both Maya Ji and Tara Moni could literally make their penises appear and disappear with the help of clapping. Although hijras today, I suggest later, do not necessarily look upon ligam potano in such mythic terms, the very mastery of this art of (dis)appearing the phallus is central to hijra status. As already suggested, this art is not to be taken literally but is rendered more meaningful in a metaphorical way whereby hijras are seen to perform various sorts of magical disappearance and appearance. As if almost literally, my hijra interlocutors' multiple and fluid lives and their apparent control and management of them always seemed like a matter of a single clap. It is as if with one single clap their heterosexual families could be made to disappear and then be brought back within a moment with further clapping. While the practice of clapping, as I already suggested in chapter 2, sets hijras apart from the normative mainstream (Pamment 2019b), clapping also works as a marker of authenticity and seniority among the hijras. For instance, it is an unpardonable offence for a cela to clap in the presence of a guru. In the event of such infraction, perpetrators are penalized. Hijras asserted that hijragiri or the occupation of the hijra is a 'play of clapping', in that it is the entitlement to that play that not only marks one as a real hijra, but also establishes one's sway within the community. *Thikri*, or clapping, is therefore a symbol of power and authenticity as well as a route to achieving magical appearance and disappearance.

Hijras today, however, view this art of phallic dissimulation in pragmatic and physical terms. In other words, the reason hijras have to master this art today is precisely because of Tara Moni's deceit and the consequent loss of the magical power of clapping, as elaborated in chapter 4. First, despite the fact that there are hijras with penises, hijras always deny it in public. When asked, their typical response is that they were born with missing or defective genitals. Because of this public claim, (janana) hijras today have to master the art of dissimulation to avoid potential embarrassment caused by public discovery of their having penises. For instance, during badhai and cholla, the acts of demanding gifts on the occasion of the birth of a newborn and collecting money from the bazaar, respectively, the wider Bangla society may at times challenge the authenticity of one's *hijraness* precisely on account of genital status. There have been instances where in the face of challenge from 'bad boys' (*bila tonna*), hijras have had to prove their lack of genitals. Furthermore, hijras also often lift up their sari in a bid to coerce the wider society to give in to their demands. On occasion, I saw hijras perform ligam potano both in the bazaar and on household premises. While for the chibry, or emasculated hijras, lifting up their sari in public poses no threat of exposure, hijras with penises require the skill of vanishing in front of the public. Given this risk of exposure, I initially assumed that only the emasculated hijras went for badhai and cholla, but contrary to my assumption, I found out that mostly janana hijras in Hridoypur undertook cholla and badhai.

Second, the constant shifts between varied masculine performances and feminine-identified practices are also evident in the way hijras conduct themselves in day-to-day settings. As already suggested in chapter 2, while hijras take on the persona of aggressive hyper-masculine collectors during cholla, they act like 'docile females' in the immediate neighbourhoods in which they live. In speaking of hijra mystique-making abilities, Mousumi once explained,

> It is not that we always tend to be docile in our interaction with our immediate neighbours, but it all depends on whom we are interacting with. If we are talking to some bad boys in the area who taunt us, we act masculine; but then when we speak to the females or older people, we act as if we are some innocent daughters of the village. We hijras are full of art and subterfuge.

This variable and context-specific gender presentation is also evident in hijra speech and tonal patterns. In her research on the use of language by hijras in India, Hall (1996) illustrates the way hijras constantly switch between masculine and feminine pronouns in their interaction with the mainstream. Although Bangla, the predominantly spoken language in Bangladesh, is uninflected by gender pronouns, such switches are evident at the level of mannerisms and variable tonal patterns. Laila, a hijra widely known for their conversational skills, once commented, 'We sometimes speak like men and sometimes like women—and at times in a mixed way and on occasion like neither men nor women.'

Third, hijras boast about their ability to hoodwink men into thinking that they are 'real' women. The reason men are so easily 'deceived', according to many hijras in Dhaka, is precisely because of this art. One particular event leaps to my mind. Although men seeking to have sex with hijras generally do not inquire about genital status, on one occasion a panthi took Ratna, one of my hijra interlocutors, behind a banyan tree in a public garden to see if they were a 'real' hijra or not. Although Ratna lifted up their sari and showed that they were a genuine hijra, ironically the man declined to have sex as he was, according to Ratna, looking for someone with a penis. Later when I wondered about how they could 'vanish' it so quickly, they volunteered to demonstrate the art to me. Other hijras cruising in that area immediately followed suit in a dazzling display of their mastery of this magical art of phallic dissimulation.

Conclusion: beyond failure and resistance—the limits of a third sex analysis

In this chapter, I sought to foreground the multiple ways in which gender is produced, reproduced and transformed by hijras. I contended that while hijras undertake a series of transformative bodily and sartorial practices to undo the phallic or Bangla masculinity, these ulti, or anal, 'male femaling' practices do not necessarily entail a hermetically sealed non-masculine status. Rather, the trajectory of the lives of hijras exemplifies movements across and between heterosexual masculinities and hijra status. Through several ethnographic vignettes, I challenged the conventional master narrative of hijra status as emanating from emasculation. By paying close attention to their actual lived practices, I demonstrated how hijras not only negotiate masculinity and femininity but also hijraness. However, such acts of transcendence need not be seen as an instance of hijras being stuck in a failed intermediate gender.

Rather, central to the assumption of a hijra subject position is the acquired ability to navigate various forms of partible and permeable lives marked by the practice of magical appearance and disappearance of both physical and social genitals.

Hijras, I elaborated in my introduction to this book, are often projected in scholarship as an intermediate 'category' that transcends the sex–gender dimorphism. I described in detail some of the conceptual and pragmatic pitfalls of a third sex lens in the study of hijras. Here, I intend to highlight once again that underlying this third sex framework is an explicit assumption about hijras being some kind of a gender failure. Conventional wisdom contends that only those failing to be sufficiently normatively masculine take up a hijra subject position. Allusions to such failure are powerfully encapsulated in Nanda's now classic expression about hijras being 'neither men nor women'. This tendency continued unabated even in the works of critical scholars who challenged Nanda. For instance, in her writing on the linguistic practices of hijras, Hall (1996) contends that attention to the linguistic practices employed by Hindi-speaking hijras furnishes further insights into the construction of hijras as a third sex. While critical of the narrative continuity of hijras as mired in the 'neither men nor women' line of analysis, Hall argues that hijras are not just 'neither men nor women', but more specifically 'deficiently masculine and incompletely feminine' (1996, 229). While Hall's projection may reflect the wider societal take on hijras, it is precisely this attribution of failure/lack/inadequacy that the ethnography I presented here squarely challenges.

Hijras, I elaborated, are clearly not 'inadequately masculine'. Rather, many of my hijra interlocutors are simultaneously successful in being hijras and masculine householding men. That is, one becomes a hijra not because of some genital defect or erectile failure. Rather, my interlocutors chose to become hijras to be able to explore various gender and erotic possibilities that are otherwise unavailable to normatively masculinized subjects. It also needs stressing that my hijra interlocutors did not yearn to be biologically female per se, although they often talked about their being 'akin to women'. Rather, the taking on of certain feminine aspects by my interlocutors was a way for them to be a proper hijra rather than being a woman. My argument here is that the adoption of a hijra status does not entail either failed masculinity or failed femininity. Instead of reading hijras through the lens of failure or deficit, hijra subjectivity is better understood as a route to varied erotic, gender and ritual possibilities, the attainment of which requires a continuous and successful mastery of various acts and arts of magical appearance and disappearance. These various practices of simultaneous gendered appearance and disappearance of the genitals, heterosexual family, masculinity and femininity—or even the sex–gender dualism in its entirety—are powerful acts. It is through exercising various forms of (ulti, or anal) agency either via the art of concealment of the (Bangla/phallic) genitals and their subsequent reappearance or through moving in and out of Bangla heterosexual masculinities and (ulti) hijra status that one becomes a hijra.

Reflecting on the various acts of (dis)appearance also moves us beyond reading hijras as some sort of a resistance group. While scholars have often construed hijras in terms of a lack and deficit, scholarship has often sought to seek epistemic validity by presenting hijras as a solid opposition to sex–gender dualism or various normative institutions (for example, Bakshi 2004; Lal 1999; Nanda 1999). My contention here is that taking hijras as a form of resistance to oppressive sex–gender regimes works to deflect our attention not only from the actual gendering practices and processes through which hijras are culturally produced and reproduced, but also from hijras as embodied subjects who produce and reproduce those very configurations of gender and sexuality. While hijras may be used as a cipher to interrogate the constructedness of both gender and sexuality, what is often lost sight of is the way hijras too can be complicit in the perpetuation of normative sex–gender regimes (as I elaborate in chapter 6). Rather than read hijraness as a disembodied metaphor for resistance and subversion, hijra subjectivity is better understood by attending to the multiple gender acts and arts that my hijra interlocutors rely on and enact day in and day out.

6 Love and Emotional Intimacy
Hijra Entanglement with Normative Bangla Men

Anyone conducting fieldwork with *hijra*s might be struck by the way they often immerse themselves in 'ulu jhulu', the hijra expression for fun. Although I initially had the impression that hijras are extremely fun-loving and happy people, I was later told by my interlocutors that this *ulu jhulu* is basically a facade, beneath which flowed a stream of despair in which hijra lives are perennially mired. In explaining to me the fount of this constant despondence, hijras pointed to their deep yearning for a lover, or *parik*. Pariks, the hijra word for partner/lover/husband, play a significant role in the lives of hijras. Although pariks are not part of *hijragiri*, they are an indispensable source of joy and anxiety for the hijras.

Although male-bodied, feminine-identified people have been amply documented and theorized within anthropology of gender and sexual diversity, very little attention has been paid to the roles their lovers or partners play in the formation of their subjectivities (Besnier 2004; Kulick 1998). One outcome of this sustained incuriosity about the partners is that these so-called gender-variant groups have become the embodiment of gender and sexual difference unto themselves. Analytically, such inattention works to rigidify hijras as instances of gender–sexual difference alone. The extent to which hijra subjectivities are formed relationally can potentially suggest new directions in understanding and explaining hijras. Such incuriosity about partners may be explained in terms of the fact that partners—and in the case of hijras, the normatively masculinized Bangla men—lack the exotic appeal that anthropologists generically find in hijras or other such groups. Partly this inattention is the result of the relative invisibility of the partners. Specifically, in the case of hijras, as I suggest later, there is an overt tendency to 'invisibilize' their partners. This invisibility of partners, I would argue, points to a broader politics of masculinity and gendering of desire within and against which hijra subjectivities are situated.

Besnier (2004) foregrounds the problematic erasure of partners in the anthropological explorations of 'transgender' people in the context of Tonga, arguing that this ethnographic silence is not a mere descriptive omission. Rather, this inattention not only works to prevent us from understanding the formation of the subjectivities of gender-variant people generally but also often contributes to their social exclusion and moral abjection. He contends that desire for normative men is central to male-born feminine-identified transgender Tongan's subjectivity and it is also on account of such desire that transgender Tongans are socially marginalized. In a similar vein, I also contend that desire for normative men is central to the formation of hijra subjectivity. And it is because of the forbidden nature of hijra desire for men that hijras enact an Ulti universe within the mainstream Bangla social world. I argue that in order to comprehend hijra subjectivity, systematic attention therefore needs to be focused on kinship, desire and partners.

In her ethnography, Nanda (1999) devotes some attention to this relational aspect of hijra selves, while Reddy (2005a) acknowledges the yearning of her interlocutors for partners; however, the accounts of these authors do not sufficiently interrogate the role of partners in hijra lives or partners' perspectives on the hijras. In other words, accounts of partners emerge only as circumstantial in their narratives and are not accorded any central importance in the constitution of the hijra selves (see, for example, Reddy 2009 for an exception). In contrast, I submit that partners are not merely circumstantial sideshows but are paramount to hijra subjectivity. In chapter 3, I elaborated hijra erotic entanglement with Bangla men and the varied spatio-cultural contexts of those encounters. Here, I highlight the affective and emotional context of hijra encounters and entanglement with their partners.

The first part of this chapter introduces hijra accounts of their partners, illustrating specifically the way hijras define and describe the Bangla men whom they desire, as well as the various selection criteria that they verbally stress. Briefly navigating through a few case stories about hijra love affairs with Bangla men, I interrogate hijra notions of marriage, kinship and affinal relations in the context of their day-to-day lives. The second part of the chapter, albeit rather brief, illustrates hijra participation in the families of their partners with a special focus on how hijras interact with members of their 'husbands'' friends and families. The main focus of this chapter, however, is not so much on the accounts of the pariks as on the hijra accounts of them. The reasons for this are twofold. First, given the focus of this book on hijra subjectivity, I felt an elaborate discussion on partners' accounts would be an analytical digression,

Love and Emotional Intimacy 159

because my primary intention is to foreground hijra views on their pariks. Second, for reasons I explain later, it was not always possible for me to interact adequately with the partners of my hijra interlocutors, a fact that perhaps explains the relative absence of and silence about partners in ethnographic work on male-bodied, feminine-identified people more generally. On the whole, what I present here is a hijra rendition of their interaction and entanglement with their partners which, as will be shown, offers unique insights not only into hijra notions of intimacy and relatedness, but also into the wider context of affect in relation to which hijra subjectivities are forged.

Who are the pariks?

While the hijra word for normative masculine or Bangla men is 'panthi', the word 'parik' is reserved for an intimate male partner, lover or husband. The relationship between a hijra and their parik can take different forms. For instance, there are pariks who live on a permanent basis with their hijra partners. Then there are also pariks who live away from their hijra partners but visit them on a regular basis. There are also long-term pariks who only receive visits from their hijra partners. The expression 'bandha parik', or bonded partner, is used to refer to those who live permanently with the hijras, as well as long-term partners with whom hijras nevertheless do not share a common household. In contrast, 'chutta', or unbound pariks, are those intimate partners who live away from the hijras, in which case either the hijras or the pariks make occasional visits.

'Parik kora', or making a parik out of a Bangla man, is a widely used expression among hijras. Hijras typically want to make a man parik when they start to 'chis' (both desire and love) a panthi. During my visits to cruising sites, several hijras I interacted with expressed their desire to make me their parik. Although there is no specific criterion in terms of which the selection occurs, most pariks are either those whom the hijras met in a cruising site or those from the areas in which hijras live. Pariks tend to be from the same social backgrounds that hijras come from. While (as already noted in chapter 3) hijras sell sex to middle-class men, those men rarely become the pariks of hijras. In fact, not a single parik I met hailed from a background starkly different from those of my hijra interlocutors.

Hijras typically desire Bangla men, that is, those who are identified exclusively with normative masculinity and heterosexuality as that is understood in this context. For example, pariks are expected to be attracted to women and it is because of their attraction to women that they are marked out as normative men in hijra conceptualization. If a panthi is attracted to another masculine-identified man, hijras would not only question the manhood of such a man, but also lose erotic and affective interest in him. In fact, men who desire other men are not in the view of my interlocutors sufficiently masculine or Bangla to be worthy of being their parik. Such men are pejoratively disparaged as 'gandu', 'khudenga' and 'khai khoara'—a range of expressions used by hijras to refer to male-bodied persons who both penetrate and get penetrated by other male-bodied persons. It is important to note that there is no organized community of men who identify themselves as parik. In other words, 'parik' is the label attributed by hijras to Bangla men whom the hijras consider as their intimate partners. Although the pariks I spoke to knew that the hijras referred to them by that term, 'parik' as a label was far from being an identitarian position that partners of the hijras took on. Intimate partners of hijras did not generally self-identify as parik in the wider Bangla society, although these male partners are identified by the hijras as parik.

Although there is no specific selection criterion in terms of which pariks are chosen, there are some marked patterns that emerged in hijra descriptions of their partners. Those descriptions, as I suggest later, did not always correspond to the realities. Among several factors, age often emerged as crucial in terms of parik selection. There were hijras who always preferred 'chudda', or older men, while others opted for 'tonna', or young men. Two of the senior hijra gurus in Dhaka had very young men as their permanent lovers. Dolly, an emasculated *hajji* hijra, lived with their parik in the old part of Dhaka. Dolly's parik was at least a decade younger than them, while Pinki, another hijra guru in their early forties, was about eighteen years older than their parik. There were also pariks from age groups roughly similar to their hijra partners. In Hridoypur, two permanent pariks who lived with their hijra partners were more or less of the same age as their hijra partners. Older hijras in Dhaka often expressed a liking for men with a 'bumper', the hijra word for moustache. In reality, however, I met only one parik who sported a shiny moustache with twirled ends.

The eternal pining for an elusive parik

One of the recurrent threads that emerged in the course of my interaction with hijras was an impassioned yearning for the perennially elusive lover. Although not all my interlocutors had pariks, almost everyone pined for one. Here I

Love and Emotional Intimacy   161

must stress that this pining for an intimate male partner stemmed not from the sexual urges alone but primarily from a deep-seated desire on the part of my interlocutors to be continually loved and to love. There was a widespread conviction among my hijra interlocutors that notwithstanding the affective love and sexual pleasure they showered their partners with, their partners would eventually jettison them. This sense of anxiety about the possibility of their being ditched by their partners was articulated not only by hijras who had been through such experiences, but also by those who had been involved in a steady relationship for a very long time. There was a tangible sense of a 'love and hate' attitude towards the partners. In the words of Payeli, one of my interlocutors, 'Partners are like air, always amorphous and slippery and difficult to catch. Even when caught, they are difficult to keep'. This constant sense of partners being elusive, especially in terms of affective reciprocation, was an inexhaustible source of despondency for my interlocutors. Because of the firm conviction of my interlocutors about partners being 'opportunistic' and 'selfish', several hijras dejectedly spoke about panthis in the worst possible terms. Dipali, a hijra from Hridoypur, once related, 'Pariks are like shoes: we have to change them every now and then.' Payeli meanwhile once contended, 'Pariks are like sweepers who we need only to sweep up our buttock holes.' Hijras in Hridoypur routinely argued that pariks are a kind of *jat* (species) of its own kind that instinctively can never be trusted. Given these deep-seated misgivings, several hijras stated that they only pretended to be in love with their pariks, as they were certain of their pariks' betrayal. Despite this pronounced accusatory tone, hijras entertained in the deepest closet of their hearts the thought that someday someone would truly love them. In other words, the selves of my hijra interlocutors were forged in relation to pariks both real and imagined. To illustrate the importance of pariks in the lives of the hijras, I present three short case stories.

'Two in one': the story of Dipali and Arman

Dipali, a hijra in Hridoypur, had a permanent parik for about nine years. Dipali, unlike most other hijras, could read and write. Dipali wrote eight diaries about Arman, their parik. In explaining to me the intensity and depth of their feelings and attachment, Dipali would often take these diaries out from a secret drawer and read them out to me. Arman was the brother of Dipali's sister's husband. When they broke up, they were totally devastated. They cut the skin of their hands, legs and scalp, the marks of which were clearly visible. They resorted to these self-injurious activities in a bid to show Arman their love for him. Dipali thought Arman would be moved by their action and come back and love them even more, but when all these efforts on Dipali's part failed to draw Arman any closer, they attempted suicide twice. Once Dipali took one hundred tablets and on another occasion, they tried hanging themself from a ceiling fan. At the time of the break-up, Dipali had six lac taka (roughly US$7,000) and six ounces of gold, all of which had been squandered on drugs and alcohol since then.

Dipali felt they could have had a bright career in the film industry as a dancer, but they had relinquished those opportunities for Arman. In addition, they had also severed all their previous ties with the *sadrali* hijras and stopped dressing up like a female to please Arman, who was opposed to their feminine sartorial presentation. Arman also wanted Dipali to stop visiting the public gardens, but they could not stop going to the public gardens, as this was the only way they could socialize with other kotis. Although Dipali explained this to Arman in the clearest possible terms, Arman was unconvinced and accused Dipali of having sex with men in the public gardens. To dispel Arman's worries, Dipali offered to have sex with Arman as many times as he wanted every day, yet Arman could never rise above his paranoia. There were also times when Arman beat Dipali up, suspecting they were seeing other men. Dipali too beat Arman up in return. They always ended up having sex after each row. Dipali contended that they loved Arman so much that they used to share the same toothbrush. Dipali used to get angry if Arman ever looked at any other hijras or women. Prior to being with Dipali, Arman had had several female partners. In retrospect, Dipali maintained that they had wasted a lot of valuable time of their life on Arman. It is on account of this experience, contended Dipali, that they lost all their faith in love and these days even though they have a partner, they pretend sincere love but in reality they live with them only for sexual satisfaction.

Perennially together: Payeli and their long-term lover, Ibadod

Payeli, another hijra in Hridoypur, fell in love with Ibadod, a man ten years older than them. Unlike Dipali, Payeli was still in a relationship with Ibadod at the time of my fieldwork. Payeli met Ibadod long before they entered the hijra group in Hridoypur. After the demise of Payeli's father, they migrated to Dhaka with their mother and lived in Premnagar, where they first met Ibadod. Later they moved to Hridoypur, leaving Ibadod

Love and Emotional Intimacy

behind. However, the fact of their separation did not weaken Payeli's relationship with Ibadod.

It was in Hridoypur that Payeli, previously known by their masculine name as Habib, had their current name conferred upon them by the sadrali hijras. In the beginning, Ibadod, who as yet knew nothing about Payeli's double life, would often visit them at their mother's house in Hridoypur, meaning that Payeli was not able to become a full-time sadrali, and had to be extra cautious in carrying out hijragiri. After about six months of equivocation, Payeli finally decided to become a full-time sadrali, that is, they publicly dressed like a female on a relatively permanent basis. Nevertheless, every time Ibadod paid a visit, Payeli would change themself back into Habib. However, Payeli got caught twice by Ibadod in sadrali mode in Hridoypur. Failing to convince Ibadod to allow them to remain a member of the sadrali group, Payeli left and reverted to masculine attire on a full-time basis, although they were still tied to the hijra group. Although this created some discontent among the hijras, Payeli was not jettisoned by the group as they obtained permission from their guru who, according to Payeli, was sympathetic to their dilemma.

In the meantime, Ibadod left for the Middle East to take up a job in a factory. Payeli once again took to sadrali mode. In 2006 when Ibadod came back to Bangladesh for three months, Payeli once again left behind their sadrali status. It was during this time that Payeli, dressed in typical masculine attire, visited my house along with Ibadod. As I ushered them into the drawing room, Payeli followed me inside and whispered in my ear to not speak a single word of Ulti and to not talk about anything to do with either Hridoypur or hijras. In addition, Payeli asked me to address them as Habib, their male-identified name.

During the time when Ibadod was away, Payeli had regular communication with him by telephone. In times of emergency, Ibadod also sent money to Payeli. When he returned to Bangladesh after two years, Ibadod was under immense pressure from his family to get married. By the end of 2006, Ibadod was married to a woman in his village. Payeli not only attended the festival, but also had a strong say in the selection of the bride. In fact, while Ibadod was abroad, he asked Payeli to go to his village and finalize this marriage. In Ibadod's village, Payeli is known by their natal name Habib and looked upon as Ibadod's closest friend. I too was invited to the ceremony but was unable to attend. Payeli, also known as Habib, went to Ibadod's village a week before the ceremony to facilitate the process and stayed an extra week after the marriage to help Ibadod and his new female bride settle. In the week prior to the ceremony and afterwards, they had sex almost every night. Payeli during this time also grew very intimate with Ibadod's wife. Ibadod introduced Payeli to his wife as his best friend. Though Ibadod emigrated a month after the marriage, Payeli remained in close contact with his wife. Back in Hridoypur, Habib was once again Payeli but then after a while they too got married to a female in their village. That Payeli had got married to a female in the village, whom they had left behind there with their mother, was, according to them, not known to the hijras in Hridoypur. Payeli categorically asked me to not tell anyone about it although such marriages, as I suggested in chapter 5, are not uncommon. The decision came as Payeli's mother was planning to go back to the village to settle there permanently. Payeli got a job in a newly set up NGO working on male sexual health in Hridoypur. Payeli therefore returned to Hridoypur and started working with the NGO while being a sadrali in the same vicinity. The last time I saw Payeli was in the middle of 2009, attending an NGO-organized hijra fashion show in Dhaka along with Ibadod and his wife.

Selection of a bride and a row between Konkona and Bijoy

Konkona, a Hindu (*chaiton*) hijra, had been involved with Bijoy, a Hindu man, for seven years. Konkona and Bijoy had been living in the same house ever since they got involved with one another. Konkona declared that they never let Bijoy feel that they were a hijra and not a woman, that is, Konkona took care of Bijoy, so they related to me, in every conceivable way a female wife takes care of a husband. In the meantime, however, there had been considerable pressure on Bijoy from his family to get married. As a friend of both Bijoy and Konkona, I was once invited to go to a house to see a prospective bride for Bijoy. Afterwards, I accompanied them back to their abode. Suddenly a fierce row erupted between Konkona and Bijoy over the fact that Bijoy was willing to marry a female from the village that his mother had chosen, rather than opting for the bride that had been Konkona's pick. Although I was confused, being under the impression that Konkona would have objections to his marrying a female in the first place, I realized that it was not the very idea of his marrying a female, but rather his apparent concession to the choice made for him by his mother that was the bone of contention. When I raised this issue, Konkona categorically stated, 'What are you saying? Is it to happen? His family will never accept me. Nor will society. What hurts me most is not that he will marry a female but that Bijoy is not listening to me. The girl I chose is perfect for him. I have lived with him and I

Love and Emotional Intimacy 165

know him!' In response to my query as to whether Konkona would maintain a relationship with Bijoy after he gets married, Konkona contended that while their life would not come to an end, they would have to deal with this reality as there would be no way to avoid it. The last time I spoke to Konkona was in 2011 and they had taken up a new job in an NGO and moved to a new location where they continued to live with Bijoy.

There are a few things to be drawn out from the three brief accounts presented here. First, all three stories, albeit only snapshots, resonate with my earlier contention that not only do hijras yearn for their pariks, but also that they experience a constant sense of apprehension regarding the parik's elusiveness. This elusiveness stems from a firm conviction that their pariks will eventually leave them and settle for female brides. While this continues to be a cause of despondency for the hijras, the hijras themselves are party to this arrangement; they seem ultimately to accept the fact that men will eventually marry heterosexually. This is further evident in the way that both Konkona and Payeli took it upon themselves to select the bride for their pariks. In the case of Payeli, however, there was no break-up and eventually Payeli's parik, Ibadod, got married to a woman selected by Payeli, and with whom Payeli too grew close. More interestingly, Payeli themself eventually entered the institution of heterosexual marriage. Although hijras desire to have partners on a permanent basis, they also often opined that what their partners did was justified on the grounds that men were ultimately meant for heterosexual marriage after all. Some hijras also contended that it was actually a sin to 'spoil' men by tying them down, as they would have no future (children) with the hijras.

Second, the accounts also underscore the importance of pariks in the lives of hijras, evidenced from the way both Dipali and Payeli not only severed all their ties with the hijra community at the beck and call of their partners, but also stopped dressing like females from time to time. In the case of Dipali, where the denouement was elegiac, we see desperation and frustration leading to a series of self-mutilating practices and a progressive disenchantment with the notion of love. The case of Dipali is not an isolated one: over the years I have heard of several hijras attempting suicide after their partners spurned them. In Hridoypur, hijras would often turn to alcohol (*khilwar*) and drugs after a break-up—followed by bouts of singing and dancing—as a way to get over the agonies of lost love.

Third, that pariks, in not only objecting to their partners' identification and association with hijras and feminine sartorial presentation, but also insisting on their hijra partners being masculine in public, demonstrate—at least in my two case stories—that they love their hijra partners not as hijras but as men. While some partners demand that their hijra partners be masculine, there are also pariks who insist on hijras being emasculated. While further research is required to find out more about whether these expectations of pariks vary in terms of private and public space, what I can say with certainty is that hijra decisions about their gender presentation and sense of self are forged in relation to their pariks' demands and expectations.

Pariks as affine: marriage rituals and celebrations among hijras

'Cia', the hijra word for marriage, figured prominently in my fieldwork. Interestingly, it was only in the context of normative or Bangla heterosexual marriage that my hijra interlocutors used this word. Even in the interactions among hijras, 'cia' is used particularly to reference marriage between a hijra and a woman—and not the marriage between a hijra and their parik. Unlike marriage between a hijra and a woman (or indeed marriage between a normative heterosexual man and a woman), marriage between a hijra and a man is linguistically unmarked among hijras. The marking of heterosexual marriage between hijras and women as 'cia' in Ulti underscores its secrecy, despite it being common knowledge among hijras. In this section, I elaborate not *cia* but marriage and partnerships between hijras and their pariks. On several occasions, I was invited to ceremonies and celebrations of marriage in Hridoypur and elsewhere. Although some of those celebrations were held in public community centres or in open space, the immediate neighbours of the hijras were told those celebrations were 'birthdays' of the hijras concerned. Despite frequent celebrations of marriage between a hijra and a parik, hijras never really explicitly used any words to reference such relations. Rather, they always spoke about such involvement indirectly by describing it as either a birthday or some other festivity.

Chottu was formally married to their long-term parik, Mannan, six months after their emasculation. Chottu had to obtain permission from their guru before tying the knot. Typically, a hijra wishing to get married has to pay compensation to the guru. It is only through paying 'sanan' or 'pakki' (hijra expressions for compensation) to the guru that such marriages are rendered legitimate. In Chottu's case, it was 500 taka (US$6) that they paid to the guru, although the amount payable to gurus varies from house to house depending on the socio-economic status of both the cela and the guru. At the time of Chottu's marriage, a small party was arranged at Chottu's house, to which only the hijras from Hridoypur and their pariks were invited. Chottu was dressed in bridal attire while Mannan was made to sit outside on the mat with hijras smearing turmeric over his face. This ritual of smearing turmeric bears resemblance to the mainstream normative Bangla marriage ritual in Bangladesh, where turmeric is applied to both the bride and the groom on two separate occasions.

Jomuna, the hijra guru of Hridoypur, took one of Chottu's hands and offered it to Mannan, saying, 'I am marrying my daughter to you. Make sure they are properly taken care of and fed.' In response, Mannan who was sitting with the pariks of other hijras nodded in agreement and promised to make Chottu very happy. Here, what is interesting is the similarity between the mainstream marriage ritual and that of the hijras. In normative marriage the father of the bride offers his daughter to the groom much like the way Jomuna the guru offered Chottu to Mannan, but in the case of normative marriage this offering is done in the presence of a *kazi*, the Islamic marriage conductor. In addition, while in normative Muslim marriage a contract is signed by both the groom and the bride along with witnesses, there was no such paperwork in the case of Chottu and Mannan. No one from the natal family of Mannan was present at the time of this marriage, in stark contrast to the normative situation.

There were, however, several instances where marriage between a hijra (especially an emasculated one) and their parik was alleged to have been officiated by a marriage registrar, or kazi. Although I did not have the good luck to observe any such marriage, several of my hijra interlocutors reportedly got married in front of witnesses and a kazi. Tina, another emasculated hijra in Hridoypur, had been married twice. Tina's first marriage took place in the office of a kazi and was registered. Sweety, a hijra guru from another area of Dhaka, also had been married by a kazi some ten years ago, though recently they had obtained a divorce through the court. The allegation brought against Sweety by their husband was that they were unable to have sex as they were a hijra. When the court raised the issue of Sweety's sexual prowess, Sweety asked the judge to marry them for five minutes so that they could show the judge their capacity. Although the marriage was revoked, the verdict was on their side, maintained Sweety. Sweety got compensation from their ex-husband as they had ample support of the local elites in the area that helped them throughout the trial. Sweety told me that since they used to teach Marwari children the Bangla language in a school in the old part of Dhaka, they got the support they needed. Rupali, a hijra whom I had met in one of the public gardens, once invited me to a marriage ceremony to be held in a community centre. I was told that a hijra named Labu had got married the other day in the kazi office in Gulshan. The reason Labu was getting married was because they had promised their parik that they would get rid of their genitals only if he married them. The panthi, Rupali continued, would make all the necessary arrangements for Labu's surgery.

Unlike the normative mainstream Bangla marriage patterns where brides marry into the families of the grooms, normative Bangla men marry into hijra houses and lineages and become known as the parik of a hijra, rather than a hijra becoming known as the partner of a parik, as is the case with the dominant Bangla model. Despite pariks being considered affines internally, a great deal of secrecy is often seen to be maintained around hijras having pariks and their presence in the neighbourhood. Both the janana and the chibry hijras in Hridoypur and elsewhere argued that the wider society was not aware of their being married. Rather, they were often deemed to be closely related friends or brothers. Every time I visited a sadrali hijra household with a parik outside of Hridoypur, both the hijra and their partners introduced themselves to me as brothers. Later, however, the hijras disclosed their relations as they grew close to me.

In view of the ethnographic descriptions here, I would like to note a few things. First, among the sadrali hijras, the marriage between a hijra and their parik is rendered legitimate only through the paying of sanan, or compensation. However, sanan has to be paid only when an emasculated hijra gets married. In contrast, jananas, or hijras with penises, could live with their partners without paying compensation to the guru. The reason for this, explained Jomuna, the hijra guru in Hridoypur, is that once one becomes a chibry, one has to be chaste in line with the prescriptions of Maya Ji. Second, the conduct of marriage under the aegis of an Islamic marriage registrar could take place only if the hijra was emasculated, although always without the kazi's being aware of the hijra status of the bride. Hijras argued that only chibry hijras could get married in keeping with the mainstream official law, as the kazi would not be able to find out. In addition, they argued that the marriage between a janana and a panthi would contradict the Islamic norm, which in the case of a marriage between an emasculated hijra and a man would not be contravened. Hijras contended that if a kazi became suspicious, he would not be able to disprove a chibry's female status. Third, that hijras often deem emasculation to be desirable in order for a marriage to be validated underscores their subscription to the Bangla hetero-gendered idioms of marriage. Yet they transcend those idioms creatively through a reversal of the conventional patri-local marital arrangements, with their pariks moving into the hijra households rather than the other way round. That hijras often undergo emasculation to be marriageable to their pariks, either because they deem it to be appropriate or because of their partners' wish, indicates a negotiation of masculinity whereby it is on account of hijras' emasculation that the masculinity of their pariks is consolidated.

Finally, I intend to reflect on the question of what exactly this Ulti convention of marriage between a hijra and a panthi enables that is otherwise not possible in the Bangla universe. What is the use of seeking ritual validation for such bonding between a hijra and a man? Besnier (2004) contends that the transformation of the socially non-mainstream male-born Tongan transgender into a morally abject other stems from these transgendered people's desire for men, which both Tongan society and the normatively oriented men consider as ridiculous and impossible. Such impossibility is also recognized by the Tongan transgender. Against this backdrop, the transgendered people become the abject other on account of their desire, as opposed to the heterosexual men, who are assumed to be the object of desire rather than initiators of such relations. In contrast, the Ulti universe not only enables the possibility of such relations, but also accommodates and acknowledges such relations, even though publicly hijras are understood to be beyond and above desire.

Several scholars on same-sex sexuality in South Asia (for example, Boyce 2006; Boyce and Khanna 2011; Osella 2012) have noted complex homo-social configuration across South Asia, whereby the fact of two male-bodied persons being together either in private or in public is not deemed to be homoerotic in popular imaginary. Rather, these authors contend that it is precisely because of such homo-social configuration that various kinds of same-sex sexual possibilities are spawned and encouraged. While such fluid social configurations allow for certain types of affect and desire to take root, the Ulti universe moves such possibilities beyond the extant homo-social arrangement by culturally recognizing and institutionalizing such relatedness. Furthermore, the entrance of a non-hijra man into the Ulti universe as a parik or affine emblematizes an elaborate dance between the Ulti and Bangla universes in which the putatively masculine pariks carry with them elements of the Ulti universe as much as they incorporate elements of the Bangla world into the Ulti. In other words, despite the Ulti universe being oppositional to the Bangla world, these two worlds are

Figure 6.1 A senior *sadrali hijra* seated next to their *parik* with *cela*s standing in the back
Source: Author.

enmeshed (Figure 6.1). To further explain this dance, I now elaborate Bangla men's participation in the Ulti universe.

'Male femaling' of Bangla men and the hijra notion of 'insiderliness'

In her ethnography, Reddy (2005a) elaborates the hijra conception of family, arguing that although her interlocutors universally expressed a desire for bonding with males, these males were external to the hijra notion of community and family. While pariks in the context of my research were also not a part of the hijra concept of community or the wider Ulti universe of male-bodied, feminine-identified people, the incorporation of the Bangla pariks into the Ulti universe complicates Reddy's categorical exclusion of the pariks from the hijra conception of family. While in Reddy's accounts pariks appear to be strange outsiders, my ethnographic material suggests that despite their Bangla otherness, such boundaries often tend to be blurred in the context of the lived lives of hijras. In one sense, pariks as Bangla men or normatively masculinized subjects are not part of the Ulti universe. Nor do the hijras expect or encourage their Bangla pariks to cross those sexual and gender boundaries. That is, while partners are an integral part of hijra lives, they still remain perennially Bangla, or outsiders. I discuss possible reasons for such tightly drawn boundaries in terms of anal receptivity and phallic insertivity in chapter 3; here, I intend to present some more ethnographic episodes as a way to complicate this supposed distinction.

Before I elaborate my observations of pariks' entanglement with hijras, it will be useful to reiterate my positionality in relation to them. As already demonstrated in chapter 3, the very fact of my being adopted as the husband or parik of Meghna, the hijra guru in Hridoypur, often made it difficult for me to elicit responses from the hijras about their erotic lives. Yet this ascribed status, despite causing some discomfort at the personal level, was also a blessing in disguise. As the putative parik of a hijra guru, it was not only the junior hijras who spoke to me respectfully, but also their pariks. The pariks of the junior hijras would not only call me 'mama' like their hijra 'wives', but also at times invite me to their houses. Generally hijras are very sceptical about introducing their husbands to outsiders. Hijras with pariks often strictly policed the interaction of their pariks not only with other hijras, but also with the wider society, especially men. In contrast, hijras in Hridoypur never had an issue with my interaction with their pariks.

This tendency to police their partners' interactional mobility, especially with other hijras, hijras repeatedly explained, was due in part to a deep sense of distrust of their partners' lack of commitment, but more importantly because of an ingrained belief that hijras would seduce the pariks of other hijras. Although I saw only a single case where the parik of a hijra was seduced by another hijra, talk about such possibilities was always on the tips of the tongues of my interlocutors. I was told that there had been several instances in the past where both the hijras and their pariks betrayed each other. Once in Hridoypur, the guru Jomuna was summoned to another hijra house for an important arbitration to which hijras from West Bengal, India, had also been invited. The reason hijras from several areas within and outside Bangladesh had to be summoned was because the parik of a senior hijra guru had eloped with one of their celas. Because both this guru and their cela were influential figures in the conduct of hijragiri and, furthermore, since the matter had been blown out of proportion and subsequent attempts to arbitrate internally had failed, senior-level *daratni*, or leaders, had to be called in. The arbitration was to happen at the meeting place (*daiyar*) of Sona hijra, one of the most senior hijras in Bangladesh. After almost three days of argumentation, a decision was reached to excommunicate the hijra who had eloped with their guru's parik. It was also agreed that no hijra house in Bangladesh or India would take this 'perpetrator' back to any of the groups. In addition, in the case of their being caught, hijras were asked to beat them up and shave their head. I cannot confirm whether the prescribed punishment was meted out to the hijra in question, but I heard of several other circumstances where hijras who slept with the parik of their gurus had to undergo similar punishment. Although I could never speak to a hijra or a parik who acted in this way, the very fact that such serious and prolonged arbitrations and penalties take place testifies to the severity of this crime among the hijras.

In Hridoypur, two emasculated sadrali hijras lived with their pariks on a permanent basis. Both Chottu and Sathi had married their pariks after six years together. Mannan and Mamun, the pariks of Chottu and Sathi respectively, were an established presence not only in the daily lives of the hijras but also in ritual settings. Mannan and Mamun were known to all the hijras of Hridoypur and beyond. During several *baraiya* festivals, for instance, both Mamun and Mannan supervised the arrangement of the chairs in the open space and food preparation, along with a few junior hijras.

In a similar vein, during *sinni*, a hijra festival undertaken in the name of a Sufi saint in Hridoypur and beyond, the presence of these two partners was particularly pronounced. In one of the sinni events organized by a senior sadrali of another area to which hijras of Hridoypur were invited, I saw not only Mamun and Mannan, but also the pariks of other hijras. There I also met a man called Kadir who held himself aloof from the crowd. Throughout the occasion, he preferred to stay busy with the packaging and preparation of the food as if he had been hired to do so, but later I was told that Kadir was the parik of Alo, the hijra who had arranged the sinni. To confirm, I asked Alo about Kadir, but in response Alo just laughed. The fact of Kadir's being Alo's parik became evident when during a photo shoot I was asked by other hijras to take a photo of Alo with Kadir. By then it was perhaps clear to Kadir that I understood that he was involved with Alo. Yet afterwards when I asked Kadir about a photo hanging on the wall of Alo's room, Kadir told me it was the picture of 'that person' (*oi lok*) when 'that person' was young. Here, 'that person' was none other than Alo, his hijra partner; but what struck me as significant was this indirect way of describing Alo as if he barely knew them. This is expressive of a general distance, both physical and emotional, that pariks are expected to maintain to set them apart from the hijras. Though pariks are expected to remain segregated from the hijras at such festivities, Mamun and Mannan were more active than Kadir. This was so as Kadir was the parik of a senior hijra guru, unlike Mannan and Mamun, who were the pariks of junior hijras. That Kadir was given more respect was also reflected in the fact that Kadir was served food along with a local imam and his disciples who came to recite the Quran and conduct a *milad* (a special prayer undertaken in the name of the Prophet during sinni) while Mannan and Mamun waited outside with the junior hijras.

Rahela, a chibry hijra, was particularly known across Bangladesh as a skilful *katial* who performed the emasculation operation. Rahela died five years ago and since then her widower, Rahman, has been acting as a ritual cutter. Although Rahman is a *panthi*, that is, a Bangla masculine man, his presence in the lives of the hijras in Hridoypur was considerable, as he had performed the operations on several hijras in Hridoypur. While Mannan and Mamun, the two notable pariks in Hridoypur, were not allowed to be present at the time of the worship of the hijra goddess during baraiya, which I elaborated in chapter 4, Rahman's presence was not only eagerly anticipated, but was necessary for the conduct of the ritual. That Rahman, an erstwhile parik of a hijra, became a ritual cutter is not an exception. There were several other katials who were pariks of hijras.

Pariks are always expected to comport themselves in a 'masculine' manner (*panthi pon*). When I asked them about why they behaved with such aloofness, they argued that they were panthis and, as such, they needed to maintain an air of apartness. Typically, pariks not only sit away from the hijras but also are served food before the hijras. In addition, they are also expected to talk less and not impinge on any of the discussions to do with the conduct of hijragiri. It was as if, despite their being physically there, they were actually not there. On another occasion during the birthday celebration of a hijra, which took place in a community centre in Dhaka, several sadrali hijras came with their pariks. Saleha, renowned for their eloquence, was the chief guest. When the cake was cut, Saleha was in the middle, next to Kajol, whose birthday party it was. Saleha's husband stayed outside throughout the party. It was as if he had not come with Saleha. It was not until the food was served that Saleha's parik came inside and sat next to them to eat. On another occasion, during a picnic organized by a hijra NGO, the majority of the hijras brought their pariks with them. Shaila, a chibry in their late forties, had performed hajj and was renowned across the hijra universe in Bangladesh. Throughout the picnic, a man was hovering around Shaila, although always at a remove. When I approached Shaila to ask about their experience of pilgrimage to Mecca, I addressed them as 'Shaila Hajji', to which the man protested and argued that it should be 'Hajji Shaila'. Later when I inquired as to who he was, Shaila spoke of him as one of their acquaintances, when he was in actual fact their parik.

While this apparent aloofness of pariks, despite their being ever-present physically in the daily lives of hijras, may be explained in terms of a politics of masculinity whereby the masculinity, or pariks' Banglaness, is consolidated through such apartness; such intentional detachment is also indicative of symbolic emasculation of the pariks. The pariks have no say in the extent to which they are allowed to interact and with whom; this is determined by the hijras alone. Despite their normative Bangla masculine trappings that hijras relentlessly insist on, pariks' activities and roles in quotidian settings run counter to the masculine images that hijras otherwise associate with pariks. Not only were the pariks of the hijras in Hridoypur soft-spoken and meek, they were often domesticated, to appropriate the oft-repeated hijra expression of 'parik pala'.[1]

Pariks who lived with their hijra partners in Hridoypur and beyond were often chronically unemployed and totally dependent on the income of their hijra partners. Hijras not only provided for their expenses, but also cooked, cleaned and mopped the floor. When asked, hijras generally argued that it was one way for them to pin pariks down. Hijras in Hridoypur with pariks often contended that if they did not provide for their pariks, then they would leave them for women. Chottu once related that the reason they 'domesticated' their parik was because they needed someone permanently to love them and that the very thought of seeing someone back in the house every night made them feel emotionally fulfilled. Sathi argued that they domesticated their parik as the parik otherwise would jettison them because of their inability to give birth to children. Several sex-worker hijras with pariks also echoed the same sentiment, arguing that although they had sex with thousands of men, they preferred to domesticate a parik for emotional support and love.

Pariks of the sex-worker hijras and those from Hridoypur, however, seemed not to be affected by their being domesticated. Rather, they all felt

---

[1] See Kulick (1998) for an account on the way putatively masculine men that form relations with Brazilian transgender sex workers are feminized by their transgender partners.

proud of their being cared for in such a royal manner. I once asked Kalam, a parik of a sex-worker hijra, what he felt about his hijra partner's profession and whether he felt bad about it. Kalam firmly insisted that he accepted it as it was generating money for him. Similar arguments were also advanced by the permanent pariks of Hridoypur. Kalam also contended that despite hijra notions about pariks being elusive and self-interested, he would never leave his hijra partner as, according to him, no woman would be able to love and care for him as his hijra wife did. In a similar vein, despite pariks being domesticated, I saw several pariks in Hridoypur take care of their hijra 'wives' consistently. After Chottu underwent emasculation, it was Mannan, their parik, who nursed them until they had convalesced. Mamun, another parik whom I have already introduced, stayed with his hijra wife not only throughout their surgery but also afterwards when they were excommunicated from the hijra group in Hridoypur because of their not seeking consent from their guru before undergoing emasculation. During this time, Mamun was the one who not only cooked food, but also washed all their clothes.

There are a few things to be noted here. First, despite all their masculine trappings, pariks are in reality more like stereotypical housewives, as opposed to the hijras, who act like the husband in a typical hijra–parik relationship. That hijras take on the persona of a Bangla husband with their pariks not only works to effeminize these normative Bangla men, but also complicates Reddy's (2005a, 170–171) assertion about hijras being akin to middle-class Indian housewives in their gendered responses to their husbands. Hijras, I demonstrated earlier, often idealize and verbalize such conventional gendered behaviours relative to their partners, but what emerges is a complete reversal of such gendered practice. Rather, as I will subsequently suggest, hijras take on the middle-class conventional Bangla housewifely role only in the context of a parik's natal family. Second, there seems to be a trade-off between pariks' masculinity and their being provided for, that is, as long as they were provided for by the hijras, the symbolic emasculation did not seem to bother these normative Bangla men. Third, despite pariks being considered non-hijra Bangla men, they were an active presence in the lives of my hijra interlocutors, not only by their being physically present in the households, but also through their participation, albeit restricted, in hijra rituals. Furthermore, permanent pariks of the hijras in Hridoypur all spoke Ulti, even though they were not allowed to express their knowledge of it in front of the wider Bangla world. While the ability of pariks to speak Ulti does not qualify them to be part of the Ulti universe, it indexes the degree of their incorporation into the Ulti universe as strictly Bangla men in opposition to which hijras construct their own sense of self. Here I remind the reader that the very fact of my being able to speak Ulti was often taken by hijras as an indication of my being either a koti in disguise or a long-term parik of a hijra. This was precisely so as Ulti, I argued in chapter 3, works to signal 'insiderliness'. Both Mannan and Mamun and other pariks not only spoke fluent Ulti, but also were adequately knowledgeable about the hijra rules and rituals, even though they were not allowed to demonstrate their acumen either to the wider Bangla world or within the Ulti universe. Finally, I want to note that despite pariks being in a position of inferiority relative to the hijras in the hijra space, they continue to be the most important people in the lives of the hijras not least because they are the ones expected to care for and love their hijra partners, but also because many important decisions in the life course of a hijra are taken in relation to partners' likes and dislikes.

Hijras in the lives of their parik's family

So far I have discussed the significance of pariks' presence in the lives of hijras. What needs emphasizing here is that my observations and interaction with the pariks were conducted in settings dominated by hijras, that is, pariks as partners of the hijras rather than hijras as partners of the pariks. This was borne out by my fieldwork in Hridoypur where it was possible on my part only to interact extensively and closely with the pariks that lived on a permanent basis with my hijra interlocutors. Pariks, I suggested earlier, are the ones who marry into hijra houses and move into hijra households, contrary to the normative patri-local marital arrangements in Bangladesh. Unlike brides, who are traditionally expected to adapt to the new ambience in their patri-local households, it is the pariks who have to acclimatize to their new surroundings.

Very few hijras I spoke to had actually visited the house of their pariks. Rupa, a sadrali in Hridoypur, had been involved with Lokman, a young, bearded, Islamic-minded bus driver in his early thirties. Although Lokman lived in Dhaka with his parents, he never took Rupa to his home. Whenever I spoke to Lokman, he denied being the parik of Rupa. Lokman instead stated that he was just one of Rupa's friends and that he liked the company of hijras more than that of women as in his youth he had been forsaken by several female lovers. Lokman maintained that although Rupa was very close to him, the reason he never took Rupa to his home was because of the possibility of his parents being scared, as a family friend of his in the neighbourhood once became a hijra after keeping company with them. It is interesting to note that the reason for Lokman's disinclination to take Rupa to his home was not that his parents might suspect his being erotically or romantically involved with them, but because of the fear of his turning into a hijra.

Mamun and Mannan, both of whom I introduced earlier, had been living in Hridoypur ever since they migrated to Dhaka. Both categorically told me that they had not been aware of what hijras really were before they got involved with them. In the early days of their involvement, both of them thought hijras to be people born with missing or defective genitals but later, as they grew close, they realized that their hijra partners were actually 'men' who transformed themselves into hijras. Both Mannan and Mamun argued that the very fact of their partners having male genitals was a source of discomfort for them, particularly when they had to go out with them. In fact, it was not until their hijra partners got emasculated that they took their 'wives' to their villages. Here it is instructive to note that while pariks who lived with hijras in hijra space often insisted on their hijra 'wives' being emasculated, pariks that stayed away demanded that their hijra 'wives' acted at least publicly like normative males. Both Mannan and Mamun maintained, to my utter disbelief and bewilderment, that their family members were totally unaware of their being married to hijras. Rather, the mothers and brothers of their families thought their 'brides' to be women. Both these pariks spoke very highly of the way their 'wives' attended to their family members whenever they visited. Notwithstanding their mothers' concerns over their not fathering children, both these pariks contended that their not being able to father children did not lead their mothers to question their hijra partners' feminine status. Although I could never speak to any of the family members of either Mannan or Mamun, there was one occasion where I could closely observe the interaction of a hijra with the family of their 'husband', to which I now turn.

Zhinuk and Rasel's Valentine festivities

Zhinuk, a professional make-up artist in the film industry and also a part-time sadrali janana, once invited me to a party that they described in English as 'marriage day' (Figure 6.2). Zhinuk is also involved with a project on hijras in an NGO and additionally moonlights as a dance teacher. The celebration, to my great surprise, took place in the house of Zhinuk's parik, Rasel. Usually, any celebration involving hijras and their pariks takes place only in hijra-dominated space. Having entered the lower-middle-class household in the old part of Dhaka, I found myself in a festive climate with children dressed in fancy clothes, and many younger and older women all around the house. Rasel's mother, along with a few other women, was busy cooking food. It was a three-room, tin-shed house. Ushered to the next room by Katha, another hijra friend of Zhinuk with whom I had made my way there, I sat on a chair next to Katha and a few other young ladies. On one side of the room was a bed occupied by a middle-aged man. I was told he was Rasel's maternal uncle who had come to their house just a few days previously to see off his son, who was going abroad. There was also another middle-aged uncle of Rasel sitting in that room. Children were running to and fro between the two rooms and in the small forecourt in front of the main gate. Rasel's sister, along with her two children, was also present to celebrate. More significantly, Zhinuk's mother was also there along with some of her guests. I was told that both their families had been intimately involved for a very long time. What I found particularly striking

Figure 6.2 A *parik* adorning his *hijra* partner with bangles in his own residence
Source: Author.

was that Zhinuk's mother behaved towards Rasel's mother in the manner of a *beyain*, a special relationship between the parents of the bride and groom, often tinged with humour. Zhinuk also introduced me to Rasel's mother as their 'shasuri', the Bangla word for mother-in-law.

Rasel, Zhinuk's parik, in whose house the party was being held, was not present from the beginning. In fact, he appeared only at the time of the cutting of the cake—and even then he was present only for a few minutes. When Rasel came, Zhinuk introduced him to me as their husband. Uncomfortable and embarrassed, Rasel kept quiet. Holding Rasel's hand, Zhinuk cut the cake with everyone standing around in a circle. Inscribed on the cake in bold letters was Z+R with the by-line 'Happy Marriage Day' and 'Happy Valentine's Day' in English. Both Rasel and Zhinuk fed each other a slice of the cake. Because their feeding of each other could not be properly photographed, Zhinuk asked me to take another photo of them with my camera. Once the photo session started, everyone was willing to get snapped except Rasel, who seemed a bit annoyed. I was told that Rasel worked in a shop nearby and had come in straight from his workplace and needed to return soon. After a while, Rasel left while the party continued. Later, when some of the guests had left, Rasel's mother came to have a word with me and Katha. In the course of the conversation, when I asked what she thought of her son's relationship with Zhinuk, she said that although Zhinuk was born a hijra, it was not Zhinuk's fault. She told me that she was totally approving of her son's relationship with Zhinuk but because Zhinuk would not be able to give birth to children, she would at some point marry her son to a woman. Zhinuk's mother also endorsed this and argued that she too might marry Zhinuk to a woman at some point, in the hope of seeing Zhinuk cured of this 'defect'.

Although hijras tend to dominate their pariks, especially when pariks permanently move into hijra households, hijras also strenuously endeavour to live up to their own notions about what good and normative Bangla housewives should do, as evidenced from the way they attend to their partners' natal family members. Also noteworthy is the fact that even when the parents and family members of the pariks approve of their relationships with the hijra, it is often on account of their understanding about those hijras being female that they do so. However, in the case of Rasel, we see an exception, although as already stated, both the parents of Rasel and Zhinuk intended to have them married off to females at some point, especially as their pair-bonding would not result in reproduction.

Conclusion

There are a few things to be reiterated here by way of a conclusion. Partners, or pariks, are an indispensable part of the lives of hijras. The constant and persistent yearning for a lover is central to the hijra sense of selfhood, even though in public it is the lack of such desire in terms of which hijras are recognized and seek to be recognized as hijras. Although pariks are in one sense located outside the hijra universe, it is in relation to the pariks that hijra subjectivities are forged. Hijraness is constructed in opposition to the normatively masculinized Bangla men and hijra subjectivity is intrinsically bound up with the Bangla men whom the hijras not only woo and desire, but also whose attention and love hijras actively and aggressively seek on a daily basis. While many pariks love the hijras as men, there are also pariks, especially those living permanently with hijras, who love them as feminine-identified, emasculated persons. That hijras are generally inclined to conform to partners' expectations about their gendered comportment, while pariks often take on tasks otherwise deemed feminine, is indicative of complex economies of emotion and affect through which multiple masculinities are negotiated and produced.

In sum, despite normatively masculine Bangla men being outsiders to the Ulti universe, the distinction between the Bangla world and the Ulti universe is not as watertight as many may assume, not only because Bangla men are also in certain contexts part of the hijra space and ritually marked contexts, but also because Bangla men often move between the Ulti and the Bangla worlds, incorporating Bangla elements into the Ulti and vice versa. That Bangla men enter the Ulti space as affines of the hijras foregrounds the cultural recognition of alternative erotic possibilities and bonding otherwise unrecognized and forbidden in the Bangla world, even though such accommodations are framed in terms of the wider protocols of Bangla hetero-erotic relatedness.

7 Contemporary Transformation of *Hijra* Subjectivities

Rita, a national-level *hijra* leader, has never been a part of a *sadrali* hijra group, that is, they never participated in either *badhai* or *cholla manga*, the two quintessential hijra occupations. From being a sex worker, they rose to national and international prominence in recent times for their HIV/AIDS activism. Once during an intense conversation involving Rita and a few other hijras working with NGOs, they remarked, 'Bit by bit, hijragiri will taper off. The guru–cela hierarchy is tyrannical. With newer opportunities, hijras will move away from badhai and cholla manga.' Poppy, another hijra also affiliated with NGOs, took slight exception to Rita's radical proposition and argued that with time hijras too should change and adopt new ways, but that these old traditions of badhai and cholla should be preserved. Taking a cue from Rita and Poppy, this chapter will identify and examine the newly emergent socio-cultural conditions and the possibilities of transformation. While the preceding chapters explicate the making of the hijra subjectivity and hijra occupation, here I am specifically interested in understanding the transformative possibilities in the wake of a series of trans-local initiatives recently being undertaken in contemporary Bangladesh. Ranging from government initiatives to NGO interventions, these recent bouts of activities have led to various forms of conflict and contestation over authenticity, cultural conceptualization of hijras, and idioms and other markers of identity. The transformations I chart in this chapter are not novel per se but are part and parcel of the themes I have been talking about throughout this book. Rather, what this chapter does is make some of those themes of transformation more explicit.

Nanda (1999) makes a passing reference to modernization and urbanization as factors responsible for the gradual de-popularization of the cultural roles of hijras as ritual performers in India. Older sadrali hijras in Bangladesh often echoed a similar sentiment linking the gradual wane of their popularity as ritual performers to the rise of videocassette recorder (VCR) and television and the advent of family planning and spread of condoms and contraceptives. While these aforesaid changes can be traced to such ongoing processes of modernization and urbanization, what I am specifically interested in here is a recent set of state and NGO interventions undertaken from the late 1990s in Bangladesh. In proposing to examine transformation, I am not suggesting that the institution of the hijras is a bounded phenomenon anchored in some synchronic 'cultural particularism' (Johnson 1998). That systems of gender and sexuality emerge in complex interplay with broader socio-historical and intra/inter/trans-regional processes has been well established (Johnson, Jackson and Herdt 2000).

In explicating the transformation of gender and sexual subjectivities in contemporary India, Bhaskaran (2004), following Ferguson and Gupta (2002), links those changes to 'transnational governmentality' (the burgeoning NGO-ization of sexual health in both the public and private spheres). She argues that the espousal of the Bretton Woods institution's economic policy prescriptions of privatization and economic deregulation in the early 1990s led to these transnational governmentalities in the Indian context. Extending Foucault's (1991) concept of 'governmentality', Ferguson and Gupta (2002) propose 'transnational governmentality' as a novel approach to the anthropology of state. 'Transnational governmentality' in their formulation does not simply embody the mere shift of the functions of state machinery to non-state entities via the burgeoning NGO-ization of social life; rather, they contend that non-state actors and apparatuses have become sites from and through which various forms of governance are exerted and exercised. Central to Foucault's notion of governmentality, as Ettlinger (2011) notes, is 'governance' of 'mentality'. Extending far beyond conventional state power, the Foucauldean notion of governmentality encompasses the governance of the population, selves, identities and practices at a distance. Adopting this approach here, I examine the newly unfolding social processes and the resultant rise of new discursive regimes within which such changes are taking place. In reflecting on these practices and processes, I do not view those external interventions as some irrepressible force but as a 'system' constantly being produced, reproduced and transformed through embodied action (Ortner 1984). More specifically, I foreground not only how hijra as a subculture is undergoing internal metamorphosis in relation to these 'external forces', but also the way those changes are the products of various agentic adaptations and appropriations by the hijras.

Following a brief introduction to the history and formation of two organizations, I first highlight a change in the idiom of hijra sociality with a specific focus on how a certain type of NGO language has become a feature of everyday hijra conversation. Although NGO activities are often dismissed as a form of digression from the authentic hijra occupation, NGOs have become a naturalized part of hijra interactional repertoire. The tension surrounding the gradual 'NGO-ization' stems from the risk of the disclosure of clandestine, or Ulti, hijra practices to the Bangla world. Following from there, I examine the efflorescence of two interrelated yet distinct developments, namely a growing sexualization of the hijras in the new public imaginary and the political economy of categorical proliferation. In the section on sexualization, I ethnographically elaborate activities related to the promotion of safe sex on an NGO premises run by hijras. I specifically argue that the very undertaking of those activities works to undermine the citadel of secrecy in which hijra Ulti erotic practices are locked away. Linked to these activities is the new conceptual praxis of hijras as rights-bearing citizens of Bangladesh. Yet, paradoxically, the advent of the rights discourse has also led to a new discursive interpellation of hijras as disabled in government conceptualization.

In the second section, I take on board the proliferation of categories as effects of broader processes of political economy and foreground novel forms of governance and disciplinary powers in the wake of this categorical proliferation. Attending to daily practices and the contextual invocation of several identity labels by the hijras, I demonstrate a complex postcolonial context continuous with the colonial classificatory imperatives. Against this backdrop, I examine the consolidation and rise of transgender as a new subject position in place of hijraness. I demonstrate that transgender indexes a new respectable regime with disciplinary prescriptions about what is and is not an authentic hijra subject position. Yet the consolidation of transgender has not led to an adoption of sex-reassignment surgeries. Rather, the hijra practice of emasculation has become popular among many not necessarily related to the hijra subculture.

The rise of hijra-focused NGOs

NGO interventions targeting the hijras began in the late 1990s in Bangladesh as part of the wider interventions into various forms of male-to-male sexualities. By 2000 two organizations were formed with exclusive focus on hijras. The rationale for setting up separate organizations for hijras stemmed from the understanding that hijras formed a distinct group. Yet, reminiscent of HIV/AIDS work across the board, the exclusive focus of these interventions was to attend to the sexual health needs of hijras via the promotion and distribution of condom and consciousness-raising about the effects of sexually transmitted diseases (STDs) and sexually transmitted infections (STIs). While there are now several NGOs working with hijras in Bangladesh, the stories hijras often related to me about the birth of these two organizations are important as they allow us to understand the initial hijra standpoints on NGO work and activism.

Formation of Sushtho Jibon

According to Bashobi, a hijra guru affiliated with Sushtho Jibon, one fine morning a few front-ranking personnel of an MSM (men who have sex with men)-based NGO approached them with the proposal to set up an office for the hijras. Unsure as to whether to agree to this offer, Bashobi met other hijras in the area and also their guru, who lived on the outskirts of Dhaka. Initially, there was considerable opposition to the idea of setting up an office, as Sonu, Bashobi's guru, vehemently objected. Sonu, often referred to as the *nayak* (leader) of the Bangladeshi hijras, took issue with this proposal on the grounds that such initiatives would jeopardize their livelihoods by tainting the hijras as people given to *gandugiri* (used here to refer to anal receptivity). In other words, their concern was rendering visible in the Bangla universe what should remain primarily clandestine (Ulti). After a series of conversations with Sonu and lobbying with their other celas, they finally gave consent to its setting up on the condition that they should always be left out of this activity. In line with hijragiri, Bashobi had to pay don (compensation) to Sonu for this initiative. During my first visit to Sonu's house, they categorically criticized the NGO activities and denied any involvement on their part. Pointing to a picture of Shabnam Mousi, a hijra from Madhya Pradesh, India, and an erstwhile parliamentarian there, Sonu argued that they were not an ordinary hijra and that hijras across India—including this powerful one—knew them. Later, Sonu told me that it was their celas and *nati* celas (disciples and grand disciples) whom I should approach to find out about this office. While Sonu publicly denounced NGO activities, paradoxically they were made the head of the board of directors, as Bashobi later confided in me. Once the office space was rented, a party to celebrate the inauguration was held with Sonu as the chief guest and it was only after receiving Sonu's blessing that the NGO started its journey.

The birth of Badhon

Joya, who was at that time the general secretary of Badhon, once narrated to me how they chanced upon a group of NGO personnel in a cruising site. Joya used to cruise in a public garden along with female sex workers. Sexual health support was available only for the female sex workers in those days. One day as some health workers arrived to recruit female sex workers for voluntary testing for STDs, they volunteered to go to the office of an NGO called CARE Bangladesh for testing. Diagnosed with syphilis, they later recruited more hijras from cruising sites for further tests. According to Joya, most of the hijras who underwent the test were diagnosed with several STDs and consequently Care Bangladesh launched a separate project to intervene in the hijra community through the formation of Badhon. While Sushtho Jibon was led by sadrali hijras, Badhon was founded through the effort of sex-worker hijras. However, soon afterwards some senior sadrali hijras had to be accommodated in order for Badhon to be functional. While Joya became the general secretary, their sadrali guru was also made a part of the initiative. The reason for the inclusion of Joya's guru and other senior sadrali hijras, they explained, was because no NGO for the hijras would be successful without the involvement of gurus.

While in a moment I will elaborate some of the practices of these NGO interventions and their effects, here I note two important observations. First, that senior sadrali hijras are an active part of the management of these NGOs is significant as sadrali hijras continue to see the formation of NGOs as a threat to hijragiri. Second, the areas these NGOs cover are modelled on the sadrali rules of *birit*, or ritual jurisdiction. That is, when an office space was rented in a particular locale, the guru of that locale was made the head of the organization. Bobby, one of the front-ranking NGO-affiliated hijras, once told me, 'Now we have to do both. On the one hand I have to conduct hijragiri and on the other the husbandry of the NGO. It requires extra skills. Not everyone in the community is capable.'

Changing idioms of hijra sociality

A striking feature of hijra sociality today in Bangladesh is the way NGOs, projects, funding and foreign tours are invoked as part of their everyday conversations. Hijras talk about these issues not only on the NGO premises, but also in their houses and cruising sites. Sadrali hijras associated with the

NGOs often contended that the NGO interventions, particularly condom promotions and sexual health clinics, have contributed to a heightened awareness about sexual health issues among hijras. For instance, Bobby once stated that in the past when hijras had any sexual problems, namely infection in the anal tract, they used to clean up their anuses with hot water or at best take some generic medicines; now with the advent of clinics, hijras can avail themselves of doctors' services. Additionally, they are now aware of the risks associated with sex without condoms. They also pointed out that hijras now also have a better knowledge about the wider world and the international community through their exposure visits and participation in conferences and meetings both nationally and internationally.

While those hijras directly linked with NGOs typically talked positively about their impact, this view was not necessarily shared by all sadrali hijra groups. Sadrali hijras in Hridoypur often fretted about the way NGO interventions gave rise to new forms of communitarian friction and income inequality. They argued that the hijra houses that now ran the NGOs were already very influential with larger birits, that is, those groups already had an average income greater than other hijra houses in Dhaka. Pointing at the habitations of differential cultural capitals and income hierarchies, Meghna, the hijra guru in Hridoypur, once related, 'It all comes down to *jhalki* [monies] at the end of the day. Now they have a two-storey building and frequently make trips abroad like *memsahib*.' Hridoypur, where I conducted much of my fieldwork, had no NGO in its vicinity until very recently. Junior hijras working in the NGOs also often expressed dissatisfaction about low pay while begrudging the sudden and quick amassing of wealth by a select cadre of hijras. Moreover, junior hijra-identified NGO workers were also of the opinion that NGOs were basically selling the marginal status of the hijras to the international community to gain funding that ends up in the pockets of a select few. Despite some sadrali hijras being critical of NGO work, several sadrali groups I spoke to at times wondered if I could link them with an NGO or even set up an NGO office myself for them.

The emergence of new discursive regimes and the sexualization of hijras in Bangla public imagination

One of the effects of NGO intervention has been the emergence of a new discourse linking the hijras to sexual desire in the Bangla public imaginary. While the existence of hijras has always been common public knowledge, hijras were never really associated with any form of desire in the popular imagination. This sexualization of the hijras is locatable within the broader epidemiologically inflected discourse on same-sex sexuality that gradually sprang up in the late nineties in Bangladesh in the form of MSM. Even though attempts were made to draw a clear distinction between the MSM framework and that of the hijras, hijras in practice often became reduced to one of the MSM variants. The rise of MSM-based NGOs and the growing interest of the wider civil society in addressing issues related to alternative sexualities and gender, especially in the context of the global AIDS epidemic and its media coverage, have all led to the emergence of a new public discourse on male-to-male sexualities in contemporary Bangladesh.

The government of Bangladesh has been quite instrumental in partnering with NGOs and international donors to launch projects for the prevention of HIV/AIDS both among the MSM groups and the hijras. One outcome of this AIDS activism has been the problematic reduction of alternative sexualities and gender identities to pathologies. In this narrow risk-based discourse on public health, hijraness has often been represented through the cipher of sexual disease. That hijras are now publicly projected as sexual is significant, as the dominant Bangla understanding conventionally posited the hijras as 'beyond and above desire', and it was on account of such cultural conceptualization that the hijras were accommodated within the Bangla social structure. This is not to suggest that hijras today publicly proclaim themselves as sexual, but the discourse of denial that was once the hallmark of hijra public presentation is slowly being challenged on account of their involvement with sexual health NGOs. What was thus an Ulti practice enshrouded in secrecy is increasingly becoming Bangla, or public—a fact that has been and continues to be a major bone of contention among the hijras. To underscore this tension and to foreground hijra involvement with sexual activities, I produce below one ethnographic episode on typical activities inside an NGO office.

Condom demonstration in a hijra NGO office

It was the appointed day of the week on which hijras gathered for a group meetup in the office of an NGO on the outskirts of Dhaka. The branch office was located across the street from the house of Sonu hijra, the famous sadrali guru in Bangladesh who had opposed NGO activities right from their inception. Bokul, an emasculated *hajji* hijra and a cela of Sonu, was in charge of this branch office. While this office was supposed to cater to the sadralis, that is, those who publicly dress up like females, those attending on that day were all dressed in normative masculine attire. The reason for this, I was told, was not only to convey to the public the image of hijras in the vicinity as people above desire, but also because of Bokul's status as a hajji and their being an active member of the Islamic preaching team and the local mosque committee. As an aside, let me mention that while Bokul dressed like a female in their house and the vicinity, during their prayers in the mosque and while preaching Islam with other devotees, they dressed like a normative masculine male. Bokul argued that sadrali, or full-time hijras, only accessed the medical services furtively, when doctors would come once or twice a week, while on other days, they catered to the needs of 'gandu', a derogatory hijra expression used to refer to those who fuck and get fucked. In this instance, Bokul, however, used 'gandu' to refer to the participants' male attire in public that contravenes the hijra convention of appearing exclusively in feminine attire in public. While I was having a conversation with Bokul, the adjoining room was packed with a vibrant gathering of young males sitting on the floor with the peer educator giving out lessons on safe sex. Dressed in typical male attire and standing in a corner with a whiteboard and a marker, they wrote 'HIV' and 'AIDS' and asked if anyone knew what these acronyms stood for. When none could say, they explained. Afterwards, they asked if anyone would like to volunteer to demonstrate safe sex. A participant came forward and said the following:

> I will now tell you about how to have safe sex with a *panthi*. We all know that panthis often object to condoms as they think condoms will lower their pleasure. And we all know they refer to *jhalka* [money] when asked to use a condom. 'Why should I put on that? I have paid you. So you must let me do you in whatever way I want,' says a typical panthi, but there are still ways to deceive them into having sex with the condoms on. And I will show you how. Whenever you have sex with a panthi, start with your mouth. Take the condom inside your mouth and then suck the penis slowly and in the process you will see that his penis is erect and also sucked. And then play.

Every time I went to these NGO premises, not only was the same demonstration repeated but more significantly the participants in the weekly gathering always turned up in normative male attire. That they turned up in male attire in an exclusively hijra-focused NGO group was significant not least because hijras are generally disapproving of non-sadrali groups, but also because hijras typically denounce sexual activities associated with such men who have sex with men in public. Although sadralis never really gathered in a routine manner to learn techniques of safe sex, the very holding of such sessions there contrived to alert the Bangla world to those hijra sexual activities that are meant to be kept clandestine.

The new visibility of hijras as rights-bearing citizens and disability as a new framework

Partly as a critique of the overarching health-driven framework of HIV/AIDS work internationally, there has been a gradual shift to a rights-based approach at least among the NGOs and wider civil society in Bangladesh working with marginal gender and sexual subjects. Particularly significant is a workshop organized in 2009 by Boys of Bangladesh, a gay group with support from Norwegian donors in which several other MSM-focused NGOs, lesbian-identified groups and hijra organizations participated. Gay groups emerged in Bangladesh from 2000 onwards primarily as an online platform, and the workshop in question was one of the first rights-focused public events organized by gay men. The idea of the gathering was to discuss the state of LGBT (lesbian, gay, bisexual and transgender) politics in Bangladesh and to explore possibilities and strategies for collective action. While the gay group embraced an LGBT identity politics as a framework to explore rights activism, the abbreviation LGBT and the associated identity politics sounded foreign and unintelligible to the rest of the groups. The gay group identified Section 377 of the Bangladeshi penal code, the anti-sodomy law inherited from the British, to be the main threat to their existence. The MSM-focused NGOs were loath to prioritize 377 as an agenda as the law did not interfere with their activities in practice. Despite these differences, a decision to form a coalition was taken and a platform launched to explore collaboration among these various groups.

While the gay group was recognizably middle class, educated and English speaking, they stood at the bottom of political activism with no social visibility, whereas the hijras were the most visible of all groups despite their being stigmatized and working class. Hijra organizations were also clearly subservient to the MSM-based NGOs, as due to a lack of social and cultural capital hijras were unable to directly connect with the donors and form organizations of their own. Furthermore, the hijra-based organizations were also dependent on the network of the MSM-based NGOs. The MSM-focused NGOs' target groups were also mainly working-class men. The MSM-focused NGOs viewed the public organizing of a workshop by a gay group as a threat to their existing dominance in the field of male-to-male sexuality. The existence of potential competitors in the field of marginal gender and sexuality generated new impetus for these male-to-male sexual health NGOs to increasingly employ rights-themed language and approaches (Hossain 2017, 2019b).

Because of the institutionalized presence of the hijras as a long-standing cultural category of people with genital ambiguity who are seen as asexual, adopting a rights approach in relation to them was, from the start, a morally legitimate cultural enterprise. MSM-focused NGOs specifically capitalized on this cultural ambiguity around the hijras by being explicitly vocal about hijra rights and making demands for their legal recognition as a third gender while being relatively silent about the repeal of Section 377. For example, hijras connected with MSM-focused NGOs have been part of public rallies and demonstrations on International Women's Day with separate banners drawing attention to their rights as human beings since at least 2000. In 2009, a hijra was elected to be the president of the sex workers' network of Bangladesh. Funded by international donors and comprising mainly female sex workers, a few hijra NGOs and associations were also part of this wider network. That a hijra-identified person got elected as the president of this network, voted for mostly by female sex workers, drew the attention of national and international media and brought hijra involvement with sex work into Bangla/public view. This was a significant development, as even in 2004 when a client was murdered by a hijra-identified sex worker named Shohagi, hijras deliberately refrained from making any show of support or defence. The guru of Shohagi, whom I interviewed, echoed the popular trope of hijras being asexual and contended that Shohagi deserved to be put behind bars for their involvement with sex work and thereby disgracing the entire hijra community.

Like the NGOs, the government was also quite enthusiastic in adopting a rights approach to hijras. In 2011, hijras were discussed in the parliament of Bangladesh and proposals to 'rehabilitate' them were tabled on the grounds of their being 'disabled'. Several projects, schemes and interventions have been launched since at least 2011 under various ministries of the government of Bangladesh. For example, a group of government officials took an initiative called the 'Integration of the Transgender (Hijra) Population into Mainstream Society' in 2011.[1] With the funding and approval of several

---

[1] See http://archive.thedailystar.net/magazine/2011/10/03/special.htm (accessed 1 January 2021).

ministries, the initiative was intended to impart various skills to the hijras to help them find mainstream employment. As part of this initiative, thirty hijras were given training in computer applications, industrial sewing and beauty care. This same group of government officials also initiated a mass awareness campaign to change people's negative perceptions about hijras by organizing seminars, rallies and advertising campaigns. They additionally organized several public rallies with demand for the legal recognition of hijras as a third gender with placards, banners and t-shirts emblazoned with similar messages. Bandhu, the largest MSM-focused NGO in Bangladesh, also organized several large demonstrations for the hijras. In 2011, holding banners, placards and festoons, hundreds of hijras dressed in colourful saris paraded along a three-kilometre-long route in Dhaka, demanding rights of employment, education and, most significantly, recognition as a third gender. On the heels of all these initiatives and activism, in November 2013 the government of Bangladesh took the policy decision to legally recognize hijras.

Although hailed both nationally and internationally as a progressive socio-legal advancement, the legal recognition of the hijra as a 'hijra sex', as I argued elsewhere (Hossain 2017), has simultaneously necessitated a mobilization of a discourse of disability.[2] In other words, hijras had to be officially defined as being sexually disabled in order for them to be worthy of recognition and rights. Thus, what was previously a minor discourse of disfigurement based on putative genital status has now been transmuted into an official discourse of disability (the class-specific construction of the hijra is further elaborated in chapter 2). Under this new regime of 'recognition', only those born with missing or ambiguous genitals qualified to be hijras in the eyes of the government (Hossain 2017). While it still remains to be seen how this new legal recognition will affect hijras' access to citizenship rights, and how hijras will negotiate this new official conceptualization of them being disabled, a range of other identificatory vocabularies were already in sight with the advent of NGOs, to which I now turn.

---

[2] The term specifically used in the gazette notification is 'hijra lingo', which can be translated as both hijra sex or hijra gender. The gazette is available at http://www.dpp.gov.bd/upload_file/gazettes/6851_39605.pdf (accessed 28 May 2021).

Categorical proliferation and the political economy of identification

NGOs that started to work on male-to-male sexualities from the late 1990s put forward varied labels at various times in collaboration with their donors. While not all labels that came into circulation as a consequence of NGO intervention have infiltrated into contemporary cultural consciousness in Bangladesh, the semantic and conceptual differences among these varied labels have often been collapsed not only in the way people in real-life situations identify themselves in response to varied organizational regimes, but also in terms of practices that NGOs may strictly associate with each of these identity labels. To put the picture in perspective, I present below an episode from my ethnographic fieldwork in 2008.

Yearly picnic of Badhon Hijra Shongho

Badhon Hijra Shongho, an NGO, organized an annual picnic in Shafipur, a popular spot located outside Dhaka. Arriving at the office of Badhon at 7:00 a.m., I saw three big buses already occupied by exuberant, would-be picnic-goers. Hijras dressed in all kinds of colourful and gaudy female-identified attire were constantly hopping in and out of the buses. The first bus had a banner strapped to its front with the name of the organization and the destination inscribed on it (Figure 7.1). Around 350 guests were invited. Although the majority of them were hijra-identified, there were about twenty to thirty non-hijra NGO staff. Arriving at the location after three hours, as people started getting down from the bus, some of the hijras dressed in female clothing rushed to a corner near a brick-built shed. Lifting up their saris, they started urinating. As those who rushed to urinate were relatively younger, senior hijras immediately picked up on this and started disparagingly shouting at the contradiction between their female attire and toilet etiquette. 'Look at those maigga [a derogatory term for men who act like women]! They are making water like panthis. Shameless gandu!'—was the comment from a hijra guru.

To my utter surprise, I saw several sadrali hijra gurus who had previously spoken in the worst possible terms about the NGOs. Roksana, a sadrali hajji hijra whom I had not expected to be present, was no less scathing in their censure of the NGO-affiliated hijra participants. Pointing to a group of 'kari kothis' (hijras in the guise of men), Roksana burst out, 'These are people with a penis and these are the ones who sleep with men. But real hijras like me

Figure 7.1 A banner pinned to the front of a bus for a picnic organized by Badhon Hijra Shongho
Source: Author.

are chaste and abstain from all kinds of erotic activities.' The group Roksana castigated remained silent; later, however, they told me that Roksana was their nan-guru, that is, the guru of their guru, and that they too were once like them and more significantly they still lived with their panthi who was also their companion at the picnic—in short, that they were not asexual at all. Pointing to Roksana's hajji status, they criticized them for not being able to refrain from a relationship.

Although initially I was not sure how those who came in normative masculine attire identified themselves, some of those dressed in male attire categorically told me that they too were hijras. One of the normatively dressed hijras told me that among those dressed like men, some were hijras while the rest were either partners of the hijras or NGO staff. Joya introduced a 'man' dressed in suit as their 'bandhobi', the Bangla expression for a female friend. Noticing surprise on my face, they commented, 'See? Even hijras can wear a suit like men.'

Most participants in the picnic frequently switched between 'MSM', 'transgender', hijra and koti. When I raised this issue, one hijra argued that there is basically no distinction among these various labels. Moni, an NGO worker whom I had known previously to be MSM-identified, turned up in female attire. Moni argued that they were basically a hijra but they identified as 'MSM' as the organization they worked with required them to identify as such. The first NGO Moni worked with required them to identify as 'transgender'. Moni then maintained that basically they were a hijra. Listening to our conversation, Kanthi, another hijra, commented, 'We all take penis in our backside and that is the main binding principle for us all. These differences are a way to do business for the NGOs. After all, more categories mean more projects and more funding.' Santha, another hijra who worked as a peer educator for an NGO, chimed in, 'Be it transgender or transvestite or transsexual or cross-dresser, we are all the same. But I prefer transgender as I am a hijra.' Kanta, another hijra affiliated with an NGO, had been to several conferences abroad. Proudly recalling their trips to India, Thailand and Australia, they argued that people like them are called transgender abroad.

There are a few things to be drawn out from this episode. First, despite sadrali hijras being dismissive of NGO activities, several of them actively participated in the picnic along with their partners. That sadrali hijras came to this public event with their partners is significant precisely because sadrali hijras tend to hide their having partners from the Bangla world. Second, what struck me as significant was the way the conventional sartorial distinction between hijras and their partners was visibly collapsed. Third, contrary to the arguments of much contemporary scholarship about reification of sexual subjectivities (Boyce 2007; Cohen 2005), NGO interventions have led to a simultaneous ossification and fluidification of identities. NGOs are trafficking in sexual–gender difference (that is, the fact that NGOs often stress distinctions of various groups and categories, as more categories and groups, as indicated by a hijra quoted earlier) in order to garner more projects and money (see also Reddy 2005b on how such distinction is banked on in the context of Indian hijras). Fourth, how one presents oneself and how one is represented depend on the context of the organization in which one works and the particular category under which an organization has received funding. In other words, an individual in the span of a day may variously identify as MSM, transgender or hijra in line with the prescriptions of the NGOs they represent. Finally, the proliferation of these several semantic monikers and their circulations represent not only a broader politics of representation continuous with the colonial proclivity to contain the apparent intransigence of the hijras (Gannon 2009), but also various discursive regimes and practices in/through which subjectivities are constituted.

Transgender, not hijra: the rise of a new respectable regime

Despite the fluidity with which people identify themselves in relation to varied spatio-organizational regimes, there is some kind of a consensus about 'transgender' being the most appropriate label to capture the hijras among NGO circles and hijra activists within Bangladesh. While hijras are variously described in the South Asian media as eunuchs, hermaphrodites and transsexuals, NGO publications and public health research in Bangladesh have increasingly employed 'transgender' as the designated term for hijras. Today, many NGO-affiliated hijras in Bangladesh, as in India, see transgender as a more respectable form of self-identification devoid of the baggage and stigma associated with traditional hijraness (see also Roy 2016).

An episode from my fieldwork illuminates the privileging of transgender over the hijras not only as a mode of self-representation, but also as a form of modern and sanitized subject position. A flyer that had been in circulation for some time was a source of several fierce rows among the hijras in Dhaka in recent times. Intended as publicity material, it was widely distributed among the general populace to warn them of 'fake hijras'. I reproduce below highlights of that flyer in translation.

> A secret story: Sapna [a pseudonym] the leader of the terrorist hijra group
>
> Brothers and sisters,
>
> This is to inform you all that there is a kind of people in Bangladesh who we call hijras, or handicapped. But they are actually neither hijra nor handicapped. They are artificial hijras. They are born as male in their family but cut off their male genitals as they grow up to become hijras. Currently the people who you think are hijra in Bangladesh are actually not real hijras. They are in fact the greatest terrorists of the country. How much does an average person with education and employment earn? A hijra earns between one and a half lac a month [roughly US$1,800]. If they are not terrorists, how do they make such a big amount of money? But if they are not into terrorism, how can some of them have three- and five-storeyed buildings? They go to shops and markets and extort. In the name of blessing the newborn babies, they get

into people's houses and demand money. If refused, they threaten to expose their genitals. Due to the fear of losing social respect, people are coerced into paying them. In fact, these hijras are big terrorists and some of them also have wives and children. So who are these hijras? They get married and give birth to two/three children and then get rid of their penises. If you do not believe what we are saying, you can investigate the matter with the help of medical examination. We have all the information about the places where such artificial excision of male genitals takes place and there are also those who hide their penises between their thighs and pretend not to have any penis.... This group [the flyer specifies a particular hijra group and a list of names with details on their whereabouts and genital status] lures economically helpless men into having their genitals excised for money. They also consume 'sukhi' pills to inflate their breasts so that they can impersonate hijras to demand money. This is one kind of business.... We, a few hijras, would like to provide you with secret information about this group and their activities.... The classified information that we have about hijras has never been published in any of the newspapers or media in the country. Dear brothers and sisters, the fear of inauspiciousness is the reason why you pay money to the hijras, but if you donate this money to the mosque and orphanage, you will earn some *sawab* [divine blessings]. So we request you to not pay any money to the hijras. The reason why we are divulging this information to you is because we are transgender [this word was transliterated]. We work to make a living and we have not had our genitals excised like them. So we are often under pressure and suffer threats from the hijras. They say that they will not let us carry on with our job if we do not get rid of our genitals. There are many like us who also make a living out of paid jobs. They don't extort or terrorize. The reason why we are providing this information is that we have now realized our mistakes and we are repentant. But we are not scared of them. We stand by you all. If you cooperate with us, the terroristic and criminal activities of these hijras can be curbed. Disseminated by: Transgender population opposed to terrorism.

There are a few points to be noted with regard to the flyer. First, the flyer can be read as an example of internal conflicts among the hijras. It can be surmised that those behind its circulation were NGO-affiliated hijras, as the flyer explicitly critiqued the hijra occupations of badhai and cholla as extortionist activities while celebrating paid employment. Second, and most interesting from the perspective of this discussion, is the way such intra-group tension is manifested in the use of 'transgender' as a label set in opposition to the regressive hijras. The use of the word 'transgender' in transliteration is also striking as it is increasingly being adopted not only as a synonym of hijra, but also as a more respectable version of a hijra subject position. Transgender thus emerges as a mode of sanitized identification indexing paid employment, modernization and progress as opposed to the stigmatized and stigmatizing hijra subject positions and their ritual occupations.

The discursive interpellation of hijras as transgender has also inaugurated a new regime of disciplinary practices, engendering new forms of tension and contestation over authentic hijra sartorial practice and status. Babuli, a hijra-identified peer educator working for an NGO, once related that while they would generally come to the NGO office in male attire, they would always be dressed in female attire when donors or people of other agencies visited the office. The reason for that, they contended, was because the organization was intended exclusively for the transgender. Moyuri, another hijra working with an NGO, echoed the same sentiment and shared with me one of the ordeals they had to face during undergoing training on HIV in a donor office in Dhaka. They contended that they were sent back from that office the very first day they went there as they were dressed in masculine attire. The project personnel categorically insisted on participants being dressed like females, as the programme was specifically designed for the transgender and not for the MSM. Since then Moyuri, along with all other participants, had attended the training in female attire, in line with the sartorial prescription about what a transgender person should look like. The very consolidation of transgender as a subject position therefore entails a strict sartorial regime in the Bangladeshi context, whereby those so identified are expected to present themselves as dressed in recognizably female attire. Significantly, the feminine public presentation works to erase the ambiguity (non-respectable and working class) that the hijra subject position conventionally embodied. The increasing alignment with a feminine gender presentation in terms of the expectations surrounding a transgender subject position in this context further bolsters the politics of respectability in hijra self-identification.

In his ethnography on transgender as a category, Valentine (2007) contends that the advent and popularization of transgender in the Euro-American context is the corollary of a systematic and essentialist separation of gender and sexuality into distinct ontological experiences. Foregrounding his interlocutors' simultaneous self-identification as gay and transgender in New York, he argues that one outcome of such artificial compartmentalization has been a growing de-sexualization of transgender as about gender only as opposed to gay, which has come to embody sexuality. That such a distinction has become naturalized is itself a product of particular socio-historical logics specific to American queer rights activism and ought to be subjected to scrutiny. In other words, Valentine complicates the dominant Euro-American proclivity for cultural disparagement of gender-variant or transgendered gay subjectivities (see also Dutta 2013).

It is instructive here to note that I deployed masculinities and male femininities instead of transgender as an approach to explore the hijras, not only because the very adoption of male femininities moves us beyond the reductionism of its socio-historical context and its uncritical transposability on to disparate settings, but also because male femininities allow for attention to be paid to the processual character of the formation of hijra subjectivities. The emergence of transgender as a mode of self-representation and as a subjectivity with stereotypical gender-variant expressions has emerged in contemporary Bangladesh within the sociopolitical context of HIV activism from the late 1990s onwards. New social and political organizing and various rights-based praxes implicating hijras are increasingly taking root around this new subject position. While in Bangladesh emergent gay subjectivities are often posited by both the NGOs and the gay groups as oppositional to transgender, transgender has become a form of disciplinary power with particular forms of normativizing gender variance whereby those so identified are expected to publicly present themselves as feminine-identified to assert their transgendered subjectivity. Furthermore, while transgender at least in theory is intended to encompass a variety of gender-variant identities, practices and expressions, in contemporary Bangladesh, as in the context of Valentine, transgender has also become characteristic of limited, monolithic expression of male-to-female 'transgender' people only.

A caveat is necessary at this point. Despite this growing tension between the concepts of hijraness and transgender, these two are not necessarily mutually excluding identities as many of my interlocutors not only identify as both hijra and transgender, but also because sadrali hijras, or those undertaking hijragiri, are also an integral part of these NGOs, as already explicated earlier in this chapter. With the increasing espousal of 'transgender' as a label by the hijras and public use of this term working to evoke connections and alliances with a global and regional transgender movement, hinting at possibilities of alignment of local hijra subjectivities with an international transgender idiom and aesthetics with their emphases on body modification via sex-reassignment surgeries, a growing number of people are opting for the conventional hijra practice of emasculation, to which I now turn.

From ritualized emasculation to genital reconstruction

Even though the rise of transgender has necessitated a full-time public (re) presentation of persons as sartorially feminine, transitioning to a normative feminine position through surgery in contemporary Bangladesh is neither practised nor even encouraged within NGO circles. Rather, NGOs working on sexual health including those exclusively dedicated to hijras categorically discountenance all forms of bodily feminization. An NGO staff member once categorically stated that there is an unwritten policy to not encourage 'feminization' of any sort. Another NGO professional I interviewed argued that 'feminization leads to one's becoming a hijra. Society does not look at the hijras positively and if we encourage people to undergo bodily changes, society would look down upon them even further.' That feminization is discouraged and viewed negatively was further evident to me when I went to a meeting organized by an NGO where various groups of people including hijras were invited. In the course of our interaction, the executive director of an MSM-focused NGO openly argued that the lack of social acceptance of hijras is the direct result of their gender practices, especially their tendency to dress and talk like females. On another occasion, when I was invited to a house party organized by an MSM-identified NGO worker overseeing a hijra project, I was surprised that not a single hijra was invited even though I was introduced to him through the hijras. Later when I inquired about the absence of any hijras, he drew my attention to his having some status in the neighbourhood, which could be jeopardized by the presence of hijras. Even the exclusively hijra-focused NGOs did not offer any such provision for feminization, nor did any of those organizations seem inclined to adopt such initiatives in the long run.

Interestingly, a growing number of people in recent times have secretly undergone emasculation in private hospitals in Dhaka and its outskirts. While this is not an entirely new development, the popularity of this practice is certainly on the rise. Although ritual emasculation is widely practised among the hijras, where a *katial* performs the operation as previously described, there were also cases where the surgery was performed by medical professionals in a hospital setting under the supervision of the hijras. In other words, hijras would undertake all the rituals surrounding emasculation but would then go on to have the operations performed in secret private medical establishments. In contrast, many these days with partial or no affiliation with the hijra groups are increasingly opting for medicalized emasculation. Once during a conversation about the future of hijragiri, Bokul hijra drew the rise of these medical establishments to my attention by stating the following: 'Who says hijras will cease to exist? Even if the sadrali hijras renounce this practice, those who want to become chibry will become so anyway.'

One of the doctors who have recently become quite popular for performing such surgeries owns a hospital situated on the outskirts of Dhaka. This doctor, whom I will anonymize as Bashir, in an interview with me in 2015 styled this surgery as 'genital reconstruction'. Trained in France and Italy, Dr Bashir stated that he had performed almost 700 such surgeries since he opened his clinic in 2006. He surgically removes the penis and the scrotum while ensuring that the urethral canal is not obstructed as is often the case when traditional ritual cutters operate on the hijras. He explained that most of his patients are hijra-identified and they typically want to have their male genitals totally removed. Not a single patient he had operated on had ever wanted a vagina constructed. According to him, a deep sense of physical and mental discomfort with their genitalia is what motivates his patients to opt for this surgery. Many of his patients had also told him that they wanted to have their genitals removed as it was shameful to have their male organs seen by their partners. He pointed out that the reason his patients want a complete removal of the male genitals rather than a vagina is because they like anal sex. He also contended that the 'feminine sexual prowess' of the hijra undergoing this surgery increases, as the removal of the scrotum significantly lessens the production of testosterone, with female hormones becoming dominant consequently.

Patients who come to access this service at his hospital, according to him, are often those hijras without any formal affiliation with the organized hijra groups. In the last few years he had also operated on a number of patients that the local hijra groups brought to his hospital after severe complications following traditional removal of the genitals. This is exactly how, argued Dr Bashir, the idea to perform this surgery occurred to him. A few years ago, a post-operative hijra on the brink of death was brought to his hospital in the middle of the night and eventually the patient survived. Although he had subsequently treated such complicated cases several times, non-affiliated[3]

---

[3] 'Non-affiliated' here refers primarily to those with no formal affiliation to the hijras; however, it may also refer to those that the hijras describe as being in *kari besh* (hijras in the guise of a man who live socially like a normative man while maintaining a surreptitious link with the hijras).

hijras also began to come to be operated on in the intervening years (see also Lorway 2017, 77–79 for a discussion on how a set of intervention techniques smooth social pathways to assuming sexual identifications). That non-affiliated hijras started to access this service was something that the local hijra group was not only unhappy about, but also vehemently opposed to. Leaders of the local hijra group on several occasions had approached him and demanded that the patients coming to his hospital for surgery be handed over to the hijra group. There had been instances when hijras came to his hospital to beat up the patients undergoing this surgery. He also stated that local hijra groups had spies deployed in the area to regularly monitor the situation.

Although the total cost of such an operation ranges from 10,000 to 15,000 taka (approximately $120–180), those coming from other areas to be operated on have to spend three times the amount as they have to pay the local hijra guru to seek their consent. Dr Bashir argued that the reason the local hijra group opposed independent patients was money. While I am not entirely clear as to the reason for this, as the local group denied such allegations to me, my feeling is that the independent undertaking of such surgery perhaps amounts to an infraction of the hijra communitarian rule that I discussed at length in chapter 4. Furthermore, several journalists had also inquired about this surgery, often threatening the doctor with exposure and bringing charges against him under Bangladeshi penal code 326, according to which emasculation or genital excision can be read as a form of bodily mutilation and therefore can be a crime. He categorically dismissed all those threats on the grounds of his being a trained medical doctor, and asserted that the service he was offering was not emasculation but genital reconstruction, which he argued was widespread all over the world.

Dr Bashir arranged meetings for me with three of his patients after I had expressed an interest in meeting them. While I met two of them both prior to and after the surgery, the other patient I spoke to had been operated on long before. I met two of his patients in the hospital and the other one in a public garden, after making an appointment by telephone. Interestingly, all three of them maintained that the main reason for their having undergone surgery was to please their partners. They also categorically stated that they did not want a vagina. One of them commented, 'What is the use? Even if I have one, that will be useless. I can never use that crack for taking a penis. Plus my partner also likes anus more than vagina.' None of them had ever been a member of a sadrali hijra group, that is, they never undertook hijragiri or appeared in public as a hijra. Nor were they affiliated with NGOs.[4]

There are a few things to be drawn out here. First, despite NGO opposition to feminization and the objections of sadrali hijra groups, there is now a growing trend among some non-sadrali, male-bodied people to become chibry, or emasculated. I say 'chibry', as all three patients of Dr Bashir I interviewed described themselves as such, despite their not having any formal affiliations with the sadrali groups. Second, the reasons offered by those patients and by Dr Bashir resonate with my contention about partners being an important cause in the decision to have the operation, as I elaborated in chapter 4. Third, that people accessing this service want emasculation rather than a vagina shows how the adoption of 'transgender' as a label for self-identification by hijras and its increasing use in the NGO context does not signal a movement towards sex-reassignment surgery. Rather, a clandestine hijra ritual is becoming popular among those without the desire or intention to conduct hijragiri, or be part of the hijra universe.

Conclusion

In this chapter, I drew attention to regimes of transnational governmentalities and disciplinary power within a fast-changing trans-local political economy. I specifically argued that the vicissitudes in hijra subjectivities are the direct effects and appropriations of those transnational processes. In locating these contemporary metamorphoses, my intention here was not to posit hijras as passive agents of those processes. Rather, what I demonstrated is that hijras actively exercised various kinds of agency in shaping and being shaped by those interventions.

In a way, the emergence of various and at times contested discourses and their effects on hijras in contemporary Bangladesh is anything but uniform. Rather, what I described is a bricolage of varied discourses inflected

---

[4] These patients I spoke to were sufficiently fluent in Ulti and other hijra mores and had claimed discipleship of senior gurus even though they had never undertaken hijragiri, nor ever wanted to in future. Furthermore, none of them had worked with any of the NGOs, although they had frequented NGO premises on a regular basis. The point here is that they all were sufficiently exposed to various hijra norms and rules but chose to become chibry, or emasculated, without any of the accompanying rituals.

through trans-local notions and practices of religion, gender, sexuality, class and political economy. In his now canonized history of sexuality, Foucault ([1978]1990) contends that the birth of the Western homosexual as a subject supplants the previously circulating discourse about same-sex sexuality being an activity or 'temporary aberration'. In contrast, the scenario I describe is not one of discursive supersession but is characterized by simultaneous and contradictory emergences of various categories, discourses and identities that are brought into being through incessant comings and goings of transnational circulation of various material and symbolic forces, both within and without (Johnson, Jackson and Herdt 2000). While the development of these varied and often contested discourses inaugurates novel forms of disciplinary regimes and governmentalities, they may also be seen to engender fresh opportunities and resources for people to negotiate and rethink their subjectivities (Wilson 2010). Here a point worth highlighting is the unequal conditions of transnational/regional political economic regimes under and within which those categories, identities and discourses are proliferating (Dutta and Roy 2014). In other words, the very nature of the emergence of those discourses, practices and categories under an inegalitarian international division of labour is such that they allow the exercise of various forms of power and governmentality over the construction of subjectivities in unforeseen ways.

In his study of the transformation of the indigenous Hawaiians in relation to the advent of Captain Cook and other European colonial powers, Sahlins (1981) suggests that the metamorphosis taking place within the indigenous Hawaiian population is not explainable merely in terms of these external forces. Rather, in the process of cultural reproduction, Hawaiians incorporated Captain Cook as part of their cosmology. Against this backdrop, Sahlins argued that the transformation is the corollary of 'failed reproduction'. Following this insight, I would argue the contemporary changes taking place within the existing arrangements of hijra occupation reflect 'transformation' resulting from my interlocutors' attempts at such reproduction. Despite the tension, conflicts and contestations, hijras, as this chapter has indicated, have embraced many of these new processes and practices. In their taking on and becoming an active and agentive part of these new processes, hijras have not relinquished the traditional structure of the hijra universe. Rather, interestingly, even the NGO work is being configured in terms of the hijra internal logics of guru–cela divide, despite piecemeal opposition from within the hijra community. While I will take up the question of the future of the hijra occupation in the conclusion of this book, suffice it to say that hijras today will have to constantly navigate and negotiate a complex emerging scenario marked by a contradiction between the traditional societal understanding of their being asexual and the emergent public re-conceptualization of them as sexual beings. Perhaps more than anything else, the answer to the question about the future of hijras as we understand it today will depend on the intricate negotiation of that question in the days to come.

Conclusion
Shifting Meaning and the Future of *Hijras*

Hijras serve as the long-running, emblematic figure of South Asian sexual and gender difference. The publicly institutionalized position of the hijras across South Asia is a testament to the continued existence of an alternative subculture that survived criminalization and eradication at different points in colonial and postcolonial history. More recently, there is a renewed interest in hijras both regionally and internationally with the legal recognition of a third gender in several South Asian countries including Bangladesh, Nepal, Pakistan and India. That a third gender has been legally recognized while same-sex sexualities remain criminalized in several countries in South Asia continues to arouse curiosity about the relationship between the hijra subject position and same-sex sexuality. The outbreak of the HIV epidemic and the crystallization of LGBT identities in the Western metropolises and their spread across the world have also led to a resurgence of interest in alternative and putatively 'native' sex/gender subjects, including the hijras.

Hijra as an alternative gender/sex and its discursive consolidation as a third gender/sex worked to destabilize the so-called sex–gender dimorphism of the Western world (Nanda 1999). Critical social science research has, however, challenged such an easy reading of the hijras as a third gender or sex by pushing us to take into account the way gender and sexual difference are embedded in other forms of social difference, including class, caste, kinship, transnationalism and desire (Cohen 1995; Reddy 2005a). More importantly, this critical body of research alerts us to the incapacity of a third sex/gender framework to account for the complex interaction among gender, sexuality and the social, economic and political context in which hijra lives are implicated. This book departs from well-trodden territory in that it goes beyond critiquing the so-called third sex/gender paradigm and brings into view structural inequalities of gender and sexuality that produce the hijra subject in the first place. In place of either a transgender or third sex perspective, too often readily employed in the analysis of gender-variant people in the Global South, this book adopts masculinity as a lens. A focus on masculinity brings into view not only the process of ideological abjection of the hijras but also the various actions and doings through which hijras craft their own subject position. Put differently, it shifts our focus away from the tendency to biologize the hijra or conceive of them through the narrow prism of genital difference (either ritual removal of the penis and scrotum or inborn condition as in intersexuality). It shows how being a hijra is an acquired subject position dependent on the successful mastery of the skills and acumen required for the conduct of *hijragiri*, or the occupation of the hijras, and their dexterous demonstration both within their own circles and among the majority mainstream.

The prevailing tendency to view hijras through the lens of emasculation, a trope often favoured in dominant ethnographic representations, works to de-sexualize the hijras. Both at the levels of intellectual and popular cultural imagination, emasculation is often equated with a lack of erotic desire and the consequent inability to experience sexual pleasure. Such a trope stems from the assumption that erotic delight not only inheres in the penis, but also that penile pleasures are superior to other forms of bodily pleasure, including that of the anus, which hijras often valorize as the apogee of erotic delight. While these alternative forms of pleasure are forbidden in the mainstream social view, it is precisely through their recognition and cultivation that one can lay claim to an authentic hijra status. From this slant, the very existence of the hijra subculture exemplifies a form of resolution of gender and erotic incommensurability. More significantly, the hijra can be seen as a counter-cultural formation that emerged not only in direct contradistinction to hegemonic protocols of masculinity, but also as an alternative subcultural community offering the possibility of varied forms of erotic pleasure and practice otherwise forbidden in mainstream society.

Insofar as the hijra can be read as an alternative cultural and erotic space in which varied forms of erotic delight can be explored and pursued that are otherwise off-limits to the mainstream, it indexes supra-locality. Hijras are a part of the Bangladeshi social world. Yet they are outside of the mainstream precisely on account of their inhabiting an alternative (Ulti) semiotic and symbolic space of desire that is neither readily accessible nor intelligible to the wider society. This alternative erotic space, however, is not without its own set of rules of appropriate sexual conduct and public engagement. For

Conclusion

example, hijras believe that only those who are part of the community as hijras are entitled to anal pleasures. This does not, however, require the hijras to be permanently detached from heterosexual affiliations. In fact, there are both hijras who are heterosexually married and those who are feminine-identified on a permanent basis; but once one becomes a hijra, one is required to 'publicly' identify receptivity as the only legitimate form of sexuality.

Marginal sex/gender subjects often figure prominently in contemporary analysis of social sciences as the perpetually suffering subjects in need either of a global rescue industry or a form of discursive salvation by scholars. It is as if the very justification for the hijras being a subject worthy of study is dependent on the extent to which they can be presented as suffering from violence, violations of human rights and lack of social acceptance. While such a proclivity is not specific to the non-mainstream sex/gender subjects, a relentless focus on suffering (at least in the sense of showcasing conspicuous forms of suffering, including everyday forms of abjection, human rights abuses and violence faced by the hijras) works to deflect attention not only from the larger social matrix in which individual experiences of suffering are embedded (Farmer 1996), but also the interlocking systems of inequalities of gender, class and sexuality that produce the hijra subject in the first place. This is particularly evident in the South Asian (and by extension, Bangladeshi) context, where the socio-cultural rationale for demand for legal changes in the status of the hijras is primarily rooted in the notion of hijras being helpless people in need of social commiseration. The exclusive social and governmental focus on genital difference as the root cause of their suffering works to erase social class and location and the politics of masculinity that produce the hijras as a sociocultural category.

The hijras in Bangladesh often talk about a trans-regional network of imagined solidarity that highlights hijra subjectivity over other markers of social and political differentiation, such as nation, religion or ethnicity. Hijras in Bangladesh also often posit India as the pristine fount of hijra ways tied to both Muslim- and Hindu-marked gods and goddesses, and their emergence in various locations both within and beyond South Asia. Moreover, various kinds of symbolic and physical movement across and between boundaries and borders are central to the formation of a hijra subject position. From this perspective, the process of becoming a hijra entails habitation of a supra-local and supra-national subjectivity that goes beyond the narrow national scale. Although the role of various material and symbolic flows in the formation of the hijra subject position is now being examined in the wake of globalization, various movements and flows have always been operative, albeit not on the same scale as during the current wave of globalization, in the way hijra subjects evolved in different historical periods, from ancient times until the present (Hossain and Nanda 2020).

A particularly pertinent issue in the wake of the various sexual and gender rights and identity movements across South Asia is the way hijra subculture is undergoing transformation. The advent of the LGBT movement in South Asia, at least in the formative days, hinted at various possibilities of transformation of existing gender/sex subjectivities. In her now classic ethnography on the hijras of South India published in 2005, Gayatri Reddy contends that hijras are increasingly being incorporated into the transnational gay world despite various class-, caste- and language-based inequalities that sharply divide the emergent gay identity from that of the hijras. Within a decade since 2005, 'transgender' emerged as the new default category for the 'indigenous' hijra. That transgender, rather than gay, became the broad-based identity template for hijras stems from and reinforces the notion that hijraness is more about gender identity than sexuality or sexual orientation. While hijras, as this book demonstrates, clearly transcend such categorical boundaries of gender and sexuality, different kinds of transformational possibilities abound for the future of the hijras in South Asia. On the one hand, the emergence of transgender engendered a space for non-hijra gender-variant groups and voices to emerge, it also created new divisions among the hijras, with transgender serving as the new and more respectable mode of self-identification (Dutta and Roy 2014; Hossain 2020; Roy 2016). The picture is further complicated by the rise of intersex activist groups in South Asia. Although hijras have long been conceived as a form of intersex, there is growing emphasis among intersex groups that they represent a constituency distinct from that of the hijras (Hossain 2020). For example, for the intersex community, differences in sex development (genes, hormones and reproductive organs, including genitals) are the primary marker of their distinction from other groups, including LGBT.

More recently, the onset of gender affirmation surgery (otherwise described as sex-reassignment surgery) in some places in South Asia and its growing, albeit still limited, use by some hijras heralds an important shift in how the landscape of gender and sexuality is being transformed across South Asia. While historically many hijras sought ritual emasculation, in recent times, some hijras are seeking partial or full vaginal reconstruction, breast implants and other hormonal replacements. However, as noted in chapter 7, although in Bangladesh surgical reconstruction of the genitals is gaining traction, it is not with the intention of becoming women in the Western sense of an MtF (male-to-female) transgender identity that people are seeking such reconstruction in Bangladesh. Rather, these hijras (and other hijra-like subject positions) seek to appropriate a particular kind of aesthetics of femininity in how their genitals look while retaining the use of the anus as the ultimate source of erotic delight, thereby making the hijra subject more complex than simply conforming to a Western biomedical notion of a transgender body.

At present, changes in the legal position of the hijras in Bangladesh have come about through a simultaneous mobilization of a discourse of disability in the way hijras are to be officially recognized. More significantly, the state is keen on positioning the hijra as an indigenous subject position delinked from sexual desire and the transnational LGBT politics and in need of rescue and social rehabilitation (Hossain 2017). Reminiscent of the colonial policy, conventional hijra occupations are targeted as being archaic as new state, private and civil-society-led initiatives aimed at finding alternative employment for hijras in Bangladesh today have proliferated. There seems to be a consensus among the policy makers on the need to eradicate the hijra way of life. The vicissitudes discussed here exemplify shift, in terms of both how the hijra subculture is changing, and societal attitudes towards their institutionalized presence. But what does the future hold for the hijras? What the hijra subculture will look like in the coming years depends not only on how those joining the hijra community will eventually craft their own subject position and shape the occupation of the hijras, but also on how the wider society evolves in its ability to deal with differences and inequalities, such as those of erotic inclination, gender identification and class position, in the face of ongoing uneven globalization.

Glossary

The words compiled below are the ones occurring most frequently in the main body of the manuscript. While the meanings of all the non-English words are spelt out inside the manuscript, I collate them here for the sake of the reader's convenience. All Bangla and Ulti words are transliterated. The translations of these words are entirely mine and reflect the context in which I heard them being used during my research.

abba	father
achol	hemline of a sari but also used figuratively to refer to motherly care and nurturance
akkhar	used as an adjective to denote great, large or big
akkhar dhur	hardcore sex
asla	the act of initiating a *cela* into *hijra* lineage
badhai	the ritual of demanding gifts at birth in exchange for blessings and performance
Bangla	the mainstream language spoken in Bangladesh
bandha parik	bonded or permanent partners of the hijras
bandhobi	a female friend
bagicha	garden
bala-musibod (or *bipod-apod*)	danger
baraiya	the ritual celebration on the twelfth day after emasculation
beyain	an address of endearment tinged with humour, used by the parents of a bride to refer to the parents of the groom and vice versa
bigrano	to ruin, used in the context of initiating someone into anal sexual practices
bila tonna	bad boys, from 'bila', bad, and 'tonna', young man or teenager
bishomokami	the literal and standard dictionary translation of heterosexual; the Bangla word is contrived and far-fetched and is rarely used

Glossary

birit	the ritual jurisdiction within which hijras carry out *hijragiri*
birit bakhor	trespassing of a *birit*
bohurupi	polymorphous
borhani	the act of frightening or shaming non-hijra people
bua	a female person employed to undertake domestic chores
bumper	moustache
butli	buttock
butli khol	the anus
cela	disciple (also *nati* and *puti* cela—grand- and great-grand-disciple, respectively)
Chaiton	Hindu
chibry	an emasculated hijra.
chibrano	the act of removing the penis and the scrotum
chilla	an Islamic religious practice in which Muslim men go from one mosque to another to strengthen their sense of faith and preach Islam; it also involves the spiritual practice of penance and solitude
chimpti	tweezers
cholla or *cholla manga*	monies or foodstuffs demanded and collected by the hijras from the bazaar
chutta parik	transient partners of the hijras
chudda	old men; often used to refer to fathers or uncles
cia	heterosexual marriage
chippu	urethral hole remaining after emasculation or, more broadly, the vagina
chipti	a synonym for chippu (see earlier)
chiput bazi or *chipti bazi*	female-to-female eroticism, (derived) from (the term) 'chippu'
chis	to desire or to have a liking for something when used as a verb but also used as an adjective to refer to someone who is excellent; can also be used to describe a situation that is pleasant
chola kola	subterfuge, hijra's mystique-making capabilities in relation to various kinds of gender and erotic practices
daiyar	a meeting place for arbitration
dan-khairat	the act of giving alms or donations
daratni	leader
darsan	beard

dorma	rice
dhol	a double-headed drum used in hijra rituals, particularly badhai
dhon	penis
dhupni	cigarette
dhurpit	sex or fucking
dhurrani	a derogatory word for a prostitute or someone with a voracious sexual appetite
dhurrani khol	a brothel or cruising site
don	compensation imposed by a guru on a cela when hijra rules and rituals are transgressed
dud beti	a so-called milk daughter with whom a hijra guru's relation is irrevocable; the word 'milk' here signifies the relation between a mother and her child who are related through milk and umbilical cord
falia	small patches of cloth used to wrap up or clean small children, especially the newborn
gamcha	a traditional coarse, thin fabric used to mop the face or body, as well as any other object
gamchali	hijras who wear gamchas and eke out a living through cooking work
gandu	a pejorative term used to refer to those who both penetrate and are penetrated by men
gaye holud	a marriage ritual in which turmeric paste is applied to the bodies of the bride and the groom
genji	a t-shirt-style garment
ghor	symbolic lineages of which hijra groups are part
gothia	sister, or hijras of equal rank
janana	hijras with a penis
jhalka	money
jhumka	scrotum
jodgman	the non-hijra mainstream, or the outside world
jok	hair
hijragiri	the occupation of the hijras, involving the rituals of badhai and cholla and mastery of various rules and skills including an ability to speak Ulti
ilu ilu	the practice of padding out bras with water-filled condoms
kacchi kora	to castigate someone

Glossary

kam	sex, as in intercourse
kari	being in the guise of a normative man; also used as a word of warning in the presence of the non-hijra populace
karkhana	the hospital where the ritual removal of the penis and scrotum occurs
katial	the ritual cutter who removes the penis and the scrotum of an initiand in keeping with sanctioned rules and rituals
kazi	an Islamic marriage registrar
khadem	custodian of a shrine
khai khowara/ kudenga	pejorative synonyms for gandu (see earlier)
khol	home or house
khilwar	alcohol
khujli	a term hijras use in relation to their being sexually excited; an itching experienced in the anus, which may only be mitigated by being penetrated
koti	an effeminate male; sadrali hijras regard koti as an Ulti word; I use the spelling 'koti' following other scholars even though the exact pronunciation is difficult to spell in English
ligam	penis
ligam potano	the art of disappearing the penis that janana hijras have to master as part of the hijra ritual. Hijras see it as a performing art, displayed to seal authenticity of hijraness, especially in their interaction with the mainstream in a bazaar setting
lilki	breasts
lutki	small
lohori or *lohori khawa*	exchange of glances and gestures, often used in the context of attracting men
lungi	a seamless tubular-shaped garment worn around the waist
magi	a 'slut'
maigga	a derogatory expression for an effeminate male
nayak	leader
neharun	female or woman
nirban	ritual acts of emasculation
norom sorom	soft; used to describe men that are softly spoken and meek
oli	a red sack used to store foodstuffs and other gifts received during badhai
orna	a patch of cloth worn across the breast by women

pan pata	betel leaves that many hijra gurus chew; betel leaves are also used in various hijra rituals
pakki	often used to refer to someone schooled in hijra mores who may be either a member of the hijra group or an outsider
pakki kora	to turn a place into a cruising site by managing the locals and the police; also used by the hijras to refer to one's being made knowledgeable about hijra ways
panthi	a masculine man or just man
panthi-pon	in the manner of a panthi
parik	husband, lover or intimate partner of the hijras
parik pala	the act of making a pet of a parik
patli	tea
pon pesha	the various rules and rituals used as part of the hijra occupation
salish	arbitration
samajik lingo	literally 'social genitalia', but often used as a translation for the English word 'gender' in NGO circles
samokami	homosexual
sanan	compensation paid by a panthi to the guru of a hijra on the event of his marriage to a hijra (also referred to as *pakki*)
sawab	divine blessings or credits
shasuri	mother-in-law
sinni	a celebratory feast in the name of a Muslim saint
sot	an internal calling or celestial power sought by hijras before undergoing emasculation
sudrani	semen
Surki	Muslim
thappu	Money
thikri	clap that hijras perform as a way to assert their hijraness during badhai, cholla and other hijra rituals
Ulti	the clandestine argot used by the hijras and the wider community of male-bodied, feminine-identified people to assert communitarian belonging
ulu jhulu	fun
vabi	the wife of a brother
vabraj	pregnant
vabrajer chibry	hijras born with defective or missing genitals
velki	fake

References

Agrawal, Anuja. 1997. 'Gendered Bodies: The Case of the "Third Gender" in India'. *Contributions to Indian Sociology* 31 (2): 273–297.
Ahmed, Durre S. 2006. 'Gender and Islamic Spirituality: A Psychological View of "Low" Fundamentalism'. In *Islamic Masculinities*, edited by Lahoucine Ouzgane, 11–34. London: Zed Books.
Alsop, Rachel, Annette Fitzsimons and Kathleen Lennon. 2002. *Theorizing Gender: An Introduction*. Oxford: Polity Press.
Alter, Joseph S. 1995. 'The Celibate Wrestler: Sexual Chaos, Embodied Balance and Competitive Politics in North India'. *Contributions to Indian Sociology* 29 (1–2): 109–131.
———. 1997. 'Seminal Truth: A Modern Science of Male Celibacy in North India'. *Medical Anthropology Quarterly* 11 (3): 275–298.
Appadurai, Arjun. 1990. 'Topographies of the Self: Praise and Emotion in Hindu India'. In *Language and the Politics of Emotion*, edited by A. C. Lutz and L. Abu-Lughod, 92–112. New York: Cambridge University Press.
Atkinson, Michael. 2008. 'Exploring Male Femininity in the "Crisis": Men and Cosmetic Surgery'. *Body and Society* 14 (1): 67–87.
Awan, Muhammad Safeer and Muhammad Sheeraz. 2011. 'Queer but Language: A Sociolinguistic Study of *Farsi*.' *International Journal of Humanities and Social Science* 1 (10): 127–135.
Bakshi, Sandeep. 2004. 'A Comparative Analysis of Hijras and Draq Queens: The Subversive Possibilities and Limits of Parading Effeminacy and Negotiating Masculinity'. *Journal of Homosexuality* 46 (3–4): 211–223.
Bandopadhay, Somnath. 2002. *Antohin Antorin Prochikavortika*. Kolkata: Papyrus.
Bartolomei, Maria Rita. 2010. 'Migrant Male Domestic Workers in Comparative Perspective: Four Case Studies from Italy, India, Ivory Coast, and Congo.' *Men and Masculinities* 13 (1): 87–110.
Besnier, Niko. 2004. 'The Social Production of Abjection. Desire and Silencing Among Transgender Tongans'. *Social Anthropology* 12 (3): 302–323.
Bhaskaran, Suparna. 2004 *Made in India: Decolonization, Queer Sexualities, Transnational Projects*. New York: Palgrave Macmillan.
Binnie, John. 2011. 'Class, Sexuality and Space: A Comment'. *Sexualities* 14 (1): 21–26.

Blackwood, Evelyn. 1998. 'Tombois in West Sumatra: Constructing Masculinity and Erotic Desire'. *Cultural Anthropology* 13 (4): 491–521.

Boellstorff, Tom. 2004a. '"Authentic, of Course!": Gay Language in Indonesia and Cultures of Belonging'. In *Speaking in Queer Tongues: Globalization and Gay Language*, edited by William L. Leap and Tom Boellstorff, 181–210. Urbana: University of Illinois Press.

———. 2004b. 'Playing Back the Nation: Waria, Indonesian Transvestites'. *Cultural Anthropology* 19 (2): 159–195.

Boyce, Paul. 2006. 'Moral Ambivalence and Irregular Practices: Contextualizing Male-to-Male Sexualities in Calcutta/India'. *Feminist Review* 83: 79–98.

———. 2007. 'Conceiving *Kothis*: Men Who Have Sex with Men in India and the Cultural Subject of HIV/AIDS Prevention'. *Medical Anthropology* 26 (2): 175–203.

Boyce, Paul and Akshay Khanna. 2011. 'Rights and Representations: Querying the Male-to-Male Sexual Subject in India'. *Culture, Health and Sexuality* 13 (1): 89–100.

Bourdieu, Pierre. [1979] 1984. *Distinction*. Cambridge: Harvard University Press.

Cameron, Deborah and Don Kulick. 2003. *Language and Sexuality*. Cambridge: Cambridge University Press.

Chowdhury, Indira. 1998. *The Frail Hero and Virile History: Gender and the Politics of Culture in Colonial Bengal*. Delhi: Oxford University Press.

Chopra, Radhika. 2006. 'Invisible Men: Masculinity, Sexuality, and Male Domestic Labor'. *Men and Masculinities* 9 (2): 152–167.

Cohen, Lawrence. 1995. "The Pleasures of Castration: The Postoperative Status of Hijras Jankhas and Academics'. In *Sexual Nature Sexual Culture* edited by Paul R. Abramson and Steven D. Pinkerton, 276–304. Chicago: University of Chicago Press.

———. 2005. 'The Kothi Wars: AIDS Cosmopolitanism and the Morality of Classification'. In *Sex in Development: Science, Sexuality and Morality in Global Perspective* edited by Vincanne Adams and Stacy L. Pigg, 269–303. Durham: Duke University Press.

Connell, R. W. 2005. *Masculinities*. Second Edition. Berkeley: University of California Press.

Connell, R. W. and James W. Messerschmidt. 2005. 'Hegemonic Masculinity: Rethinking the Concept'. *Gender and Society* 19 (6): 829–859.

Cornwall, Andrea and Nancy Lindisfarne. 1994. 'Dislocating Masculinity: Gender, Power and Anthropology'. In *Dislocating Masculinity: Comparative Ethnographies*, edited by Andrea Cornwall and Nancy Lindisfarne, 11–47. London: Routledge.

Crichlow, Michaeline and Piers Armstrong. 2010. 'Introduction: Carnival Praxis, Carnivalesque Strategies and Atlantic Interstices'. *Social Identities* 16 (4): 399–414.

Das, Rahul Peter. 1992. 'Problematic Aspects of the Sexual Rituals of the Bauls of Bengal'. *Journal of the American Oriental Society* 112 (3): 388–432.

Davies, Sharyn Graham. 2007. 'Hunting Down Love: Female Masculinities in Bugis South Sulawesi'. In *Women's Sexualities and Masculinities in a Globalizing Asia*, edited by Saskia Wieringa, Evelyn Blackwood and Abha Bhaiya, 139–158. London: Palgrave Macmillan.
Douglas, Mary. [1966] 2002. *Purity and Danger: An Analysis of the Concepts of Pollution and Taboo*. London: Routledge.
Dutta, Aniruddha. 2013. 'Legible Identities and Legitimate Citizens: The Globalization of Transgender and Subjects of HIV-Aids Prevention in Eastern India'. *International Journal of Feminist Politics* 15(4): 494–514.
Dutta, Aniruddha and Raina Roy. 2014. 'Decolonizing Transgender in India: Some Reflections'. *Transgender Studies Quarterly* 1 (3): 320–337.
Ekins, Richard. 1996. 'The Career Path of the Male Femaler'. In *Blending Genders: Social Aspects of Cross-dressing and Sex-changing*, edited by Richard Ekins and Dave King, 39–48. London: Routledge.
Ettlinger, Nancy. 2011. 'Governmentality as Epistemology'. *Annals of the Association of American Geographers* 101 (3): 537–560.
Farmer, Paul. 1996. 'On Suffering and Structural Violence: A View from Below'. *Daedalus* 125 (1): 261–283.
Ferguson, James and Akhil Gupta. 2002. 'Spatializing States: Towards an Ethnography of Neoliberal Governmentality'. *American Ethnologist* 29 (4): 981–1002.
Foucault, Michel. [1978] 1990. *The History of Sexuality, Vol 1: An Introduction*. Translated by Robert Hurley. New York: Random House.
———. 1991. *The Foucault Effect: Studies in Governmentality*, edited by Graham Burchell, Colin Gordon, and Peter Miller, 87–104. Chicago: University of Chicago Press.
Gannon, Shane Patrick. 2009. 'Translating the Hijra: The Symbolic Reconstruction of the British Empire in India'. PhD thesis, University of Alberta.
Garber, Marjorie. 2008. *Vested Interests: Cross-dressing and Cultural Anxiety*. London: Routledge.
Gilmore, David D. 1993. 'The Democratization of Ritual: Andalusian Carnival after Franco'. *Anthropological Quarterly* 66 (1): 37–47.
Gopinath, Gayatri. 2007. 'Queer Regions: Locating Lesbians in Sancharram'. In *A Companion to Lesbian, Gay, Bisexual, Transgender, and Queer Studies*, edited by George E. Haggerty and Molly McGarry, 341–54. Malden: Blackwell.
Greenberg, David F. 1995. 'The Pleasures of Homosexuality'. In *Sexual Nature Sexual Culture*, edited by Paul R. Abramson and Steven D. Pinkerton. Chicago: University of Chicago Press.
Grosz, Elizabeth. 1994. *Volatile Bodies: Toward a Corporeal Feminism*. Bloomington: Indiana University Press.
Halberstam, Judith J. 1998. *Female Masculinity*. Durham: Duke University Press.

Hall, Kira. 1997. '"Go Suck Your Husband's Sugarcane!" Hijras and the Use of Sexual Insult'. In *Queerly Phrased: Language, Gender and Sexuality*, edited by Anna Livia and Kira Hall, 430–460. New York: Oxford University Press.

———. 2005. 'Intertextual Sexuality: Parodies of Class, Identity, and Desire in Liminal Delhi'. *Journal of Linguistic Anthropology* 1 (1): 125–144.

Hall, Kira and Veronica O'Donovan. 1996. 'Shifting Gender Positions Among Hindi-speaking Hijras'. In *Rethinking Language and Gender Research: Theory and Practice*, edited by Victoria Bergvall, Janet Bing, and Alice Freed, 228–266. London: Longman.

Hansen, Thomas Blom. 1996. 'Recuperating Masculinity: Hindu Nationalism, Violence and the Exorcism of the Muslim "Other"'. *Critique of Anthropology* 16 (2): 137–172.

Harvey, Keith and Celia Shalom. 1997. Introduction to *Language and Desire: Encoding Sex, Romance and Intimacy*, edited by Keith Harvey and Celia Shalom, 1–20. London: Routledge.

Heaphy, Brian. 2011. 'Gay Identities and the Culture of Class'. *Sexualities* 14 (1): 42–62.

Hennessy, Rosemary. 2000. *Profit and Pleasure: Sexual Identities in Late Capitalism*. London: Routledge.

Hinchy, Jessica. 2014. 'Obscenity, Moral Contagion and Masculinity: Hijras in Public Space in Colonial North India'. *Asian Studies Review* 38 (2): 274–294.

———. 2019. *Governing Gender and Sexuality in Colonial India: The Hijra, c1850–1900*. Cambridge: Cambridge University Press.

Hocquenghem, Guy. 1978. *Homosexual Desire*. London: Allison and Busby.

Hossain, Adnan. 2012. 'Beyond Emasculation: Being Muslim and Becoming *Hijra* in South Asia'. *Asian Studies Review* 36 (4): 495–513.

———. 2017. 'The Paradox of Recognition: *Hijra*, Third Gender and Sexual Rights in Bangladesh'. *Culture, Health and Sexuality* 19 (12): 1418–1431.

———. 2018. 'De-Indianizing Hijra: Intraregional Effacements and Inequalities in South Asian Queer Space'. *Transgender Studies Quarterly* 5 (3): 321–31.

———. 2019a. 'Sexual Nationalism, Masculinity and the Cultural Politics of Cricket in Bangladesh'. *South Asia: Journal of South Asian Studies* 42 (4): 638–653.

———. 2019b. 'Section 377, Same-sex Sexualities and the Struggle for Sexual Rights in Bangladesh'. *Australian Journal of Asian Law* 20 (1): 1–11, https://papers.ssrn.com/sol3/papers.cfm?abstract_id=3516500 (accessed 28 April 2020).

———. 2020. 'Hijras in South Asia: Rethinking the Dominant Representations'. In *The SAGE Handbook of Global Sexualities*, Vol. 1, edited by Chiara Bertone, Zowie Davy, Ana Cristina Santos, Ryan Thoreson and Saskia Wieringa, 404–421. London: SAGE.

Hossain, Adnan and Serena Nanda. 2020. 'Globalization and Change among Hijras of South Asia'. In *Trans Lives in a Globalizing World: Rights, Identities, and Politics*, edited by J. Michael Ryan, 34–49. New York: Routledge.

References

Hussain, Delwar. 2013. *Boundaries Undermined: The Ruins of Progress on the Bangladesh/India Border*. London: Hurst.

Jackson, Peter. 2000. 'An Explosion of Thai Identities: Global Queering and Reimagining Queer Theory'. *Culture, Health and Sexuality* 2 (4): 405–424.

Jaffrey, Zia. 1997. *The Invisibles*. London: Weidenfeld Publishing Group ltd.

Johnson, Mark. 1997. *Beauty and Power: Transgendering and Cultural Transformation in the Southern Philippines*. Oxford: Berg.

———. 1998. 'Global Desirings and Translocal Loves: Transgendering and Same-Sex Sexualities in the Southern Philippines'. *American Ethnologist* 25 (4): 695–711.

———. 2009. 'Transgression and the Making of "Western" Sexual Sciences'. In *Transgressive Sex: Subversion and Control in Erotic Encounters*, edited by Hastings Donnan and Fiona Magowan, 167–190. New York: Berghahn Books.

Johnson, Mark, Peter Jackson, and Gilbert Herdt. 2000. 'Critical Regionalities and the Study of Gender and Diversity in South East and East Asia'. *Culture, Health and Sexuality* 2 (4): 361–375.

Kakar, Sudhir. 1990. *Intimate Relations: Exploring Indian Sexuality*. Chicago: University of Chicago Press.

Kalra, Virinder S. 2009. 'Between Emasculation and Hypermasculinity: Theorizing British South Asian Masculinities'. *South Asian Popular Culture* 7 (2): 113–125.

Khan, Shahnaz. 2016. 'What Is in a Name? Khwaja Sara, Hijra and Eunuchs in Pakistan'. *Indian Journal of Gender Studies* 23 (2): 158–164.

Khan, Shivananda. 1999. 'Through a Window Darkly: Men Who Sell Sex to Men in India and Bangladesh'. In *Men Who Sell Sex: International Perspectives on Male Prostitution and HIV/AIDS*, edited by Peter Aggelton, 195–212. London: UCL Press.

Khan, Sharful Islam, Nancy Hudson-Rodd, Sherry Saggers and Abbas Bhuiya. 2005. 'Men Who Have Sex with Men's Sexual Relations with Women in Bangladesh'. *Culture, Health and Sexuality* 7 (2): 159–169.

Khan, Sharful Islam, Mohammed Iftekher Hussain, Gorkey Gourab, Shaila Parveen, Mahbubul Islam Bhuiyan and Joya Sikder. 2008. 'Not to Stigmatize but to Humanize Sexual Lives of the Transgender (Hijra) in Bangladesh: Condom Chat in the AIDS Era'. *Journal of LGBT Health Research* 4 (2–3): 127–141.

Kippax, Susan and Gary Smith. 2001. 'Anal Intercourse and Power in Sex between Men'. *Sexualities* 4 (4): 413–434.

Krishnaswamy, Revathi. 2002. 'The Economy of Colonial Desire'. In *The Masculinity Studies Reader*, edited by Rachel Adams and David Savran, 292–317. Oxford: Blackwell.

Kulick, Don. 1998. *Travesti: Sex, Gender and Culture among Brazilian Transgendered Prostitutes*. Chicago: University of Chicago Press.

———. 2006. 'Theory in Furs: Masochist Anthropology'. *Current Anthropology* 47 (6): 933–952.

Lai, Franco. 2007. 'Lesbian Masculinities: Identity and Body Construction among Tomboys in Hong Kong'. In *Women's Sexualities and Masculinities in a Globalizing Asia*, edited by Saskia E. Wieringa, Evelyn Blackwood and Abha Bhaiya, 159–180. New York: Palgrave Macmillan.

Lal, Vinay. 1999. 'Not This, Not That: The Hijras of India and the Cultural Politics of Sexuality'. *Social Text* 17 (4): 119–140.

Leap, William L. and Tom Boellstorff. 2004. 'Introduction: Globalization and the "New" Articulation of Same Sex Desire'. In *Speaking in Queer Tongues: Globalization and Gay Language*, edited by William L. Leap and Tom Boellstorff, 1–22. Chicago: University of Illinois Press.

Levine, Phillipa. 2000. 'Orientalist Sociology and the Creation of Colonial Sexualities'. *Feminist Review* 65 (1): 5–21.

Liechty, Mark. 2002. *Suitably Modern: Making Middle-Class Culture in a New Consumer Society*. Princeton: Princeton University Press.

Lorway, Robert. 2017. *AIDS Activism, Science and Community across Three Continents*. Cham: Springer.

Marmon, Shaun. 1995. *Eunuchs and Sacred Boundaries in Islamic Society*. Oxford: Oxford University Press.

Marsden, Magnus. 2007. "All-male Sonic Gatherings, Islamic Reform, and Masculinity in Northern Pakistan'. *American Ethnologist* 34 (3): 473–490.

Mazumdar, Ajay and Niloy Basu. 1997. *Bharater Hijreh Samaj*. Calcutta: Dip Prokashon.

Moodie, Megan. 2010. '"Why Can't You Say You Are from Bangladesh?" Demographic Anxiety and Hindu Nationalist Common Sense in the Aftermath of the 2008 Jaipur Bombings'. *Identities: Global Studies in Culture and Power* 17 (5): 531–559.

Mookherjee, Nayanika. 2004. '"My Man (Honour) Is Lost but I Still Have My Iman (Principle)": Sexual Violence and Srticulations of Masculinity'. In *South Asian Masculinities: Context of Change, Sites of Continuity*, edited by Radhika Chopra, Caroline Osella and Fillippo Osella, 131–159. New Delhi: Women Unlimited.

Morton, Donald E. 2001. 'Global (Sexual) Politics, Class Struggle, and the Queer Left'. In *Postcolonial Queer: Theoretical Intersections*, edited by John C. Hawley, 207–238. New York: State University of New York Press.

Murray, Stephen O. and Will Roscoe, eds. 1997. *Islamic Homosexualities: Culture, History and Literature*. New York: New York University Press.

Najmabadi, Afsaneh. 2008. 'Types, Acts or What? Regulation of Sexuality in Nineteenth Century Iran'. In *Islamicate Sexualities: Translations Across Temporal Geographies of Desire*, edited by Kathryn Babayan and Afsaneh Najmabadi, 275–296. Harvard: Harvard University Press.

Nanda, Serena. [1990] 1999. *The Hijras of India: Neither Man nor Woman*. London: Wadsworth.

Nandy, Ashis. 1989. *The Intimate Enemy: Loss and Recovery of Self under Colonialism*. Oxford: Oxford University Press.
Ortner, Sherry. 1984. 'Theory in Anthropology since the Sixties'. *Comparative Studies in Society and History* 26 (1): 126–166.
Osella, Filippo. 2012. 'Men's Sociality across the Indian Ocean'. *Asian Studies Review* 36 (4): 531–549.
Osella, Filippo and Caroline Osella. 2006. *Men and Masculinities in South India*. London: Anthem Press.
Osella, Caroline, Filippo Osella and Radhika Chopra. 2004. 'Introduction: Towards a More Nuanced Approach to Masculinity, Towards a Richer Understanding of South Asian Men'. In *South Asian Masculinities: Context of Change, Sites of Continuity*, edited by Radhika Chopra, Caroline Osella, and Filippo Osella, 1–33. New Delhi: Women Unlimited.
Pamment, Claire. 2010. 'Hijraism: Jostling for a Third Space in Pakistani Politics'. *The Drama Review* 54 (2): 29–50.
———. 2019a. 'Performing Piety in Pakistan's Transgender Rights Movement'. *Transgender Studies Quarterly* 6 (3): 297–314.
———. 2019b. 'The *Hijra* Clap in Neoliberal Hands: Performing Trans Rights in Pakistan'. *The Drama Review* 63 (1): 141–151.
Pattanaik, Devdutt. 2002. *The Man Who Was a Woman and Other Queer Tales from Hindu Lore*. New York: Harrington Park Press.
Peletz, Michael. 2009. *Gender Pluralism: Southeast Asia since Early Modern Times*. London: Routledge.
Potts, Annie. 2000. '"The Essence of the Hard On": Hegemonic Masculinity and the Cultural Construction of "Erectile Dysfunction"'. *Men and Masculinities* 3 (1): 85–103.
Preston, Lawrence W. 1987. 'A Right to Exist: Eunuchs and the State in Nineteenth-Century India'. *Modern Asian Studies* 21 (2): 371–387.
Raheja, Gloria Goodwin. 1989. 'Centrality, Mutuality and Hierarchy: Shifting Aspects of Inter-Caste Relationships in North India'. *Contributions to Indian Sociology* 23 (1): 79–101.
Rahman, Momin, 2014. *Homosexualities, Muslim Cultures and Modernity*. London: Palgrave Mcmillan.
Ramaswami, Shankar. 2007. 'Togethering Contra Othering: Male Hindu-Muslim Inter-relations in Proletarian Delhi'. *South Asian Popular Culture* 5 (2): 117–128.
Rashid, S. F., O. Akram and M. Anam. 2012. 'Sex, Pornography and Medicines in the Markets of Dhaka'. In *Technologies of Sexuality, Identity and Sexual Health*, edited by Lenore Manderson, 95–115. London and New York: Routledge.
Reddy, Gayatri. 2003. '"Men" Who Would Be Kings: Celibacy, Emasculation and the Reproduction of Hijras in Contemporary Indian Politics'. *Social Research* 70 (1): 163–200.

———. 2005a. *With Respect to Sex: Negotiating Hijra Identity in South India*. Chicago: University of Chicago.
———. 2005b. 'Geographies of Contagion: *Hijras, Kothis*, and the Politics of Sexual Marginality in Hyderabad'. *Anthropology and Medicine* 12 (3): 255–270.
———. 2009. 'The Bonds of Love: Companionate Marriage and the Desire for Intimacy among Hijras in Hyderabad, India'. In *Modern Loves: The Anthropology of Romantic Courtship and Companionate Marriage*, edited by Jennifer S. Hirsch and Holly Wardlow, 174–192. Ann Arbor: The University of Michigan Press.
Rogers, Martyn. 2008. 'Modernity, 'Authenticity' and Ambivalence: Subaltern Masculinities in a South Indian College Campus'. *Journal of the Royal Anthropological Institute* 14 (1): 79–95.
Roth, Debra. 2004. 'Engorging the Lesbian Clitoris'. *Journal of Lesbian Studies* 8 (1–2): 177–189.
Roy, Jeff. 2016. 'Translating Hijra into Transgender: Performance and Pehchān in India's Trans-Hijra Communities'. *Transgender Studies Quarterly* 3 (3–4): 412–432.
Rubin, Gayle S. 1992. 'Thinking Sex: Notes for a Radical Theory of the Politics of Sexuality'. In *Pleasure and Danger: Exploring Female Sexuality*, edited by Carole S. Vance, 267–319. London: Pandora.
Sahlins, Marshall. 1981. *Historical Metaphors and Mythical Realities: Structure in the Early History of the Sandwich Islands Kingdom*. Ann Arbor: The University of Michigan Press.
Saria, Vaibhav. 2019. 'Begging for Change: Hijras, Law and Nationalism'. *Contributions to Indian Sociology* 53 (1): 133–157.
Sarti, Raffaella and Francesca Scrinzi. 2010. 'Introduction to the Special Issue: Men in a Woman's Job, Male Domestic Workers, International Migration and the Globalization of Care'. *Men and Masculinities* 13 (1): 4–15.
Sinha, Mrinalini. 1995. *Colonial Masculinity: The 'Manly Englishman' and the 'Effeminate Bengali' in the Late Nineteenth Century*. Manchester: Manchester University Press.
Sinnott, Megan. 2007. 'Gender Subjectivity: Dees and Toms in Thailand'. In *Women's Sexualities and Masculinities in a Globalizing Asia*, edited by Saskia E. Wieringa, Evelyn Blackwood and Abha Bhaiya, 119–138. London: Palgrave Macmillan.
Skeggs, Beverly. 1997. *Formations of Class and Gender*. London: Sage Publications.
Srivastava, Sanjay. 2004. 'Introduction: Semen, History, Desire and Theory'. In *Sexual Sites, Seminal Attitudes Sexualities, Masculinities and Culture in South Asia*, edited by Sanjay Srivastava, 11–48. New Delhi: Sage Publications.
Staples, James. 2003. 'Disguise, Revelation and Copyright: Disassembling the South India Leper'. *Journal of the Royal Anthropological Institute* 9 (2): 295–315.
———. 2011. 'At the Intersection of Disability and Masculinity: Exploring Gender and Bodily Difference in India'. *Journal of the Royal Anthropological Institute* 17 (3): 545–562.

Stephens, Elizabeth. 2007. 'The Spectacularized Penis: Contemporary Representations of the Phallic Male Body'. *Men and Masculinities* 10 (1): 85–98.
Taparia, Swadha. 2011. 'Emasculated Bodies of *Hijras*: Sites of Imposed, Resisted and Negotiated Identities'. *Indian Journal of Gender Studies* 18 (2): 167–184.
Towle, Evan B. and Lynn M. Morgan. 2002. 'Romancing the Transgender Native: Rethinking the Use of "Third Gender" Concept'. *GLQ: A Journal of Lesbian and Gay Studies* 8 (4): 469–497.
Ung Loh, Jennifer. 2014. 'Narrating Identity: the Employment of Mythological and Literary Narratives in Identity Formation among the *Hijras* of India'. *Religion and Gender* 4 (1): 21–39.
Valentine, David. 2007. *Imagining Transgender: An Ethnography of a Category*. Durham: Duke University Press.
Walle, Thomas Michael. 2004. 'Virginity vs. Decency: Continuity and Change in Pakistani Men's Perception of Sexuality and Women'. In *South Asian Masculinities: Context of Change, Sites of Continuity*, edited by Radhika Chopra, Caroline Osella, and Filippo Osella, 96–130. Delhi: Women Unlimited.
Werbner, Pnina. 1990. 'Economic Rationality and Hierarchical Gift Economies: Value and Ranking among British Pakistanis'. *Man* 25 (2): 266–285.
Wieringa, Saskia E. 1999. 'Desiring Bodies or Defiant Cultures: Butch-Femme Lesbians in Jakarta and Lima'. In *Female Desires: Same-Sex Relations and Transgender Practices across Cultures*, edited by Evelyn Blackwood and Saskia E. Wieringa. 206–229. New York: Columbia University Press.
Wilson, Ara. 2006. 'Queering Asia: Western Exports, Asian Imports'. *Intersections: Gender, History and Culture in the Asian Context*, 14, http://intersections.anu.edu.au/issue14/wilson.html (accessed 28 December 2019).
———. 2010. 'NGOs as Erotic Sites'. In *Development, Sexual Rights and Global Governance*, edited by Amy Lind, 86–98. London: Routledge.

Index

abuses and violence, faced by the *hijra*s, 207
acceptance of hijras, in Bangladesh, 61
akkhar dhur, 136
akkhar lilki (large breasts), 140
akkhar panthi (real masculine man), 101, 149
　akkhar panthi-pon, 149
alcohol (*khilwar*), 113, 165
anally penetrated, desire of, 23, 28, 89, 101–102, 104
anal receptivity, as the apogee of sexual pleasure, 6, 22, 99, 103–104, 107, 171, 184
androgyny
　Gandhian, 11–12
　metaphorization of, 12
　metro-sexuality, 13
anthropological debates, on hijras, 3
anti-colonial movement, Gandhi's call for the feminization of masculinity in, 11
Antohin Antorin Proshitovortika (2002), 109
anus power
　anal receptivity as the apogee of sexual pleasure, 99, 104
　as apogee of erotic gratification by hijras, 104
　assertiveness of hijra's anal receptivity compared to penile insertivity, 103
　butli khol, 98–99
　and politics of pleasure, 98–105
　superiority of anus over vagina, 110
　versus vagina, 96–98
arial/akkhar ligam (huge penis), 99
asla. *See* initiation, rites of

authentic 'hijraness'
　anal receptivity in, 104
　negotiation and contestation of, 79

badhai (acts of demanding gifts at birth), 21–22, 28, 38–40, 56, 111, 139, 181
　as celebration of (male) masculinity, 73
　hijra exchange relations during, 69
　hijra performance of, 63–67, 69
　obscenities, use of, 73
　performance of, 124
　rethinking of, 62–72
　verbal slurs and masculine anxiety, 72–75
　vilification of father who sired the child, 74
　working-class acts of donation to hijras, 72
Badhon Hijra Shongho
　formation of, 185
　yearly picnic of, 192–195
bagicha hijra, 29
*bagicha koti*s, 32–34, 38, 43, 50
Bahuchara Mata (mother goddess), 115
bandhobi, 193
Bangla hetero-gendered protocols, 90
Bangla koti, 31, 88–89
Bangla sexuality, hetero-patriarchal and phallocratic model of, 103
bantut bantut, 138
baraiya festival, 34, 60, 172
　'gaye holud' ritual, 124
　respect to Maya Ji and Tara Moni on occasion of, 122
　ritual bath and worship, 123

Index

ritualized celebration of, 112
twelve-day liminal period, 121
welcoming of 'newborn' hijras, 121–125
barging into people's houses, hijra acts of, 66, 68
Bedraj Mata (mother goddess), 115
begging, acts of, 70
bel (wood apple) tree, 121, 140
Besnier, Niko, 3, 158, 169
bila panthi (not a nice man), 85
bila tonna (bad boys), 153
biological maleness and femaleness, properties of, 10
bipod-apod/bala-musibod (bad times/danger), 70
birit (ritual jurisdiction), 40, 68, 75, 79, 117, 185
   bakhor, 79, 118
   birit manga, 68, 113
   distribution of, 147
   trespassing of, 75
bishoo dhurrani, 38
bodily and sartorial transformation, practices of, 138–142
bodily metamorphosis, paradoxes of, 127–130, 142
bodna, 120
bohurupi (hijras as polymorphic beings), 151
borhani, 75
Brazilian transgendered sex workers, 6, 138
breasts enlargement
   breast implants for, 208
   techniques used for, 140–141
Bretton Woods institution, 182
bride, selection of, 164–166
British colonialism
   centrality of the body in, 11
   civilizing mission, 11
   colonial masculinity, 12
   Gandhian anti-colonial androgyny, 12
   governance of India, 2
   notions of
      gender and sexuality, 2
      hijras, 2, 8

policy to ban rehabilitation of hijras, 79n3
butli khol (anus), of a hijra, 98–99

CARE Bangladesh, 185
castration, hijra practices of, 11, 30, 116, 131–132
*cela*s (disciples), 26, 82, 184
   socio-economic status of, 166
chibrano, 112, 117–119, 121, 127
chibry (emasculated hijra), 48, 62, 100, 129–130
   traits of, 129
chilla, practice of, 61
chimpti (tweezers), 141
chipti bazi. *See chiputbazi*
chiputbazi, 108
chis panthi (nice man), 85
chola kola (mystique-making capabilities), 151
cholla manga (hijra collection of money from the bazaar), 21–22, 38–40, 45, 75–80, 139, 181
   birit (ritual jurisdiction), 75
   as source of income for the *sadrali hijra*s, 75
chol pani bondh, 46
cia, 166
circumcision, hijra practices of, 23, 131–132
clapping (*thikri*), practice of, 74–75, 152–153
   loss of the magical power of, 153
class-cultural
   abjection of hijras, 22, 53
   anxiety, 58
   politics, 20, 52
   solidarity and conventions of neighbourliness, 58–62
class-specific demonization, of hijras, 58
code of conduct, of hijras, 37, 45–46
   infringement of, 46
coercive subordination, concept of, 78
Cohen, Lawrence, 11–12, 51, 83, 103–104, 116

communitarian rules and rituals, of hijras, 24
compensation, for changing gurus by hijras, 43
condoms
  demonstration in a hijra NGO office, 187–189
  promotion and distribution of, 184, 186
contraceptive pills, ingestion of, 139–140
crafting of hijra subjectivities, 4, 18, 51
cultural abjection, of hijras, 3, 53
cultural demand for hijras, as performers, 55, 181
cultural performers in Indian society, ritual role of hijras as, 55–56, 66, 90
cultural reproduction, process of, 203
cultural 'truth' about hijras, 13

Daily Star (English-language newspaper), 55
dan-khairat, 69, 78
*daratni*s, 42, 171
dargarani, practice of, 141
darsan potano, practice of, 141
demanding, hijra acts of, 78
desire and pleasure, economy of, 4
de-sublimating sexuality into spirituality, theory of, 146
dhol (drum), 123
  hijras worship of, 68, 113
dhon, 129
dhupni, 59
dhurpit, 82, 91, 107–108
dhurpiter chaya masi (porn video), 82
dhurpiter khutni (sex talk), 84–86
dhurpit turpit (sex), 86
*dhurrani hijra*s, 29, 34, 38–39, 50, 86, 91, 105
  guru–cela hierarchy, 38
  as sex workers, 38
dhurrani neharun (female prostitutes), 98, 108
dingi (food shop), 95
Dipali and Arman, story of, 161–162
disability, framework of, 189–191

disgust, sense of, 82
division of labour, 203
  between guru and chelas, 46
don (compensation), 36
donation to hijras, working-class acts of, 72
dua (prayer) to Allah, 70

Eid al-Adha, 70
Eid al-Fitr, 70
emasculation
  act of, 116
  contradiction, authenticity and ritual power, 125–127
  cultural politics of, 130–132
  functional factors and stories of, 116–118
  hijra practice of, 3, 12
  hyper-masculinity of, 127–130
  renunciation in Hindu-dominated India, 131
  ritual of. *See* ritual excision, of the scrotum and the penis
employment, for hijras, 191, 196–197, 209
  career in the film industry, 162
English sex, hijras as providers of, 96–98
erotically devalued body parts, reclamation and restoration of, 6
erotic and bodily gratification, 5
erotic asceticism, valorization of, 83
erotic delight, forms of, 5, 99, 103–105, 110, 206, 209
erotic desire and practices, 87, 98
  hijra conceptualization of, 103
  lack of, 206
  politics of pleasure, 98–105
  renunciation of, 3
erotic economy, 88, 89–91, 104, 106, 109
erotic encounters, with middle-/upper-class Bangla men, 94–96
erotic pluralisms, 16
erotic transaction and register, in the public garden, 91–92
erotic transgression and taboo, in hijra sexuality, 105–109

Index

ethnographies of hijras, 9, 52, 67, 83, 115, 146
eunuchdom, Islamic institution of, 131
eunuchs, 2, 9
    patronage of, 131
    as royal regalia as harem guards, 131

fake hijra, 50, 76, 79, 118, 195
*falia*s (small trappings), 62
Farsi language
    as hijralect, 87
    hijra's use of, 87
    as official language of Mughal sultanate, 87
female-born, male-identified people, 17
female femininity, traits of, 142, 146
female-identified name, 143
female-marked sartoriality, 139
female sex workers, 93, 107–108, 185, 190
female-to-female same-sex desire, 110
feminine attire in public, hijra convention of appearing in, 188
feminine-gendered performance, 32
feminine-identified
    name, 150
    people, 16–17, 22
feminine sexual prowess, of hijras, 200
feminine traits
    adoption of, 145
    idealization of, 145
feminine virtue, protection of, 74
femininity
    aesthetics of, 209
    aspects for hijras, 146
    cultural devaluation of, 12, 17
    docile femininity, 144
    hijra-defined notion of, 142–146
    male femininities, 12–16
    stereotypical traits in describing, 142
feminization of masculinity, 11
film industry, career in, 97, 100, 162, 177
forceful abduction and castration of men, 28, 116
Foucault, Michel, 182, 203

gamcha (traditional Bangladeshi towel), 34, 37
gamchali hijra, 29, 34–37, 50, 149–150
    dressed like females, 37
    sex work, 37
gandu/gaira/do-porotha (double-decker), 137
gandugiri (anal receptivity), 184
gangs of hijras, 1
garden koti, 32–34
gatecrashing of marriage ceremonies, by hijras, 66
gay (upper- and middle-class hijras), 52
gay-identified group, 33
gay identity, 208
'gaye holud' ritual, 124–125
gender affirmation surgery, 208
gender and sexuality
    notions of, 2, 6, 80, 208
    among hijras, 135–138
    structural inequalities of, 16
gender-(dis)appearing, art of, 151–154
gender categories of hijras
    koti/hijra, 136
    neharun (woman), 136
    panthi/parik (man), 136
gender identity, construction of, 11
gender-transient gods and goddesses, 115
gender-variant people, subjectivities of, 16, 158, 206
genital defects, 30, 118, 155
genitally disfigured, 70
genitals, surgical reconstruction of, 200, 209
genital status, disclosure of
    embarrassment and discomfort associated with, 100–101, 102, 104
genji (t shirts), 34
*ghor*s, 40–42, 123
Ghunguriya (hijra house), 44
gift exchange, in Bangladesh
    acts of giving and receiving, 69–70
    cultural logics of, 58, 69, 72
    dan-khairat, 69
    during Eid festivals, 70

gift exchange, in Bangladesh (*continued*)
  hierarchical gift economies, 69
  systematics of gifting in Muslim-majority Pakistan, 69
  theories of, 58, 68
Global South, analysis of gender-variant people in, 206
*gothia*s, 36, 41, 82, 85, 144
governmentality, concept of, 182
Gulshan Lake, 92
guru–cela relationship, 34, 38, 40–41, 125, 181
  based on mutual respect and reciprocity, 46
  chol pani bondh, 46
  division of labour, 46
  on initiation rites, 41–44
  and logics of guru–cela divide, 203
  milk daughter (*dud beti*), 47–48
  misconduct in, 45
  modelled on mother-daughter relationship, 46
  reciprocity and power in, 44–47
  role reversal' in, 45
  social system of, 46
guru ma, 144

hajji
  hijra, 128, 160, 187, 192
  pilgrimage, 60
*hakim*s (religious doctors), 129
Hall, Kira, 33, 51, 67, 87, 154–155
health activism, 149, 151
hegemonic masculinity, 10–11, 14
hermaphrodite (hijra) populace, 55–56
hetero-erotic masculinity, 151
heterosexual marriage, 97, 125, 147, 149–150, 165–166
heterosexual masculinities, 2, 135
  and hijras, 146–151
  privileges of, 5
hierarchical gradation, of body parts, 6
hijra asexuality, ideals of, 23, 83, 89, 107
hijra bodies, deficiency of, 58

hijra culture, ban on, 79n3
hijra encounters and entanglement, with their partners, 158
hijra erotic economy
  engendering sexuality versus sexualizing gender, 89–91
  female-to-female eroticism, 109
  principle of pleasure in, 104
hijra-focused NGOs
  Badhon Hijra Shongho, 185, 192–195
  rise of, 183–184
  Sushtho Jibon, 184
hijragiri, 41, 44, 62, 75, 113, 157
  apotheosis of, 27, 30
  conduct of, 206
  occupation of, 124
  ritual conduct of, 39
hijra guru, 26, 59, 62, 82, 116, 128, 148, 166
hijra houses, types of
  Ghunguriya, 44
  Machuya, 44
  Shambajariya, 44
hijra identity, 52
  clapping, practice of, 74–75
  construction of, 11
  Islamic identification, 124
  markers of, 74
  in public place, 74
hijra identity, construction of, 112
hijralect, 87
hijra/men relationship, dynamics of, 14
'Hijra Panic Grips City Dwellers' report (2009), 55
hijras
  as an alternative erotic space, 5–7
  anal thinking and, 5–7
  anthropological debates on, 3
  communitarian rules and rituals, 24
  demand for money as 'extortion',
    'criminal' and a 'public nuisance', 56
  ethnographies of, 9
  feminine-identified, 14

Index

forceful abduction and castration of men to enhance their member base, 28
gangs of, 1
hetero-gendered framework, 5
in Hridoypur, 18–21
identity formation of, 13
kinds of, 48–49
lack of a penis among, 6
marginalization of, 3, 8, 11
markers of differentiation, 27
meaning of, 2–3
with missing or defective genitals, 28
as neither men nor women, 2
notion of gender among, 135–138
as people born with defective or missing genitals, 2
as phenotypic male, 9
public (re)presentation of, 4
Reddy's projection of, 131
relations with their pariks, 24
as rights-bearing citizens of Bangladesh, 183
self-identification as Muslims, 132
in Hindu-dominated India, 131
societal understandings of, 4
superior ability as pleasure-givers relative to women, 97
theorization of, 4
as third gender/third sex, 2–3
as universal source of fertility, 3
vulnerability to HIV/AIDS, 25
hijra's anal receptivity, compared to penile insertivity, 103
hijras being helpless people, notion of, 207
hijra sex, 105, 107, 191
hijras fucking men, issue of, 106
disgust associated with, 106
hijras–Islam relationship, 131
hijra sociality, features of, 185–186
hijra social organization, guru-centricity of, 45
hijra subjectivity, formation of, 83–84, 158, 198
role of class in, 52, 80

hijra-to-hijra eroticism, taboo associated with, 106
hijra to hijra sex, 105, 107
hijra versus koti, debate over, 31–32
Hindi language, hijra's use of, 87
Hindu
husband–wife relationships, 46
masculinity, 12
mother goddesses, hijras' association with, 67
scriptural valorization, 83
Hindu-born hijras
in Bangladesh, 132
in India, 132
Hindu-marked cosmology and practices, 132
HIV/AIDS epidemic, 16, 83, 181, 184, 189
hijra vulnerability to, 25
koti–panthi (penetrated–penetrator) model, 103
media coverage of, 187
outbreak of, 205
prevention work in India, 103
homo-hetero binary, 90
homosexual prostitutes
representation of hijra sexuality as, 90
role of hijras as, 90
hormonal replacements, 208
Hridoypur hijra group, 47
human rights, violations of, 207
husband–wife relationship, 46, 125
hyper-masculinity, 129
embodiment of, 133
notion of, 14

ideological abjection of the hijras, process of, 206
ilu ilu, practice of, 32, 140
impotency, idea of, 2
income disparity, 55, 79
Indian
caste-based social structure, principle of, 69

Indian (*continued*)
  elites, colonial principles by, 11
  hijra culture, 115
  selfhood, in postcolonial India, 11
initiation, rites of, 41–44
  asla khawa, 42
  ideas of motherly care and nurturance, 42
  sponsoring guru, 42
inserter/insertee models, idealization of, 103
insiderliness, hijra notion of, 170–176
'Integration of the Transgender (Hijra) Population into Mainstream Society' initiative (2011), 190
intermediate beings, hijras as, 35n2
International Women's Day, 190
intersex activist groups, rise of, 208
Islamic
  beliefs and practices by hijras, 132
  lifestyle of hijras, 61
  marriage, 167–168

*janana*s (hijras with penises), 23, 48, 62, 99, 101, 111, 125–126, 144, 151, 153
  art of magical disappearance of their penises, 79
  *chibry cela*s of, 126
  Maya Ji and Tara Moni, 112–115
jholki, 93, 186
jhumka (scrotum). *See* scrotum, removal of
jodgman, 62, 79, 88, 119
Johnson, Mark, 57, 88, 104, 137–138
jok, 142

kangali voj, 70
kari besher koti, 48
kari koti (a koti in the guise of a male), 31, 141, 192
karkhana (place of operation), 120–121
katial, 119, 173, 199
kazi (Islamic marriage conductor), 167
khai khowara, 105

kinship networks, 22
Konkona and Bijoy, story of, 164–166
koti groups, 26, 30
  bagicha koti/garden koti, 32–34
  Bangla koti, 31
  versus hijra, 31–32
  in hijra argot, 31
  kari koti, 31
  koti-pona, 31
  male-born, feminine-identified, 27
  mannerisms of, 31
  middle-class gay men as, 33
koti–panthi framework, of male-to-male sexuality, 103–104
kudenga, 105
Kulick, Don, 6, 88, 101, 138, 157

Lacanian phallus, 24
language, hijra use of
  Farsi, 87
  to forge and affirm identity, 88
  Hindi, 87
  Ulti, 87
'lavender' languages, of sexual minorities, 87
legal statute, to grant hijras the right to carry out badhai/cholla, 78
lesbian sex, 108
LGBTI (Lesbian, Gay, Bisexual, Transgender and Intersex) movement, 25, 189, 205, 208
ligam forkano (hijra expression for erection), 101
ligam potano (physical art of magically (dis)appearing the penis), 24, 115, 152
lives of hijras, 15
lohori khawa, 92
long bata, 111
'love and hate' attitude, 161
love, notion of, 165
Luna hijra, disciples of, 114n2
lungi, 34
lutki ligam (small penis), 99

Index

Machuya (hijra house), 44
magical disappearance of their penises, art of, 79
male and female same-sex desires, 91
male-bodied, feminine-identified people, 25, 27–28, 34, 51, 138, 142, 157
  desire for normative masculine men, 29, 31
  in public gardens, 88
  Reddy's analysis of, 27
male-born feminine-identified transgender, 158
male femaling, 154
  of Bangla men, 170–176
  male femininities and, 12–16
  practices of bodily and sartorial transformation, 138–142
male femininities, 29
  domesticated by hijras, 24
  gender discourses and practices, 15
  heuristic utility of, 13
  and male femaling, 12–16
  utility of 'male femininity' approach over that of third sex framework, 13
  Western male-to-female transgender practices, 13
male genitals, ritual sacrifice of, 3, 9
male-identified name, 37, 143, 145, 148, 163
male masculinity, celebration of, 73
male-to-female (MtF) transgender identity, 209
male-to-male sexual intercourse, 5, 190
  HIV/AIDS activism and, 103–104
  gender and sexual variance of, 28–29
  homo-social configuration of, 29
  koti–panthi (penetrated–penetrator) model of, 103
  men who have sex with men (MSM), 105, 187, 194
  public discourse on, 187
manhood
  hijra understanding of, 136–137
  loss of, 6

marker of hijra identity, in public space, 74
markers of differentiation, 27, 29
marriage ceremonies
  in Bangladesh, 124
  Bangla hetero-gendered idioms of, 169
  cia, 166
  demand for money by hijras, 66
  gatecrashing of, 66
  heterosexual marriage, 150, 166
  between a hijra and a man, 166
  between a hijra and a woman, 166
  hijra notions of, 158
  hijras blessings to newlyweds with fertility, 66
  Islamic marriage, 167
  between a normative heterosexual man and a woman, 166
  presence of a *kazi*, 167
  rituals and celebrations among hijras, 166–170
masculine anxiety, 72–75
masculine hegemonies, 2, 7
masculine honour of the household, threat to, 74
masculine-identified
  men, 14
  names, 59, 143
'masculine' men
  desire of, 28–29, 31, 37, 89
  manners of, 149
masculine potency, 150
masculinity
  Bangla-defined, 23
  construction of, 130
  feminization of, 11
  formation of, 15, 24
  hegemonic notions of, 14
  hegemonic protocols of, 206
  hetero-erotic, 151
  male femininities and 'male femaling', 12–16
  politics of, 2
  and renunciation in South Asia, cultural logics and politics of, 112

masculinity (*continued*)
  societal norms of, 136
  South Asian, 15
Maya Ji goddess, 67, 112–115, 121–122, 168
  art of 'vanishing the phallus', 152
  ideal of asexuality, 125
  mythic tale of, 126–127
  power of, 127
mazaar (shrine), 38
memsahib, 186
men who have sex with men (MSM), 105, 187
metro-sexuality, 13
middle-class
  gay men as kotis, 33
  households, hijras' encounter with, 57
  imagining of hijras, 54–58, 62
milad, 173
milad mahafil, 70
milk daughter (*dud beti*), 47–48
misconduct, in relations with a guru, 45
morality tales, of hijras, 54–58
mother-daughter relationship, 46
motherly care and nurturance, ideas of, 42
mullah, 60
murad (vow to undergo emasculation), 111
Muslim-born hijras, 130
  in Bangladesh, 132
  in India, 132
Muslim-majority societies, 61
Muslim-marked rituals, observance of, 132

Najmabadi, Afsaneh, 6
Nanda, Serena, 3, 67, 83, 90, 115, 116, 131, 155, 181
natal familial ties, severance of, 147
*nati cela*s (grand disciples), 40–41, 85, 184
nayak (leader), of the Bangladeshi hijras, 184
neharun, 30
neharun dhurrani neharun (women fucking women), 108

neharun neharun dhurpit (female female sex), 108–109
neharun-pona (female), 143
'newborn' hijras, welcoming of, 121–125
night kam (sex work in the public gardens), 21, 37, 86
nirban (rebirth), 112, 131
non-governmental organizations (NGOs), 24, 32–33, 60, 86, 149, 183
  Badhon Hijra Shongho, 185, 192–195
  CARE Bangladesh, 185
  hijra-focused. *See* hijra-focused NGOs
  rise of MSM-based, 187, 189, 199
  Sushtho Jibon, 184

obscenities, hijra use of, 73
Oedipal anxieties, 3, 130
oli, 68, 113
orna, 34

pakki, 20, 148, 166
pakki kora, 91
pancake (cosmetic face powder), 141
'Panic Attack by Hijra at Uttara: Two Hurt' report (2010), 56
panthi, 30, 85, 89–90, 92, 99, 101–103, 136–137, 143
panthi pon, 149, 173
panthi thekano, 92
parik (a masculine-identified husband), 37, 85, 86, 157, 159–160
  as affine, 166–170
  bandha parik, 159
  eternal pining for, 160–161
  hijras in the lives of, 176–177
  parik kora, 159
parik pala, 144, 174
patli, 59
Payeli and Ibadod, story of, 162–164
penetrator–penetrated relations, 5, 103, 138
  indigenous model of, 104
penile pleasures, 6, 23, 110, 206
penile prowess, methods used to weaken, 28, 140

Index

penis (*ligam*), 136
  arial/akkhar ligam (huge penis), 99
  loss of
    cultural valorization of, 7
    due to ritual sacrifice, 3, 7
    Hindu mythological narratives on, 3
    and renunciation of erotic desire, 3
  lutki ligam (small penis), 99
  magical disappearance and appearance of, 152
  staying power of, 129
  vanishing the phallus, art of, 151–154
phallic dissimulation, art of, 107, 109, 135, 152–154
phallic pleasure, economy of, 4
pleasure and desire, in context of hijras, 2–4, 98, 104
power inequalities, 6
  conceptualization of, 103
prayer (*azan*), 60
prejudices against hijras, 54
profanities, use of, 74, 82
public gardens, hijras sexually servicing at, 21, 32–34, 38–39, 88, 92, 94–95, 140, 148, 162, 168, 185, 201
public nuisance, 56
  hijras as source of, 57
public vilification, of hijras, 52
purity–impurity, Dumont's postulation of, 69
*puti cela*s (great-grand-celas), 34, 40–41

queer rights activism, in America, 198
queer theory, culturalist, 52–53
Quran, 173

Raheja, Gloria Goodwin, 69
  disquisition on exchange relations, 69
'real' hijras, 26, 38, 126, 152, 154
Reddy, Gayatri, 26–27, 44, 50–52, 83–84, 115, 131–132, 158, 170, 194, 208
rehabilitation of hijras, 79n3
Renshen (Chinese breast-enhancement cream), 140

renunciation and asceticism
  Hindu ideal of, 12
  hijra practice of emasculation and, 12
renunciation of reproductive heteronormativity, practice of, 146
rights-bearing citizens, hijras as, 189–191
ritual excision, of the scrotum and the penis, 3, 112, 129, 146, 206
  commandments for undergoing, 116
  cultural risks associated with, 112
  fear, secrecy and the operation related to, 119–121
  Hijra cosmologies and, 112–115
  katial, 119
  paradoxes of, 112
ritual practice of emasculation. *See* ritual excision, of the scrotum and the penis

sacredness, hijras' sense of, 115
sacrificing animals, practice of, 70
sadra, 39
sadrali hijras, 21–22, 27, 36, 38, 86, 91, 102, 149, 162, 181, 185
  acquisition of ritual acumen and practices, 40
  association with putatively missing or defective genitals, 27
  breast enlargement, practice of, 140
  cholla manga as source of income for, 75
  classification of, 48–50
  internal social structure of, 39–40
  mobility of, 55
  as most authentic of the hijra groups, 27
  occupations of, 39
  performance of badhai in the poor households, 55
  possession of ritual knowledge and skills, 27
  reputation of, 38
  ritual conduct of hijragiri, 39
  self-identify of, 39, 68
  view on the social universe, 29–30
Sahlins, Marshall, 203
salwar kameez, 38, 95, 123

samajik lingo, 135
same-sex sexualities, 25, 205
    discourse on, 187
sari-clad hijra, 134
sawab (divine goodwill), 70, 196
scrotum, removal of, 3, 30, 48, 98, 112, 119, 121, 128, 136, 200, 206
selfhood, hijras' sense of, 22, 80, 84, 115
self-identification, 208
    proliferation and the political economy of, 192
semen retention and anxiety, theme of, 130
sex–gender difference, 52
sex–gender dualism, 156
sex–gender subjectivities, 16
    formation of, 52
sex–gender variance, valorization of, 130
sex lives, of hijras, 85
    erotic desire and practices, 98
    erotic transgression and taboo in, 105–109
    hijra to hijra sex, 105
    lakeside sex, 92–94
    money for sexually servicing, 93
    at public garden, 94
    sexual experiences with
        Bangla men, 93, 94–96
        foreigners, 96
    sex with men in public space, 93–94
sex-reassignment surgery, 183, 202, 208
sexual behaviours and identities
    anal receptivity, 103
    anus versus vagina, 96–98
    complexities and fluidities of, 5
sexual conversation, with hijras, 84–86
    dhurpiter khutni, 84
sexual disease
    associated with hijraness, 187
    infection in the anal tract, 186
    sexually transmitted diseases (STDs), 184
    sexually transmitted infections (STIs), 184
    syphilis, 185

sexual fantasies, 99
sexual-gender difference, 194
sexual health
    clinics, 186
    NGO-ization of, 182, 199
sexual health materials, 86
    promotion and distribution of condom, 184
sexual health needs, of hijras
    consciousness-raising about the effects of
        sexually transmitted diseases (STDs), 184
        sexually transmitted infections (STIs), 184
    promotion and distribution of condom, 184
sexuality in Europe, history of, 57
sexualization of the hijras, 183
    in Bangla public imagination, 186–187
    discourse on same-sex sexuality, 187
    effects of NGO intervention on, 186
    new discursive regimes and, 186–187
sexually transmitted diseases (STDs), 184
sexually transmitted infections (STIs), 184
sexual practice, of hijra, 83
sexual renunciation and androgyny, ideals of, 11, 83
sexual stratification, idea of, 106
sexual transactions, commoditization of, 94–95
sex work, 68, 86
    by 'dhurrani' hijras, 38
    by gamchali hijras, 37
    monies earned through, 75
sex-worker hijras, 94, 99–101, 107, 140, 174–175, 185
Shambajariya (hijra house), 44
Skeggs, Beverly, 57
social differentiation, 52
    vectors of, 84
social marginalization, of hijras, 3, 8, 11
social rehabilitation, of hijras, 209

Index

social standing of the hijras, in India, 83
social universe, sadrali view on, 29–30
societal denigration, 104
sociocultural institutionalization of hijras, in South Asia, 2
socio-cultural milieu, 52
socio-economic status, of a hijra group, 79
somatic masculinity, 127
sona, 129
sot, 120
South Asian masculinities, 15
spatial location of hijras, in Dhaka, 54–58
special status of hijra, in Indian society, 116
sponsoring guru, 42–43
stereotypical feminine trappings, 145
stigma associated, with hijras, 31, 54
sudrani (semen), 98, 108, 129
Sushtho Jibon, formation of, 184
syphilis, 185

Tara Moni (hijra goddess), 112–115, 122
   art of 'vanishing the phallus', 152
   deceit and the consequent loss of the magical power of clapping, 153
   mythic tale of, 126–127
   ritual embodiment of, 127
   sins of, 126
telephone conversations, for dating men, 143
testosterone, 200
thappu, 38, 50
thikri. See clapping (*thikri*), practice of
thirdness, cultural accommodation of, 8
third sex/third gender framework
   analysis, limits of, 154–156
   construction of hijras as third sex, 155
   inadequacies of, 83
   limits of, 7–12
   markers of, 11
   and masculinities as an alternative approach, 7–12
   socio-political power relations in formation of, 8
   status of, 3, 8

'third sex' gaze, exotification of, 8
two-gender system, 8
utility of a 'male femininity' approach over, 13
tolerance of hijras, in India, 130
Tongan society, 169
transgender people
   de-sexualization of, 197
   discursive interpellation of hijras as, 197
   global code for hijras, 17
   male-born feminine-identified, 158
   male-to-female 'transgender' people, 198
   rise of, 195–198
   from ritualized emasculation to genital reconstruction, 199–202
   sex workers, 6
   use in study of hijras, 16–17
   Western biomedical notion of, 209
trans-local initiatives, 181
transnational governmentality, 25, 182
travesti, 101, 138
two-gender system, notion of, 8

Ulti (clandestine language), 22–23, 31–32, 37, 86, 96, 110, 169, 184, 206
   versus the Bangla world of hetero(a)sexuality, 86–89
   idiolects, 87
   as language of desire, 88
   and 'lavender' languages of sexual minorities, 87
   as medium for secretive communication, 88
   use of, 86
ulu jhulu, 32–33, 60, 87–88, 157

vabi (wives of brothers and friends), 145
vabraj ('pregnant' in the hijra argot), 62
vabrajer chibry, 26, 48–49, 125
vaginal reconstruction, 208
Valentine, David, 16
vanishing the phallus, art of, 115, 151–154
velki jok, 142
verbal insolence, 67

verbal slurs, use of, 72–75
vilification of father, who sired the child, 74
virile masculinity, Hindu cultural politics of, 132

waria, 138
Werbner, Pnina, 69
Western homosexuals, 203
Western male-to-female transgender practices, 13

wifely duties, 143
working-class
    donation to hijras, 72
    hijra populace, 20, 58
    migrant workers, 59
    neighbours, 61

Zhinuk and Rasel's Valentine festivities, 177–179
zones of pleasure, 6